VENTURE CAI

STRATEGY

How to Think Like a Venture Capitalist

Part I: Background

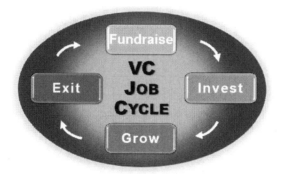

Part II: Practice

VC Razor Publishing
906 Shady Lane
Chapel Hill, NC 27517

info@vcrazor.com
www.vcrazor.com

Printed in the United States of America

VENTURE CAPITAL
STRATEGY
How to Think Like a Venture Capitalist

Brief Table of Contents

INTRODUCTION

Intended Audience

The goal of this book is to teach you how to think like a venture capitalist. As the professionals charged with deciding whether to invest in startups, VCs have refined an opportunistic philosophy with specific tools and methodologies for assessing opportunity and risk. They are optimistic contrarians, and we can learn from them.

The primary audience for this book is business school students who will have careers that are deeply influenced by technology, whether in consulting, banking, finance, marketing, operations or general management. Learning how to think like a VC is relevant for students going into large corporations, startups and everything in between.

Students will benefit two-fold. First, you will develop decision-making skills and an opportunistic outlook that blends micro and macro perspectives, placing any given decision within the context of a *portfolio* of other decisions and opportunities. These are helpful tools for entrepreneurs and managers alike.

> *Thinking like a VC will help you make better opportunistic decisions.*

Secondly, you will learn how venture capital plays an integral role in the commercialization of disruptive technologies in our economy. Almost all of us are touched as consumers by venture-backed companies: Apple, Google, Amazon, Facebook, LinkedIn, Twitter, and more recently Uber, AirBnb, Instagram, Dropbox, Spotify...the list goes on and on. Over 40% of U.S. public companies started after 1974 are VC-backed, meaning they received venture capital before they went public.[1]

Similarly, with less fanfare, nearly every business is in a competitive race to adopt the latest technology solutions, often coming from venture-backed companies such as Salesforce.com, Square and Slack. There are thousands of venture-backed startups out there solving all sorts of

---

[1] "The Economic Impact of Venture Capital: Evidence from Public Companies," Gornall and Strebulaev, Nov. 1, 2015, Stanford GSB No. 15-55, http://bit.ly/vcr001.

business problems. This book will teach you some of the things you should know before you become their first big customer.

If you are or will be in an industry that is heavily influenced by technology, your industry will be disrupted in some way in the next decade, and it will likely be the result of a venture-backed startup. Understanding the venture capital investment process will give you insights into the risks and rewards of working with venture-backed companies. You may want to know, for example, that the startup with whom you are signing a multi-year strategic partnership will likely be raising another $50M from VCs in pursuit of explosive growth that may have serious implications for your relationship.

Another audience for this book is entrepreneurs. The framework I develop in Part II of this book, which I call "VC Razor," is a toolbox for assessing the viability of your startup ideas. You are your first investor, investing your precious time, money and mental energy. You will benefit from learning to think like an investor.

When you first have an idea, you are rewarded with intellectual stimulation—it's fun to play startup! But soon the stakes get real, and you will be faced with tough Go/No-Go decisions. Will you quit your day job? Should you hire a coder for $10,000? Are you ready to begin servicing customers? Thinking like a VC will help you make informed decisions.

VCs have fascinating jobs on the razor's edge of innovation. These are the people who funded the amazing companies listed above: Apple, Facebook, Amazon...I'll warn that there is an occupational hazard in studying venture capital: you may wish you could become a VC!

Venture capital is a small but influential part of our overall economy.

Some argue that VCs get too much attention, considering they represent a tiny segment of our economy. The total capital invested per year is well under 1% of GDP, and less than 1% of all new companies in the U.S. are VC-backed. However, I will argue that VCs deserve even more of our attention, not necessarily because of their economic impact, but because they embody the American spirit and have honed an opportunistic mindset from which we can all benefit.

Lean Startup and VC Razor

Published in 2011, Eric Reis' book *Lean Startup* coined the title phrase and in so doing crystalized Steve Blank's work over the prior decade around the concept of *customer development*. Since 2011, *Lean* has taken the startup world by storm, particularly in higher education. In addition to Reis and Blank, many others have contributed to what I will call *Lean Methodology*, or simply *Lean*.

Lean shifted the focus of teaching entrepreneurship from business planning to customer discovery. It's a lesson in empathy. Entrepreneurs need to fully understand their customers' needs. However, this perspective taken to the extreme can be problematic. Steve Jobs, for example, believed just the opposite. He famously declared that he knew what customers wanted better than they did themselves. His success at Apple is an excellent counterpoint to Lean methodology.

That said, most of us are not Steve Jobs. It is important to understand both the rules *and* the exceptions so that we can make calculated decisions about when we want to be exceptional. The rule, according to Lean, is to empathize with your customers.

With VC Razor, I propose another perspective from which founders should consider their startup: from the lens of the investor. VC Razor is a framework that complements customer empathy with *investor* empathy. While Lean helps refine product/market fit (how well a startup's offerings satisfy its customers), the *Razor* takes a more holistic view to investigate the viability of the entire startup, not just its relationship with its customers. For a startup to be successful, we need happy customers *and* happy investors.

Where I'm Coming From

In the winter of 2002, I had a life-changing experience that ultimately led to an unorthodox career in academia and this book. I had no idea at the time that it was going to be so impactful. I was in the middle of my first year of graduate school at the University of North Carolina, pursuing an MBA, a surprising place to find myself considering how I had spent my 20s.

I had moved to Los Angeles just after college to pursue a music career. Within a few years I was touring the west coast with my band, the Zookeepers, performing 500 shows in 8 states, plus one particularly memorable gig in a 12th century castle in Switzerland called Schlooss Thun.

Figure: The Zookeepers rocked the castle, Schloss Thun, Switzerland

By my early 30s, the band had evolved into a small business with a reluctant sole proprietor: me. I was the booking agent, manager and producer. Through savings from my day job, I had purchased most of the equipment through which we performed, the van that carried us over 150,000 miles and the basement recording studio where we produced four independently released CDs. I hired the musicians who toured and recorded with me. I created the marketing materials. I did the taxes.

I had become a small businessperson in a hit-driven California industry. Unfortunately, after a decade in Los Angeles, I burned out before I ever hit. When I was in my early 30s considering next steps, an old friend suggested business school.

About 18 months later, I was a 1st-year MBA student at UNC's Kenan-Flagler Business School. I stumbled across a seemingly innocent little event that would change my life. The Venture Capital Investment Competition (VCIC) was in its fifth year, limping along after the dot-com bubble-burst. Interest in venture capital was nearly dead after the crash, and only a handful of students signed up for the competition. My team and I did not take it seriously. We pretty much just showed up. That's when my socks were blown off.

In the competition, students get to be venture capitalists for the day. Real startups come to pitch for funding. Playing the role of the investors, we, the students, had a mock VC fund from which we would invest in one of the startups. We had to choose one of the four.

We had been given four business plans from local startups that were attempting to raise venture capital. My team had (barely) read the plans the night prior and prepared a list of questions for each entrepreneur. It was clear to us which plan was the best. By this time in our MBA program, we had read many cases and completed several "integrated exercises" that incorporated all aspects of the b-school curriculum: finance, marketing, operations, management, etc.

When we arrived at VCIC, we already knew which startup would get our funding. We had applied our newly gained business acumen to tear apart the business plans just as we had torn apart dozens of case studies. And then at the event, we met the founders. Game changer!

It turns out, people matter. You can study all the theory in the world and not be prepared for the hair standing up on the back of your neck because you just don't trust someone. There is no textbook that will fully explain the myriad variables involved with navigating a complex conversation with another human being, perhaps one who is much smarter than you, or not nearly as smart, or seems to be hiding something, or is oversharing, or is an amazingly compelling salesperson, or stumbles while explaining things...

> *Theory is important, but people matter more.*

It was an integrative exercise incorporating disciplines like marketing, finance, and operations, with the addition of *real human beings*. These were real founders pitching their real startups and doing their best to answer our real questions just as they'd answer to real VCs.

Prior to this event in our business school classes, we had always discussed businesses as "cases," which were either historical or theoretical. And *on paper*. They had been part of a teaching module designed to impart a specific lesson, often somewhat contrived, or at the least, conveniently choreographed.

At VCIC, it was a maelstrom of variables by comparison. These were not meticulously written cases that made a clear point. These were current business plans, the real deal, being thrust upon the real world with no predictable outcomes. There were no right answers. The students were immersed into the ambiguities of an entrepreneurial endeavor, sharing in the uncertainty with the founders.

The only people in the room who seemed to understand what was going

> *The only ones who understood every-thing: the VCs.*

on were the VCs, the venture capitalists, who were there to judge our performances. They were watching it all as if they'd seen it a hundred times. I thought, *they must be onto something.*

Confession of My Conceit

I am an unlikely candidate to write this book. I am neither a successful tech entrepreneur nor a venture capitalist, nor do I hold a Ph.D. in entrepreneurial finance or strategic innovation.

I have been running entrepreneurship programs and teaching startup classes at the University of North Carolina's Kenan-Flagler Business School for over a decade. In this capacity, I have had the benefit of interacting with hundreds of venture capitalists and startups. More specifically, I have facilitated classes and events in which students, startups and investors interact. This book is a distillation of the lessons I have learned through those experiences.

As a professor, I have had the unique perspective of an objective observer. I've met VCs from all over the world and from funds of all sizes. I've worked with senior partners and young associates. On the startup side, I've seen what gets funded and what gets a pass. I've met serial entrepreneurs and first-timers.

Each of the individuals I've met has a story to tell from a particular perspective. I have attempted to incorporate all of these perspectives in this overview of a disparate industry, as a transparent reporter of my observations. Having never been a venture capitalist nor a tech entrepreneur, I can say definitively that I am not relating my own story or my own bias, other than the bias of an educator.

I have necessarily generalized in a way that you may find uncomfortable at times. That is a good sign! Feel free to break the rules and be exceptional. In fact, understanding and then selectively breaking rules is a key part of being an optimistic contrarian and "thinking like a VC."

I tell my students that one of the challenges of teaching entrepreneurship is that I must necessarily convey the norms and the averages. Yet, success in this field is usually the result of exceptionalism. I'll share the rules, I tell them, and you have to decide which ones you want to break.

> *Think like a VC...*
> Understand the rules, and know when you need to break them to be exceptional

Why Write Another Venture Capital Book?

Over the years as I have run VCIC and taught classes about how VCs think, I have struggled to find materials for my students. I have been frustrated by the simultaneous abundance and lack of available content.

There is an abundance of terrific blogs written by VCs and founders, often teaching specific lessons derived from specific situations. Many VCs are prolific writers and have covered a wide variety of topics of the VC investment process.[2] However, most blog postings have a very specific relevance, and they are not organized into a coherent body of work. In other words, they go too deep in the weeds. The forest is lost for the trees, to mix the metaphors.

Similarly, there is also an abundance of textbooks that treat venture capital as a topic of finance. Wrong forest! Venture capital is undeniably a subset of *private equity*. However, approaching the industry from that perspective ignores the vast majority of what VCs actually do. If you would like to study venture capital as a finance subject, there are many other books that will serve you better than this one.

---

[2] Two great examples are Foundry Group's Brad Feld (www.feld.com) and Union Square Venture's Fred Wilson (www.avc.com).

Treating venture capital as a topic of finance overemphasizes the importance of numbers. For VCs, number play a large role, but just as important is the "story about the numbers." In this regard, I will argue that VCs are more like journalists and filmmakers than financiers.

What I have not been able to find is a holistic overview of venture capital as a *topic of strategy*, explaining its place in the broader entrepreneurial ecosystem. It is not simply entrepreneurial finance! VCs play a very important strategic role in commercializing technologies. Just as importantly, they employ specific strategies that we can learn and apply to our own entrepreneurial circumstances.

> *This book treats VC as a topic of strategy, not finance.*

In this book, we will focus on how venture capitalists make decisions, i.e., how to think like a VC. To do so, we'll need to understand the context of their behavior as *capitalists*. But most VCs consider themselves company builders, not financiers. We will spend most of our time focusing on the *venture* side of venture capitalism, so to speak.

Structure of This Book

The first part of the book covers the VC ecosystem and what we'll call the *VC Job Cycle*. We'll briefly discuss the origin of venture capital and then delve into the specific job duties of venture capitalists. We'll learn that VCs' jobs are both incredibly interesting and extremely challenging. This will give us the context in which VCs operate.

With a firm grasp of where they are coming from, we will then dissect the VC decision-making process. In Part II, I'll lay out an analytical framework distilled from my work with hundreds of VCs at VCIC events. I call the framework *VC Razor*, with a nod to *Occam's Razor*, a 14th century principle that advocates taking the least complicated path. Today you might just say, keep it simple, stupid.

Part I: Background

A. VC Industry

1. A Brief History

Contents

Optimistic Contrarians

Americans are optimistic contrarians. Most of our ancestors had some gripe with the way things were working back home and decided they'd rather make a go of it somewhere else. They were optimistic about creating a better life in America.

The concept of America was a new one, and it was not perfect out of the gate. We've had a lot of ups and downs over the last 250 years, but I believe we've been anchored in perpetual optimism that things continue to get better. Change is good. Just as we marched to the Pacific Ocean, we have always marched toward *progress*, even when we may not have exactly known what we meant by *progress*, and even when we knew there would be casualties.

By European standards, America's march toward progress is downright reckless. Nowhere else can you find a similar drive to achieve. I believe that only in America could venture capital have been born, and only after a couple of hundred years of refinement of the American dream.

> *Venture capital is a truly American invention.*

It's like we'd been reducing the capitalism sauce for centuries to make VC. Part of the reduction was the American settlement of California.

California has always been literally and figuratively *way out there*. It is a place that dreamers go. Every American could benefit from living at least a few years in California. I spent my 20s there, chasing a dream that put me on nearly every backroad in the state, from San Diego to Humboldt County, Death Valley to Silicon Valley, Yosemite to Venice Beach.

California is geographically and culturally enormous and has a proportional influence on the rest of the country. A seminal event in this chapter's brief history of venture capital was the discovery of *gold in them thar hills*. In the mid-19th century, Americans had the opportunity to head west again. Just as they'd crossed the Atlantic to get to the new world, they again donned their optimistic contrarian hats and headed across the continent.

It's easy today to think that 49ers were get-rich-quick schemers. But there was nothing *quick* about getting across the country in 1849. The Transcontinental Railroad would not be complete for two more decades. Once they arrived at their destination, new Californians were met by an ample amount of hard manual labor with no guarantees of success.

Think like a VC...
In pursuit of a big opportunity, be prepared to work harder than you've ever worked with no guarantee of success.

The 49'ers had embarked on a life-threatening journey that included indeterminate amounts of hard work, all of which could very well lead to nothing. Sounds like a startup to me.

Back in the 1800s, California represented the opportunity for Americans to escape rigid east coast hierarchies, old money and old power structures, just as the American colonies had been an escape from the fossilized hierarchies of Europe. Escapism, opportunism and freedom were themes reinforced by the gold rush, creating a new kind of wealth and a new kind of capitalism. All money was new money. California was anarchy by European standards.

Gold induced the first huge wave of American westward migration. The great Dustbowl the second. In between and ever since, California has been populated by dreamers who in one way or another wanted to take advantage of its amazing natural resources: gold, sunshine, fertile land, oil and, oh yes, other dreamers. Lots of other dreamers.

> *California has had numerous influxes of dreamers.*

Hit-driven Industries

Since statehood in 1850, California has been home to numerous boom and bust industries, or what I prefer to call *hit-driven* businesses: gold, oil, defense, aerospace, entertainment and even real estate.

A hit-driven industry is one in which big winners pay for lots of losers. Numerous bets are placed on opportunities that have the potential to be hits, with the full understanding that a large percentage will not work out. Failure is part of the plan.

Think about the film industry, for example. One big hit pays for all the flops that a studio releases in any given year. In oil, one gusher covers many explorations that don't pan out. Even the phrase "pan out" is derived from the California gold rush and panning for gold.

Following the gold rush by a few decades was California's oil boom. By the early 1900s, California was the top oil-producing state in America. Today, there are still thousands of oil wells in Los Angeles, and California remains third in crude oil production.

Figure: Venice Beach in 1925 (Photo: USC Digital Libraries)

Meanwhile, motion picture pioneers D.W. Griffith and Cecil B. DeMille had discovered southern California's sunshine, and the film industry was taking off in the 1920s. Soon came sound and *talkies*, and many cite the *Jazz Singer* in 1927 as the beginning of the Golden Age of Hollywood.

Around the same time, just after World War I, both Lockheed and Douglas Aircraft started manufacturing airplanes in southern California for the army and civilian airlines. While the film industry struggled with the advent of World War II, the defense and aeronautical industries began a boom that would last a half century, through the Cold War and the Korean and Vietnam conflicts.

If that were not enough, along came the moon race of the 1960s, further cementing California in the American economy and the American psyche. The American Dream was succeeded by the California Dream, a novel concoction of risk, hard work, innovation and high reward never before accessible to such a large proportion of the population.

Failure as Part of the Process

A key element of hit-driven industries is the embrace of failure. Failure is not just an option; it is a necessity. As a part of the California Dream, if nobody is failing, we're not trying hard enough.

Think like a VC...

Embrace failure as a part of the process. If you never fail, you are not trying hard enough.

This embrace of failure is not ubiquitous in America, but thanks to the California Dream, Americans are far more tolerant of failure than the risk averse cultures of Western Europe and Asia, for example, where you'll find things like life-time job security and honor suicides.

In America, we admire our friends who move out to California to try to make it big. We know that the odds are against them, and we welcome them home if they return rebuffed. The process is not necessarily a shameful one.

By the 1950s, thanks to a century of hit-driven industries like gold, oil, entertainment, aviation and aerospace, California had been attracting a certain kind of dreamy, ambitious, cutting edge talent. It was in this unique petri dish of culture and infrastructure that the next wave of hit-driven innovation came, thanks to the silicon wafer.

Silicon Valley

One hundred years after gold was found in the California hills, a new untapped resource was discovered, buried under a metaphorical mountain of corporate stagnation. The old model for commercializing technology had stopped working, and a goldmine of opportunity awaited the early VC pioneers who could unlock the potential.

Unlike the breakthrough technologies of the preceding century—trains, electricity, automobiles, telephones, etc.—which required immense amounts of capital, the new technologies of the mid twentieth century, thanks in large part to that preexisting infrastructure, could be launched for a fraction of the cost in dollars and time. The advances that had already been made opened the doors to even faster innovations, but the old corporate and capital structures were behind the times.

This faster, cheaper trend was memorialized by Gordon Moore in the '60s when he observed and prognosticated with *Moore's Law* that advancements in computing would double in speed and halve in size every 18 months. While Moore was referring specifically to computer chips, the rule loosely holds true for the broader concept of bringing new technologies to market today.

> *Moore's Law: size/speed will halve/double every 18 months.*

Traitorous Eight

Back to the late '50s in our California petri dish of opportunism and individualism, we find eight scientists, coincidentally including the aforementioned Moore, working hard on silicon chips for a Nobel Laureate physicist William Shockley, who was a legendary genius and total jerk. When these scientists, dubbed the *Traitorous Eight,* couldn't take working for Shockley anymore, they began looking for a way out. They found their escape thanks to Arthur Rock, a New York banker who recognized an unusual opportunity.

At first, Rock was trying to help the team find a new employer. When that did not work, Rock began to look for an investor to back this talented group to start their own company. This was a new idea made possible by extremely unusual circumstances. How often do eight elite scientists all leave a company at one time looking for something new?

Rock famously pitched the idea to (and was rejected by) over 40 investors. Eventually he found an investor in 1957 in Sherman Fairchild of Fairchild Camera and Instrument, and a $1.5 million deal was inked to launch Fairchild Semiconductors. It was a great success.

A decade later, after an incredible run, but feeling like they were being shorted by their deal with Fairchild, Moore and another Traitorous Eight alum Robert Noyce peeled off again to start Intel, again financed by Rock, who by then had moved to California and started one of the first firms that would look like today's VC firms.

In addition to being an interesting anecdote, the Traitorous Eight story was a seminal point in creating the underlying philosophy of venture capital, i.e., how to think like a venture capitalist. Two key elements were born at that moment: a free market for talent and the sharing of equity with that talent.

> *Traitorous Eight help set VC culture: equity sharing and free market for talent.*

Free Market for Talent

With a creation story that celebrates traitorous behavior, not to mention the free love movement of the '60s, perhaps it is no surprise that California's VC culture includes a philosophy that the best talent should be free to move to the best opportunity, from company to company. The belief is that the market will determine the highest utilization of talent, and that all companies will ultimately benefit from access to the best talent. This rising tide will lift all boats.

This *free love* ethos for talent is in stark contrast to traditional corporate employee retention strategies. From a corporation's perspective, clearly you do not want your top talent to have the ability to leave and then compete against you.

In the topsy turvy world of startups, recruiting the best talent into a highly risky environment may need to include giving them professional flexibility. Many attribute Massachusetts' waning tech industry at least in part to the proliferation of non-compete employment contracts that benefit older firms and penalize startups. Where do the top techies go? Silicon Valley.

Sharing Equity

Of course, in a free market for talent, companies must compete for the best performers, who are free to choose the best opportunities. The best long-term payoff comes from being a part owner, from owning equity in your company.

This may harken back to California's gold rush mentality. Forty-niners took on a lot of risk and worked extremely hard, but they had a literal pot of gold as the motivation. The Traitorous Eight stumbled across their pot of gold. They were really just looking for a new job. It hadn't occurred to them that they could start something new themselves, something they owned.

Owners of businesses behave differently than employees. Owners have incentives to work harder, to get more done. It is a foundational principle of venture capital that the founders and key talent must share in the ownership so that they will be devoted to making a startup a success.

VCs believe that the most value will be created if everyone's incentives are aligned to maximize the value of the company, and that is only done if the *operators* share in the upside. This was a radical departure from business as usual at Bell Labs or Texas Instruments, two of the leading technology companies at the time.

Think like a VC...
Look for opportunities to grow and share the pie: include talented people who will make the pie bigger and be sure to split the pie with them.

Fast Forward 50 Years

In the half century since its inception, the VC industry has grown significantly through a series of booms and busts. The early '80s saw a VC boom created by amazing returns from the likes of Apple and Genentech. Then there was Black Monday and the recession of the late '80s.

By the mid-'90s, the industry was climbing again thanks to the early Internet. After an incredible six year run up, the dot-com bubble burst, but the industry recovered and continued an upward trajectory. The next bump in the road was the great recession of 2008.

Table: Number of VC investments from 1980-2014

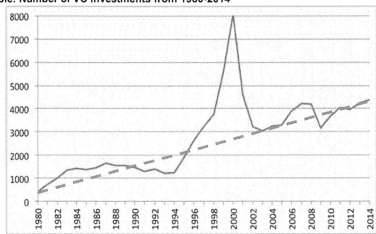

Source: www.aristosventures.com/venture-capital-update.html

Currently we are seeing the highest valuations in VC-backed companies in history. In 2017, the five largest companies in the United States (based on market capitalization) were all originally VC-backed.

Venture capital has also cycled through a variety of "hot" industry sectors. In the '80s, it was lots of hardware, biotech and even some dabbling in retail (Home Depot, Staples). Things transitioned through software and then all things dot-

> *Top five U.S. companies by market capitalization in fall of 2018*
>
> **1. Apple**
> **2. Amazon**
> **3. Alphabet**
> **4. Microsoft**
> **5. Facebook**

com through the '90s, with plenty of biotech and even some telecommunications sprinkled in there. In the last decade or so, we've seen mini-bubbles in cleantech, social networking and the sharing economy. As of this writing, artificial intelligence, the Internet of things (IoT), blockchain and mobility are hot spaces.

Figure: VC industry focus through the decades

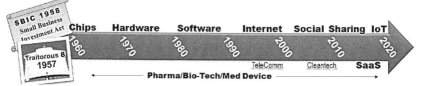

The phrase *venture capital* immediately connotes Silicon Valley, and with good reason. The Valley continues to dominate the industry, representing nearly 50% of all investment dollars in the U.S. New England, another birthplace of VC, is a distant second, with less than 33% of the activity.

Figure: Amount of VC investments by region in (NVCA, 2014)

If you are wondering what some of the biggest names in the industry are, below is a list of firms that did the most deals in the first quarter of 2016.[3] You'll notice that most are based in California, and all of them have offices in the Valley.

Number of deals Q1 2016

Firm	State	#
New Enterprise Associates	CA	23
Kleiner Perkins Caufield & Byers	CA	20
First Round Capital	PA	17
DreamIt Ventures	PA	14
Canaan Partners	CA	14
Lightspeed Management	CA	13

---

[3] The number of deals is not an indication of financial performance, but this list gives you an idea of some of the most active VC firms.

Polaris Venture Partners	MA	13
True Ventures	CA	12
GE Ventures	CA	11
Wavemaker Partners	CA	11
Khosla Ventures	CA	10
Menlo Ventures	CA	9
Upfront Ventures	CA	9
Andreessen Horowitz	CA	9
Google Ventures	CA	9
Intel Capital	CA	9
Bessemer Venture Partners	NY	9

Source: PWC MoneyTree

A Brief History Summary

I've included this brief and incomplete history of the venture capital industry as a backdrop to our investigation into the behavior of venture capitalists. I've posited that venture capital is a truly American experiment, and further, embodies a hit-driven California spirit. Several cultural norms resulted from the VC origin story of the Traitorous 8 in Silicon Valley: failure as part of the process, sharing of equity and a free market for talent.

> ### WHAT WE COVERED
>
> ### A Brief History
>
> - Optimistic Contrarians
> - Hit-driven Industries
> - Failure, Part of the Process
> - Silicon Valley
> - Traitorous Eight
> - Free Market for Talent
> - Sharing Equity
> - Fast Forward 50 Years

Chapter Questions

1. Who were the Traitorous Eight and why is their story relevant?
2. What defines a hit-driven industry? What are some examples of California's hit-driven industries?
3. Why would VCs want to share the upside with startup founders?
4. Why do VCs believe in a free market for talent?

2. What is Venture Capital?

Institutional	Equity investments	High growth startups

Contents

The phrase "venture capital" is often used loosely in the mainstream to mean "any funding for any new company." However, venture capital is a well-defined type of investment class that resides within a broader category called private equity, which essentially means, "part ownership of companies whose stock is not traded publicly." Here's my attempt at a somewhat approachable yet specific definition of venture capital:

> *Razor Definition, Venture Capital:*
> *Institutional equity investments in high growth startups.*

Let's unpack this, starting with the first word, *institutional*.

Institutional

This refers to where the money is ultimately coming from. VCs are not investing their own cash, by and large. Rather, they are professional money managers investing *other people's money*, mostly from large *institutions*, such as pension funds, university endowments, banks, insurance companies and other corporations.

Institutions: university endowments, state employee pension funds, financial institutions, other corporations.

These institutions have cash they need to invest, and often they want to diversify their investments beyond traditional public stocks and bonds. They opt to put a small percentage of their portfolio into higher risk investments called *alternative assets*, most commonly real estate, hedge funds and private equity. Venture capital, again, is a type of private equity.

The money that fuels venture capital is coming from these large, often financial, institutions. VCs are paid a fee plus a share in the profits for managing these funds, and they have a legal obligation (often called a *fiduciary duty*) to act in the best interest of these institutions, who are the *limited partners* (LPs) of the VC fund.

Angels vs. VCs

VCs are often confused with *angel investors*, individuals who invest *their own money* in startups. Many angels employ investing techniques similar to venture capitalists, though usually at an earlier stage, often called the *seed* stage. While they have some similarities to VCs, angel investors have nobody to answer to and may choose to invest in a startup for a variety of reasons not connected to financial returns. Angels have no fiduciary duties.[4]

---

[4] Famed VC Ben Horowitz of Andreessen Horowitz has an excellent blog post from 2010 entitled "Angels vs. Venture Capitalists," http://bit.ly/vcr002

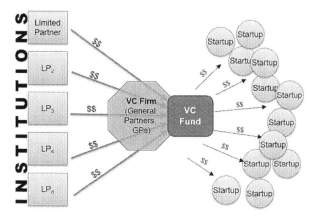

The term angel investor was coined back in the heyday of the movie industry. Movie producers would find *angels* to put up the money for a film project. After the dot-com bubble, many newly minted tech millionaires found themselves with a lot of extra cash, and a new larger angel class was born.

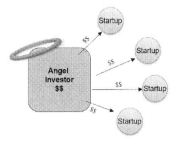

Figure: Angel investors: investing their own capital

Tech angel investors have become more sophisticated through the years, often organizing themselves into groups that run the gamut from loosely affiliated individuals to legal entities that look a lot like small early stage VC funds. However, the capital generally comes from the members, not from institutions.

VCs, on the other hand, have numerous institutions to whom they are beholden. Hence, startups who receive money from VCs are said to be receiving their *first institutional money*, which refers to this distinction.

Startups who raise their first institutional round receive a level of credibility along with the cash. Because VCs are professional investors

> In addition to cash, startups gain credibility with their "first institutional" round.

with a fiduciary duty to return capital, their investments are generally regarded with a higher degree of objectivity and credibility.

Bottom line, VCs are pros.

Equity Investments

When VCs make an investment in a startup, they are buying shares of stock in the company, also known as *equity*. This is very similar to you or I buying shares of stock of a public company on a public stock exchange, with some important differences.

Private vs. Public

First, venture capital stock purchases are *private*, not public. Hence the moniker *private* equity. While public equities are bought and sold on public exchanges like NASDAQ or the New York Stock Exchange, private equities are, well, private. Aspects of the deal, such as the share price and investment amount, do not have to be disclosed to the public, though sometimes press releases indicate some of that information.

Illiquid: Unlike public stock, private equity is an *illiquid asset*, meaning that it cannot easily be exchanged for cash or some other *liquid* asset. Public equities are traded *publicly* thousands of times a day. The price of each transaction is published. One may liquidate one's position for cash at almost any time.

Private equity is more like a house. It takes an extended amount of time to sell, and the price will need to be negotiated. VC-backed startups are even more illiquid than a house. Ultimately, for investors to get a return, they'll need to liquidate this illiquid asset, either by selling it to a larger company, or in rarer cases, by *going public* via an IPO, initial public offering.

Active Role: Another difference between public and private equity is that VCs will take an active role in their investments, lending their expertise and connections to help a startup succeed. Since VCs are purchasing a significant percentage of ownership, perhaps 20-50%, they usually take seats on the board of directors. As board members, VCs have a voice in major strategic decisions.

Newly Created Equity: The last difference I want to point out here is that VCs are purchasing *newly* created *preferred* shares. Two key words here: *newly* and *preferred*. Public stocks are *traded*, meaning you can buy my shares and vice versa. No new shares are created in that transaction; we are simply trading them, which is why it is called the New York Stock *Exchange*. We exchange shares for cash.

> *Three ways VC differs from public stock: 1) illiquid; 2) active participation; and 3) issuance of new stock.*

In venture capital, new shares are created by the startup and sold to VCs with the cash going into the bank account of the startup. This means that the pool of stock has increased, thereby *diluting* the ownership of the founders and early investors.

For example, two founders incorporated their startup and each owned 500 shares of a total of 1,000, or 50% of the company. To raise money, they created 500 new preferred shares and sold them to VCs. The founders now each own 500 out of a larger pool of 1,500, resulting in their ownership being diluted from 50% to 33%. (Simultaneously, the *valuation* of the startup increased by the amount of cash received from the VCs.)

The other keyword, *preferred*, refers to special rights that VCs will have above and beyond *common* shareholders, such as liquidation preferences, voting rights, anti-dilution, pay-to-play and dividends. These rights have evolved through the decades to give VCs certain advantages and protections.

Table: Examples of benefits of "preferred" shares

Board Seats	VCs generally seek board seats as well as a say in choosing independent board members.
Liquidation Preference	Upon exit (sale of the startup or IPO), VCs get a multiple of their investment (often 1X) prior to splitting the equity pie.
Anti-Dilution	On a down round, early VCs will receive extra shares to compensate for dilution.
Dividends	Upon exit, VCs will receive an additional percentage of their investment, often 7-8% accrued annually.

More Info	A fantastic resource for the intricacies of preferred shares is Brad Feld and Jason Mendelson's *Venture Deals, Be Smarter than Your Lawyer and Venture Capitalist,* Wiley, 2013.

While these rights are extremely important to understand before signing a deal with VCs, for our purposes, it will suffice to understand that VCs are not regular shareholders like you or I might be in a public company.

Equity vs. Debt

So we understand when a VC wires money to a startup, it is in exchange for preferred shares of private equity. VCs are buying a percentage of the company. We should also be very clear that this is an investment, not a loan. It is co-ownership. The founders and the VCs enter into a complex long-term relationship that is intended to last until the company is sold or goes public, called an "exit event," which refers to the investors having the opportunity to *exit* the investment (convert an illiquid asset into a liquid asset).

> *An "exit" refers to investors "exiting" the investment when the startup is sold or goes public.*

There is good and bad news for startups considering an equity partnership, i.e., taking cash from a VC. On the good side, it's not debt. You won't have to pay it back, and you can't go bankrupt by missing a payment to your VC. In fact, there will be no payments from the startup to the VCs. Again, you're in it together until the exit, at which time, you split the proceeds from selling the company.

It is nice not to have to make debt payments, and it is nice not to have to pay back a loan if the startup goes belly up. If things go poorly, the VCs will lose their investment.

The bad news? This is not debt. You can't just pay it back and be done with your creditors. These investors own a sizeable percentage of your startup, and you cannot easily be rid of them. This can be a bummer if things go incredibly well, as the investors will get a much bigger slice of the pie than a bank would have gotten.

Quick example: if you borrowed $1M and then took your company to a $20M exit, you could simply pay off the $1M and pocket $19M.

However, if you sold half your company for that $1M, it's going to cost you half of the proceeds at exit, or $10M in this case. This is why bank loans are sometimes referred to as *cheap money*.

> *Debt is considered cheap money if things go well.*

On the flipside, if your company flopped, you'd still personally owe the bank $1M because it is very unlikely that they were willing to lend you any cash without a personal guarantee. The only thing worse than having a failed startup is having a failed startup with an additional $1M loan to pay off.

There is another potential drawback if you are planning to bring in equity investors. As mentioned above, they will require an exit, also called a liquidity event: the sale of the startup to another company or by going public. As we'll see later, an exit is the only way equity partners can get their required return on the investment. They are not interested in a perpetual profit-sharing scenario. They need to invest, grow and exit. This can, but does not always, present a conflict for founders who plan to run their companies for decades to come.

> *Think like a VC...*
> Be prepared to maintain long-term relationships. Be in it for the long haul!

The last bit of bad news is that you can't easily get rid of investors if the relationship sours. You are in it together for the long haul (witness Benchmark Capital suing former Uber CEO Travis Kalanick). True, it is conceivable that you could buy them out, but that probably won't work for a number of reasons we'll discuss later. As a rule, equity partners are stuck together until the exit. So choose wisely!

Equity to Fuel Growth

As mentioned above, equity is considered expensive money. If you can grow organically by reinvesting your revenues or borrowing from a bank, you should probably do so. However, growth can be very expensive, and, of course, risky. That's where equity comes in.

The old-fashioned way to start and grow a business is a long slog of acquiring paying customers and growing slowly and steady over time, living off a meager (but growing) salary and plowing most the money the company makes back into the business (called *retained earnings* by accountants). With any luck, the business grows relatively steadily over time, perhaps with some fits and starts.

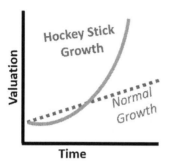

Everything changes with venture capital. The whole point of equity investing is to accelerate growth. The tired but true cliché is that VCs are looking for *hockey stick growth*. The hope is to find growth inflection points, where an injection of capital can have a disproportionate effect on the slope of the curve.

Figure: Hockey stick vs. normal growth

However, this curve is misleading. With equity investments, you actually have discrete funding moments, called *rounds*, which create a bumpy road in terms of the actual growth trajectory. These equity rounds follow a typical pattern:

- The initial cash and sweat equity that **founders** supply to get going (called *skin in the game)*,
- Often followed by investments from ***friends and family*** (and sometimes *fools)*,
- Moving on to **angel** and seed investors, and finally,
- *Institutional* investors (**venture capitalists**).

Traditionally, venture capitalists enter the picture when the investment size is in the $2M-25M range, though some smaller VC firms specifically target *seed stage* investing, and some larger firms have *side funds* to invest in earlier stage deals. This first round of VC funding, i.e., the *first institutional round*, is dubbed *Series A*, and will be followed by *Series B, C*, etc., until exit. A Series A first institutional round can be as low as $1M but is more typically in the $5-15M range, with some exceptional outliers as high as $100M.

Figure: Rounds of equity financing

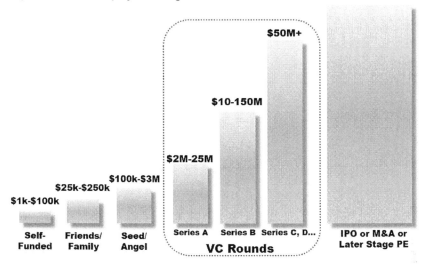

Early stage refers to most any startup near the left of this pattern, with *later stage* referring to startups that fall to the right, say Series C and later, getting close to an exit. Some firms, for example, called *mezzanine funds*, only invest in rounds just before the exit. In so doing, they have a risk/reward profile that can look more similar to private equity firms than to early stage VC firms, i.e., lower risk, lower return, but more capital deployed per deal.

High Growth Startups

As we mentioned above, venture capital has a hit-driven business model, very similar to the entertainment business, in which one hit covers many duds, and a megahit can boost the entire industry. In the VC industry, the megahits are called *unicorns*, startups that have reached *valuations* over $1B. For the industry to work, the financial success of the unicorns must far exceed the losses from all of the busts.

For a startup to have any chance of becoming a unicorn, it must be able to grow very, very quickly. This generally requires some sort of *disruptive* technical innovation, as in, some new way of doing things that completely disrupts an industry. Think of what Uber is doing to the taxi industry, for example, or what happened to the travel industry a decade or so ago.

So VCs are hunting unicorns. To make it particularly challenging, unicorns and flops look nearly identical in the infant stage. Amazon and Webvan looked much the same in 1999.[5] Distinguishing between

> *VCs are professionals using other people's money to hunt unicorns.*

potential unicorns and everything else is the subject of Part II of this book, in which we study the *VC Razor* framework for analyzing startups as potential investments.

Perhaps a more useful metaphor for explaining the VC investment process is a moonshot. VCs are shooting for the moon. They are looking for rocket ships (startups) for which VCs will supply the fuel (cash) to get to a moon landing (exit) for the investment to pay off.

In some ways, this metaphor better describes the process. The first round of capital is akin to a blastoff, which may get a startup out of earth's atmosphere, but more fuel will be needed to finish the trip to the moon. This can create conflict between founders and investors.

A somewhat conservative entrepreneur who survived blastoff might well hit outer space and want to slow down to acclimate. Getting into earth's orbit is a fantastic achievement! Normal survivalist behavior would dictate a measured approach to preserve the growth already achieved.

Meanwhile VCs are on the horn from Houston (Silicon Valley in this metaphor), imploring you to hit the button to deploy the next booster rocket (*round* of investment). *To the moon or bust,* you can hear them chanting down in Houston.

> *Moon Metaphor*
> *Startup = space ship*
> *Venture capital = rocket fuel*
> *Rounds = booster rockets*
> *Exit = moon landing*

---

[5] Webvan (online grocery delivery) was one of the more famous implosions of the Internet bust. Shut down in 2001, it reportedly lost over $800M, http://bit.ly/vcr003

Feel free to skip this section as I go on a little digression about how the VC industry behaves like the (old) music industry. In learning to think like a VC, it is important to understand the shortcomings as well as strengths.

As I have mentioned, I traveled around California in a former life with my band, the Zookeepers. I had moved to L.A. from the east coast and pretty quickly accumulated enough rejection letters from record labels to cover a wall of shame in my rented house in Silver Lake.

It wasn't until I went to business school and learned about venture capital that I fully understood the depth of the *hit mentality* of the record industry. Back in the day, I thought labels were short-sighted not to invest in hard-working road bands like mine. Growing a solid fan base was not their goal, weirdly, I thought.[6]

> **Think like a VC...**
> Focus on high growth, not sustainability. Caution: this can be a risky philosophy unless you have a "portfolio" of opportunities.

VCs are similarly disinterested in growing modest, sustainable businesses. In fact, a company that grows a healthy 5% a year is in some ways worse for a VC than a company that simply implodes on a moonshot. VCs have derogatory names for these otherwise seemingly healthy businesses: the *walking dead*, or worse yet, *lifestyle businesses* (when you say these phrases, it is appropriate to make a face like you can smell dog poop).

I submit that in learning to think like a VC, we may or may not choose to adopt their hit-driven focus. Rather, we should note the emphasis on opportunity and the utilization of a portfolio to reduce risk. In so doing, we may want to place a few bets on potential hits. As you'll see below, the math can be compelling!

---

[6] I prefer to believe that this was why I never got a record deal. Nothing to do with my talent, right?

Back to our music industry example, it does not take a math major to appreciate the hit formula. Let's say you own a regional record label and you have five hard-working, well-known bands. They tour constantly and sell tens of thousands of CDs (travel back in time with me). One CD release might cost you, the label, around $100,000 to produce and market.

If a band sells 50,000 units, you can net $400,000 (assuming $10/CD wholesale, $500,000 - $100,000). That is a 4X return on your $100K and a very solid return in conventional business terms. If you could repeat that success, you'd do it over and over again and would have a fantastic business. But you would not get to the moon.

Now let's say a late night talk show host takes a liking to one of your bands. Imagine he thinks one of your band's names is goofy, and he starts repeating it over and over again. This is basically what happened in the '90s to Hootie and the Blowfish, a solid regional act selling tens of thousands of CDs. Then David Letterman semi-accidentally made stars out of them.[7]

In 1995 alone, their CD *Cracked Rear View* shipped over 10 million units. Let's do the math. We're talking $100 million dollars on the same $100,000 recording. Heck, we can even put a few million into marketing, and we are still looking at over 30X return.

Shooting the moon: 30X on a few million vs. 4X on $100,000.

As the label, guess what you are looking for in the next band you sign? You can't help yourself. Do you want another solid act working their butts off 150 nights a year to move 50,000 units, calling you at 3AM when the van breaks down?

Or do you want a band with hit potential?

Don't you want to figure out the formula for hits? Don't you want to become a hit factory? Can you even remember why you were working

---

[7] I am remembering and recounting this through a skewed and admittedly semi-bitter lens.

so hard on those marginal acts? Can you believe you now think of those successful acts as *marginal*?[8]

The entertainment industry's business model, just like venture capital, is built around placing a lot of bets on {bands, TV shows, movies, startups} that have hit potential. When one starts getting traction, the machine kicks into gear and they double and triple down in hopes of creating a megahit.

Another way of saying this is that the returns are, by design, disproportionately represented by the hits. In the example above, Hootie brought in $100M. It would take somewhere around 250 of the other $400K-a-pop bands to bring in that much.

When your label has a hit artist, all the other artists, whether they are selling 50,000 or only 100 units, start to look the same.[9]

> *From a returns perspective, there are the hits, and then there's* everything else.

West Coast vs. East Coast

The hit-driven mentality described above varies in degrees across the industry, largely depending on geography. Silicon Valley is hands down hit mecca. Just as L.A. is the hit factory for the entertainment business, Silicon Valley is the hit factory for tech startups.

Different regional VC ecosystems have different cultures. Just as Nashville is a key music hub that is known to be very friendly to songwriters, Boulder is a key VC hub that is founder friendly. New York is hip and driven by finance. Boston is smart and somewhat conservative.

Ultimately, the commonality across all VC firms is that they are building portfolios of startups that have high growth potential. West coast firms are likely swinging harder for the fences in terms of finding actual

---

[8] OK, last bitter footnote from me. For the record, we weren't even marginal. We sold tens of *hundreds* of CDs, probably more like scores of dozens.

[9] For another "math of a hit" example, see Google on p. 39.

unicorns and duds. East coast firms are often building a less risky portfolio hoping for many doubles and triples and fewer strikeouts.

West coast venture capital tends to be higher risk/reward than east coast or regional firms.

To stick with the moonshot metaphor, west coast is aiming at the moon and is fine with littering space with some ghost spaceships. East coast is hoping to get more satellites into orbit with fewer rockets plummeting into the ocean.

Careers in Venture Capital

One of the challenges of learning to think like a venture capitalist is getting the bug to *be* a VC. Sounds like an amazing industry, and as you'll see in the next chapter, an amazing job. By all accounts, it is. The VCs I work with at VCIC events have very high job satisfaction.

The bad news for aspiring venture capitalists is that it is an extremely difficult industry to break into, in large part simply as a function of numbers. There are very few VC firms, and each firm only employs a handful of people. Using banks as a comparison, there are nearly 7,000 banks in the U.S. and fewer than 1,000 VC firms. Over 2.1M people work at banks. Fewer than 7,000 work at VC firms.

The flat structure of VC firms also creates a challenge to young graduates looking to break in. Each firm is a partnership, and some firms have no employees beyond the partners. There are basically three levels of full-time employees at VC firms: partners, non-partner VCs (called principals, analysts or associates) and administrative support staff. Many firms only have the top and bottom level, leaving no employment opportunities.

A mid-sized firm might have a handful of partners, 2-3 mid-level VCs and support staff. The result is very, very few job openings any given year. Further, even if you land a job as an associate, there is generally no "partner track." Analysts, associates and principals rarely move up to a partner level in the same firm.

Still, there are some jobs, and I encourage any student to be exceptional and shoot for the moon. If you would like to pursue a career in venture capital, here are the two key take-aways that I've heard scores of VCs share with students:

1. Get involved in a promising startup. Be selective and find a great early-stage startup where you can make a difference. Earn your way into a strategic role. Perform like a star. Get to know the startup's investors.
2. Develop some domain expertise in a disruptive field, such as computer science, biotechnology or physical sciences. Guess where the next big innovation may come and position yourself in that space.

What is VC Summary

Put it all back together and we are back to where we started this section: venture capital is defined as institutional equity investments in high growth startups. VCs are professional money managers using someone else's money to hunt unicorns.

Understanding that VCs are professional money managers gives us an important context for exploring how they do their jobs (and make decisions). Like all money managers, their primary job is to make more money. The "C" in VC is for *capitalist*. It boils down quite simply. They must return more capital to the institutions that gave them the money in the first place.

Further, because these investments are deemed high risk by institutions, higher returns are required. So VCs must *outperform the market*, i.e., yield better returns for their investors than traditional assets, like public stocks and bonds.

Like other money managers, VCs will do this by creating a portfolio of investments, in this case, startups. They will attempt to achieve a portfolio effect: higher returns with reduced risks. VCs' have an added challenge with their portfolios: illiquidity. VCs need to exit each startup to return liquid assets to their institutional investors.

WHAT WE COVERED

What is VC?

- Institutional
- Equity Investments
- High Growth Startups
- The Math of a Hit
- West vs. East Coast

Chapter Questions

1. In a few bullets, list some differences between debt and equity from a startup's perspective. Why might a founder prefer debt to venture capital?
2. How is the west coast different from other regions of the United States in terms of a hit-driven approach to venture capital?
3. How might one hit in your portfolio overshadow other successes?
4. What is flawed about a startup founder's pitch to raise enough capital to get to break-even?
5. Define venture capital.
6. What are some differences between public stocks and venture capital?
7. How are VCs and angel investors different?
8. What are "preferred" shares?

B. VC Job Cycle

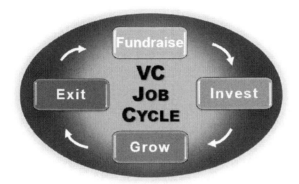

3. Fundraise

Contents

On the one hand, as VCs, we are on the vanguard of innovation. We invest in exciting technologies that can and will change the world. [10] However, from a different perspective, we are money managers who cling to conventions and are very, very slow to change. Raising money is the old school part of venture capital that hasn't changed fundamentally since the industry got started over a half century ago.

---

[10] Since you and I are learning to think like VCs, I'm going to use the first person plural, "we," moving forward.

This is no surprise if you look upstream and see where the money is coming from. Pension funds and insurance companies are not exactly big risk takers. Hence, VCs set up their funds just like private equity funds were doing back in the 1950's. VC funds are limited liability partnerships in which the VCs are the GPs (general partners) and the pension funds, banks, endowments and other investors are the LPs (limited partners).

As the title implies, the LPs have a limited role. They will have no active participation in our partnership and will have no liability beyond the cash they've invested. All they do is supply cash and get cash in return.

Fundraising Strategy

It can be surprising to learn that, as VCs, we pitch to our investors in much the same way as startups pitch to us. Just as startups must put together a fundraising strategy and pitch to numerous investors, we also go on a roadshow to present our firm as an investment opportunity for institutions.

> **Think like a VC...**
> Become an expert presenter. You'll need pitching skills just as much as the founders who pitch to you.

Both VCs and startups present a specific amount being raised and a strategy for the "use of funds." While startups are presenting a series of milestones on the way to a successful exit, we pitch a particular fund size and strategy that should match the competencies of our partners.

The main variables that determine the size of the fund are the number of partners, the number of deals each partner can handle and the stage of financing that the firm will target. Earlier stage generally will need less capital. Later stage needs more.

Let's say, for example, that we have three partners and we would like to invest in early stage startups, say $5-7M per startup. If we believe that each partner can handle one new deal per year for the next five years, we'd be

> *Fund size factors:*
> *# of partners,*
> *# of deals per partner,*
> *average $$ per deal.*

looking at a total of 15 startups in our portfolio. At $7M/startup, we'd need to raise about a $100M fund for this strategy.

Change the strategy to be a little bit later stage, which would require more capital per startup, and we might need to raise a $150M fund to average $10M per startup. Add a partner, and we may be able to increase our portfolio size by 1/3, up to 20 startups. Now we might be looking at a $200M raise.

As GPs, we are constantly working our LP network to gauge the temperature of the fundraising market. That is, we are asking our LPs and prospective LPs what they'd want to see. Just as startups create an MVP (minimum viable product) and test it with early customers, we will start floating the idea of our new fund to LPs to gauge interest. We'll iterate our fundraising strategy based on their feedback.

Just as founders test their products with customers, VCs test their fund strategy with prospective LPs.

The fundraising process officially begins with our announcing that we are raising a new fund, identifying the target fund size and strategic focus. Ideally, before we've even announced, we'd like to have a soft commitment from an *anchor LP,* one that will represent a large stake in the fund, perhaps in the 10-20% range.

The fundraising process can go quickly if we already have a great track record for returns to LPs and the public markets are up, or it could take more than a year if markets are in a downturn or we are relatively new to venture capital or are trying a new strategy.

Why does it matter if public markets are up? Isn't this *private* equity? Yes, but remember that our LPs are institutions that mostly invest in traditional stocks and bonds. They will allot a relatively low percentage of their entire portfolio to crazy things like venture capital. If the markets are down, the denominator has moved, increasing their exposure to VC, and they will not have an appetite for a new investment in our VC fund.

Different LPs will get on board for different amounts and potentially for different reasons as they balance their portfolios. Just as a startup should be careful about choosing its equity partners (see Equity vs. Debt, p. 24), VCs need to be careful about choosing their LPs. These will be long-term relationships that will necessarily go through ups and downs.

While fundraising, VCs pitch different levels depending on the LP and its capacity. For example, a $5B pension fund may not be able to commit to writing a check smaller than $20-50M as a function of their size. They only have so many professionals to track their investments. With $5B to manage, they need to write bigger checks. Meanwhile, a $200M *fund-of-funds* may be able to commit $5-15M. In this example, the pension fund might be our anchor investor, putting up $30M of our $150M fund, while the fund-of-funds is in for $15M. Each will have a commensurate stake in our investments (20% and 10%).

If we have done a great job selling our story and are lucky enough to have good timing, our fund may get *oversubscribed*, meaning we received commitments for more capital than we targeted. This is a good problem to have, but it still can be a problem.

Remember our strategy to invest in 15 early stage startups with our three partners? If we raise a larger fund, we will either need to get more partners, invest more per startup or work harder to put the money to work.

> **Think like a VC...**
> Be very wary about deviating from your original investment strategy. There will be many temptations to stray.

It is a good problem, and a validation of our fund's value proposition, but it is not the awesome situation it may appear to be on the surface.

Top quartile VC firms, those that perform in the top 25% of the industry, regularly oversubscribe. They will generally stick pretty close to their target and simply cherry pick the LPs that they would prefer to work with, LPs that can write big checks and are not too intrusive. For the rest of the industry, it can be difficult to pass up the extra cash, and many firms will increase the fund size by 10-20% and adjust their strategy accordingly.

Let's keep it simple and assume we reached our fundraising goal. We are now ready to start investing in startups! Ironically, to announce that we are open for business as VCs, we must first announce that our *fund is closed*. The terminology is confusing. The fund is now closed to any more LPs, but it is finally *open* for investing in startups.

> *VCs begin investing out of a fund once it is "closed."*

If we have yet to reach our goal of $150M but already have a very hot prospect for a startup investment, we have a couple of options. We could close the fund at a lower level, though this is not ideal, as it will mean we will need to alter our strategy (and receive lower fees, addressed below). The better choice, if our LPs are amenable, is to announce a *partial close* at the lower level, indicating that we are still fundraising to reach our goal. This will allow us to start making investments using capital from our current LPs.

Capital Calls

After we have closed or partially closed the fund, we still don't have any cash in our bank account. Rather, we have *commitments* from LPs: the promise that cash will be delivered when called upon. After we have identified a startup and are ready to invest, we put out a *capital call* to our LPs, who are then obligated to wire their specific percentage of the investment to us. We'll aggregate the funding from all the LPs into a single account and wire the full investment to the startup.

Figure: Capital call

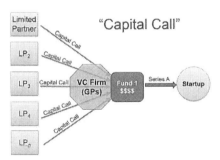

Since different LPs will have committed different amounts to the VC fund, they will be wiring us different amounts on a capital call commensurate with their percentage stake in our fund. Our $30M anchor LP, for example, upon receiving a capital call for a $2M investment, would send 20% of $2M, or $400,000. Our 10% fund-of-funds would wire $200,000. As the VC firm, we would collect and aggregate the entire round before wiring the full $2M to the startup.

All our LPs are motivated to honor capital calls thanks to very severe penalties in our term sheets which could result in an LP losing all of their investments to date as well as any right to continue investing in our fund. The harshness of these penalties makes sense considering the importance of capital calls. The whole system falls apart if anyone can stop wiring cash.

Our LPs are taking quite a leap of faith about when their capital will be put to work. They are also taking a leap of faith about when it will be returned. We are not planning to return any capital until after an exit, which will be several years in the coming.

10-year Fund Life

LPs are signing on for a very interesting *"we don't know when we'll put the money in or get it back"* arrangement. To contain some of this uncertainty, the standard agreement that has not changed since the industry began is to put a ten year window on the fund. LPs are thus signing up for a ten year ride, having committed to respond to every capital call for the next decade.

Think like a VC...
Add time limits to your investments. You can always extend them. Limits provide a mechanism to check-in and reconsider.

For a fund to go through its entire cycle in 10 years, it must follow a somewhat predictable pattern: new investments (*Series A*) for the first few years only, *follow-on rounds (Series B, C, etc.)* for the middle years and exits for the last few years.

Figure: 10-year fund life

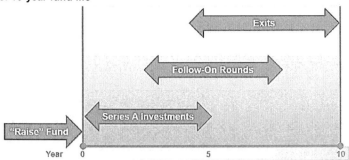

Capital calls may happen anywhere along the way, for new or follow-on rounds. At this point, it might cross your mind, why would an LP sign up for this? Aren't endowment fund managers looking for consistent, predictable returns? How can an LP commit to an investment when they don't know when the cash will go in or come out, other than they expect to be out by the end of 10 years or so? Do any of these people even have these same jobs in 10 years?

The answer is pretty clear if you break down the risk and reward potential. Let's start on the risk side. First, the fund manager is only putting a small percentage, less than 5%, of their entire fund into this asset class. Even if the entire amount were to be lost, it would be a relatively low percentage of the entire fund.

Second, there is almost no chance that the entire VC investment will be lost. Each VC firm has a portfolio of startups, and while each startup is quite risky, the overall portfolio has a good chance of at least breaking even. So for LPs, the downside is quite limited.

On the other hand, the upside can be fantastic if they happen to get into the next WhatsApp, Facebook or Google. The relatively small bet on the VC sector could actually move the needle on the overall returns for the entire endowment.

LP perspective: there is little chance a VC firm will fail completely and some chance it'll hit big.

Let's do some math on an example of unicorn return, making some guesses based on Google. It was reported that Sequoia Capital and Kleiner Perkins (KPCB) invested $25M for 20% of Google in 1999.[11]

Five years later, Google IPO'd to the tune of something like $26B. After some waffling, the stock went up, further increasing returns for VCs and LPs alike. There are a bunch of unknowns because this was *private* equity, and the details of the deals are not public information, but we can take a stab that the returns on that original $25M were somewhere in the $4-10 billion range, or half that for each venture firm.

Figure: Google as an example of a unicorn exit

Looking at 1999, I'm guessing Sequoia was investing out of their eighth fund (Sequoia VIII, $250M) and KPCB was on either VII or VIII ($300M or $550M respectively). No matter how you slice it, both firms *returned the fund* many times over. $4B to Sequoia VIII would represent 16X *on the fund!*

On page 31, I walk through the mathematics of a hit record and assert that from a record label's view, there are the hits, and then there is everything else. Notice in the graphic below how the Google exit would dwarf everything else in the portfolio. This includes busts, of course, but in my image below, I also include two other "return the fund" exits!

---

[11] Here's a fun walk down memory lane, a press release announcing Google's $25M investment from Sequoia and Kleiner Perkins, bit.ly/google25m.

Figure: Hits and everything else

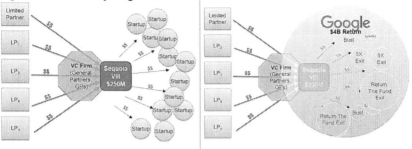

An LP who put $10M into Sequoia VIII would have gotten $160M back *on that one deal.* For fun, I looked up one of Sequoia's LPs, Duke Endowment, which was just north of $3B back in 2004. Google alone potentially contributed 5% to Duke's Endowment that year, an incredible bump for a little gamble.

Good news for Duke, they were also in Kleiner Perkins! (Eugene Kleiner, BTW, was one of the Traitorous Eight, p. 13.) Other LPs included the endowments from the universities of Michigan, Chicago, California, Vanderbilt, Yale, Harvard, MIT, and Georgia Tech. These LPs may have seen their entire endowments get a bump near 10% thanks to this very small bet. Careers were made.

> *LP return on Google: $10M in, $160M out (speculating).*

Multiple Funds

We've gotten ahead of ourselves with returns here. Back to the context of fundraising, with a fund limit of 10 years you might wonder how VCs remain employed for decades. Simple (conceptually), they just have to keep raising more funds! A successful venture capital *firm* will raise numerous venture capital *funds*, which usually carry the firm name with a number attached, like Sequoia I, Sequoia II, etc.

I'm sure it is no surprise that both KPCB and Sequoia were able to raise many funds given a track record that included Google, not to mention other winners in their portfolios. Both firms continue to be bastions of the industry, with LPs clamoring over themselves to invest. Together the two firms have raised, wait for it, 80 funds! Recent ones include KPCB XVI (2014, $450M) and Sequoia Capital US Venture XIV (2012, $553M).

Figure: A VC firm needs to raise a Fund II to continue making new investments

Mega and Micro Funds

If you noticed that the fund sizes seem, well, sizable, you're onto something. There has been an industry trend over the decades of fund sizes growing and growing. It is no small feat to put a half billion dollars to work *in startups*. Up until 2008, it seemed that megafunds approaching $1B each were going to be the norm. The industry was taking a lot of flak for not really investing in startups anymore, waiting for other investors to bring along new companies until they are big enough to handle a $10-50M cash infusion.

In recent years there has been a barbell trend. Megafunds over a half billion dollars continue to get raised, but there is also a trend of smaller funds, sometimes called micro-funds, often defined as $50M or under. Some larger funds also earmark a percentage of the big fund, sometimes called a *side* seed or opportunity fund, for early stage investing.

Fee Structure

Just as other professional fund managers charge fees, so do venture capitalists. There are two sources of income for a VC firm, the *management fees* and the *carry*, and the most common fee structure,

> *Most common fee structure is 2/20.*

similar to other private equity and hedge funds, is 2/20, meaning 2% management fees and 20% carry.

Management fees supply the baseline cash that keeps the firm in operation. These expenses include salaries for GPs and all other employees, rental costs for office space, travel expenses and any other overhead. You might think of these fees as the *keep the lights on* source of income. These fees will vary, but on average are in the 2% range.

Micro funds, thus, need to be scrappy. A $25M fund, for example, would only produce $500K in annual management fees. It is easy to see why small VC firms do not have much support staff. There is barely enough there to pay for office space and salaries for the partners.

More important to the long-term welfare of the general partners is the *carry*, or *carried interest*. This is basically a profit sharing arrangement that splits any capital after the firm has returned to limited partners their entire investment. Carry can vary dramatically depending on the track record of the venture firm, but 20% seems to be an industry benchmark.

In our Google example above, let's conjecture that Sequoia received somewhere near $4B into its Sequoia VII fund, which was a $250M fund. After the first $250M was distributed to LPs, the next $3.75B was split between LPs and GPs. Sequoia already had an amazing track record, and reportedly had carry in the 30% range. That would result in the partners at Sequoia receiving nearly $1B. I cannot find an exact number of partners, but I would estimate 15 or so, maybe 20. Even at 20, that's an average of $50M each, though it would not be divided evenly. [12]

Even if my assumptions are off by an order of magnitude, the point remains the same. Things can go very, very well.

Corporate VC

There is another class of venture capital that has very different fundraising needs (or lack thereof). *Corporate venture capital* refers to the investment arms of major corporations. No LPs or GPs. Just the mother ship and some specialized employees. Venerable corporate venture names include Google Ventures, Intel Capital, Dell Ventures,

> There is one type of VC fund that doesn't have to deal with LPs: corporate VC.

---

[12] Here's an interesting blog by Bill Burnham taking a more robust stab at these calculations: bit.ly/google4b.

Qualcomm Ventures and Johnson and Johnson Development Corporation.

While all corporate VC funds depend on the corporation for funding, they run a spectrum of independence when it comes to how they make investment decisions. At one end are funds that operate entirely independently, deploying capital like traditional VC funds with a singular focus: financial returns. These entities may report directly to the CFO and be considered financial instruments.

At the other end of the spectrum are strategic investors. These corporate venture funds pick startups that have some strategic value to the larger company. In these cases, venture capital is used as a substitute for traditional R&D in the search for disruptive innovation.[13]

Traditional VCs often refer to these corporate investors as *strategics.* Further, traditional VCs sometimes view these investors with skepticism because strategic investors notoriously overpay for startups. This tension is predicable since strategic investors have the potential for two types of return: financial and strategic. Traditional VCs are financial only. In the extreme, corporate venture capital can look like a pipeline for M&A, and indeed there are some similarities between M&A jobs and venture capital (see *Sidebar about VC vs. M&A*, p. 89).

Fundraise Summary

VCs are GPs who get commitments from LPs seeking a high ROI. A VC *firm* aspires to raise numerous VC *funds*, each of which has a 10-year life and will have its own portfolio of startups. LPs do not actually *invest* until there is a capital call, and they don't get any money back until there is a *distribution* from a *liquidity event*. Once the firm *returns the*

WHAT WE COVERED

Fundraise

- Fundraising Strategy
- Capital Calls
- 10-year Fund Life
- Peek at Return Potential
- Multiple Funds
- Mega and Micro Funds
- Fee Structure
- Corporate VC

---

[13] "New Game for Corporate R&D and VC," Igor Sill, 2012, http://bit.ly/vcr004.

B. VC Job Cycle

fund, the carry is split between LPs and GPs, most commonly 80/20.

Chapter Questions

1. How long is the life of a venture capital firm? Fund?
2. What are LPs? What is a capital call?
3. When is a VC fund considered "closed?"
4. About how many years into a VC fund would you expect the VCs to stop making investments in new startups?
5. How are VCs raising a fund similar to founders raising capital for a startup?
6. What factors are considered when VCs are determining the size of a fund they would like to raise?

Case Study: VCIC Ventures, Fund I

Jeff was a tech whiz who had started a social networking company that raised $30M in venture funding before being acquired for $300M. After exiting his startup, Jeff dabbled in angel investing and discovered that he really enjoyed finding and mentoring promising young entrepreneurs. He felt that he had a winning formula for angel investing, but he was frustrated that he could not participate in later rounds as his successful angel investments began to grow and raise venture capital. He started exploring the idea of raising a venture fund so that he could continue to be involved in the startups he had nurtured.

Mark was a principal at a well-known VC firm. Whenever he found a promising startup, he would have to find a partner at the firm to champion the deal at the Monday partner meetings. It was Mark who had brought Jeff's original startup to his firm, but it was someone else at the firm, a partner, who received most of the credit. As always, the partners also received the financial rewards of the successful exit.

Jeff and Mark had hit it off since the beginning and kept in touch even after the acquisition. When Jeff had the idea of starting a new VC firm, Mark was the first person he approached. He figured Mark knew how a good VC firm should operate, and perhaps he would be ready to go out on his own.

The two decided to join forces to start an early stage fund. In putting together an investment strategy, they built off of Jeff's successful angel track record and Mark's understanding of how a VC

---

firm operates. They decided that they would target 2-3 new investments per year with a total of about 12 investments in their portfolio. Since their winning formula was in finding very early companies, they targeted $250,000 to $1M as their first money into each startup, reserving another $2-4M for later rounds. With 12 total investments and $4M as the target total investment in each, they decided to raise a $50M fund, called *VCIC I*.

They went with the traditional 2/20 fee structure, in which they would receive an annual 2% of the *assets under management* ($50M), or $1M per year. In addition to their salaries, the operating budget included rent for an office near a local accelerator, salary for a part-time administrative assistant, extensive travel and outsourced bookkeeping and HR.

TO PONDER: If you were a colleague of Jeff and Mark and wanted to join their firm, how might you pitch yourself to convince them to include you as a third partner in their new fund? How would a third partner change the fund size?

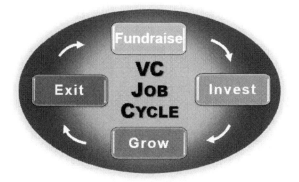

4. Invest

Contents

Recall our definition for venture capital is *institutional equity investing in high growth startups*. We've discussed the institutions that trust us to manage a small portion of their capital, and we've looked closely at the hit-driven model that defines the type of high growth startups we can invest in. But how do we find them?

Deal Flow

With our fund closed, we are ready to invest! It is time to go unicorn hunting, a process lovingly referred to as *sourcing deals*. In this capacity, VCs are like the old-fashioned A&R reps of the big music labels. *Arts and repertoire,* A&R guys were the talent scouts.[14] It was their job to scour

---

[14] Just like venture capitalists, the vast majority of A&R reps were men.

the clubs to find the next hot band, sign them up and develop them into stars.

VCs similarly must work their channels to find the next great startup. This is a surprise to many entrepreneurs, who fantasize that VCs are kicking back in La-Z-Boy chairs, smoking cigars and dolling out cash like the *Godfather* or the sharks on the TV show *Shark Tank*.

Most VCs will tell you that venture capital is a service business. They don't *just* provide capital. They also provide advice and connections. They have reputations for *adding value* beyond the checks that they write. Their ability to attract the best startups is based on their reputations.

As any talent scout will tell you, good acts don't just fall in your lap. You have to hustle. Case in point is the *unsolicited submission*. Just as A&R guys hated ye ole unsolicited demo tape, VCs similarly begrudge anything coming *over the transom*.[15] VC firms receive hundreds of random pitch decks. Bigger firms may have interns or young analysts take a quick look at these, but for the most part, time spent going through these submissions is not well spent.

Figure: My band's demo tape, circa early '90s

VCs maintain extensive networks to create *deal flow*. Startup referrals can come from any of the various constituencies VCs regularly work with: startup attorneys, serial entrepreneurs, industry experts, portfolio company employees, M&A professionals, investment bankers, angel investors and, of course, other VCs.

VCs spend a lot of time at industry events to keep these networks active. National conferences, venture showcases and even some high profile startup competitions—all of these events are opportunities for VCs to work the rooms to nurture relationships with experts within their ecosystem who might eventually be helpful for sourcing deals,

---

[15] A phrase borrowed from the publishing industry, referring to manuscripts tossed into the publisher's window by wayward authors.

performing due diligence, finding a strategic partner for a portfolio company or even exploring exit opportunities.

If you ever see a VC as a guest speaker, on a panel, judging a competition or teaching a class, note that that they have incentives to take part in these activities beyond giving back to their alma mater and communities. VCs need to build their reputations and expand their networks. These events help VCs brand themselves as trustworthy and accessible members of the startup ecosystem.

Syndicate Partners

> *A* syndicate *is a group of VC firms in one deal.*

Just like the music business, in which record labels could find themselves in a bidding war over the hottest bands, VC firms often must compete to get *in the deal* for the hottest startups. However, unlike the music business, VC firms sometimes come together in a deal by *syndicating,* meaning more than one VC firm participating in a round of equity.

Somewhat counter-intuitively, *syndication* has become a ubiquitous industry practice. It would seem like a tricky decision for a VC to bring in another VC firm on a deal. If our firm found a great startup and thought we could make a lot of money, why would we want to share that upside?

It turns out that the benefits of syndication outweigh the downside of shared success. Perhaps the most important benefit: to get to unicorn status, the startup will ultimately need to raise more than we can likely supply ourselves, which means we'll eventually need more investors anyway. If that is the case, it is a good idea to bring them in early so that they are part of the entire process with incentives aligned with our own.[16]

In addition to the likelihood that we'll need the extra cash, we could use extra *help* turning the startup into a unicorn. The more VC firms we have behind this startup, the greater our chances of success, one could

---

[16] I don't want to get into the math yet, but later stage investors have incentives to lower the valuation in later rounds. Early stage investors want to see valuations increasing to compensate for early stage risk. "Last money in dictates the terms."

argue. Each firm has a network of portfolio companies, serial entrepreneurs, potential acquirers and a whole range of industry experts who could be helpful. At the very least, we'll have more people pulling for us and fewer rooting against us.

There is another crucial benefit to bringing in a syndicate: confirmation that we aren't crazy. Hunting unicorns is tricky business, and like many creative endeavors, there is a very blurry line between genius and crazy. If we can find another VC firm willing to join us in an investment, we have solid validation that we are onto something good. We also have a CYA (cover-your-ass) plan to take to our LPs in case the whole thing blows up. (A VC once told me, "You'll never get fired for syndicating with Sequoia.")

While you might deduce that VCs would want to invest alone, it turns out that they almost always syndicate at some point before a startup exits. Exactly when to bring in syndicate partners can be a source of internal conflict for a VC, whose duty is to maximize returns for LPs. One common tactic is to take an early, smaller round in its entirety with the plan to begin courting syndicates for the following, bigger rounds.

Benefits of syndication:
1. *Shared capital risk*
2. *More resources*
3. *Sanity check*

Firms often invest different amounts in the round and may have different levels of involvement. Generally, one firm *leads the deal*, meaning that firm does the bulk of the due diligence. Sometimes firms will co-lead.

Often the *lead investor* is the firm that discovered the startup, but it is not a hard rule. It is also common for the firm that makes the largest investment to be the lead, but again, this is not set in stone. Lastly, the most prestigious firm in the syndicate will often take the lead.

For other VC firms to be a valid source of deal flow, you must become a VC that others want to work with. This theme will reappear numerous times in this book. This is a people industry built on reputations. To get into the best deals, you need a great reputation.

Accelerators

Another very important development in VC deal sourcing over the last decade has been the emergence of the startup accelerator. In 2005, Y-Combinator launched the first class of what would become known as an accelerator by combining seed stage investing with offerings that formerly were associated with business incubators.[17] TechStars followed a couple of years later, and today there are hundreds of accelerators, over 450 in 2015 according to *Entrepreneur* magazine.

The accelerator model has evolved, but at its core it usually includes a seed investment, usually $25,000-50,000, in exchange for a small amount of equity, usually 6-8%. Startups usually join in cohorts and spend 10-12 weeks together in an open working space. Mentors are brought in regularly to help each startup team. The theory is that the program will *accelerate* the development of these early stage companies. The programs usually end with a *demo day* attended by angel investors and VCs.

Startups coming out of accelerators are usually still a bit too early for a Series A, having received maybe $50,000 to date and probably needing less than $100,000 to hit the next milestones. Many accelerators have follow-on seed investment funds to further support strong graduates. While it is early for VCs, we'll often attend demo days to network and start early relationships to be in a good position for a Series A should one materialize.

> *Top Accelerators:*
> *Y Combinator:*
> *$120K for 7%;*
> *TechStars: $20K for*
> *6% + $100K*
> *convertible debt.*

---

[17] Here is a nice write-up from Paul Graham, co-founder of Y-Combinator, about how they got started, old.ycombinator.com/start.html.

Once we have found a startup that we are excited about, we begin the *due diligence* process in which we attempt to uncover everything we can to make sure this investment will be a good one. We'll want to see all of the financials of the startup; talk with key customers to gauge how well the startup is meeting their needs; reach out to our own industry experts, sometimes for a fee, to get their opinions about the startups offerings; and even run background checks on the founders.

> *Due Diligence: research performed by investors once they are interested in a startup.*

This process can easily take months, but if markets are *frothy* (lots of deals are happening quickly), or we are particularly enthusiastic about an investment, due diligence can be compressed into weeks, sometimes even days.

If we are considering building a syndicate, we'll send the pitch deck around to other VCs to get their feedback. If we are *leading the deal*, we will do most of the due diligence. If we are joining a syndicate led by another firm, we will likely take a backseat in this process, doing minimal due diligence to piggyback onto the efforts of the lead firm.

Term Sheet

Somewhere in the due diligence process, when we become confident that the deal will happen, we will *put down a term sheet*. This is a contract that lays out the general terms of the deal we are offering the startup, with the caveat that there will be more due diligence and more specifics to be worked out before the final deal is inked.[18]

The venture capital term sheet is akin to the home-buying contract. When a real estate sign says *under contract*, it means that the seller and buyer have signed a contract that spells out their intentions to have a transaction, though there are still some details to be worked out. The

---

[18] For an example, you can download a model term sheet from the National Venture Capital Association, https://nvca.org/resources/.

actual sale of the home has not been executed. That happens on closing day.

Similarly, a term sheet is a contract that is a part of the process, not the end of the process. The terms in the term sheet will be negotiated between investors and startups, and the signed document will serve as a road map for the process to follow.

> *A term sheet is part of the process, not the end.*

Term sheets are loaded with, wait for it, *terms*, many of which have far reaching implications. For a comprehensive run-down of deal terms, I highly recommend the aforementioned *Venture Deals, Be Smarter than Your Lawyer and Venture Capitalist*, by Brad Feld and Jason Mendelson of the Foundry Group. It is a very practical approach for founders to learn more about term sheets before negotiating with VCs.

For now, let's focus on the two fundamental terms: *investment size* and *valuation*. These are the two items in the term sheet that spell out exactly what percentage of the company is being purchased by the new equity partners.

Investment Size and Valuation

If you've ever seen the show *Shark Tank*, you've seen offerings like these:

X% of the company being sold for $Y

or

For $Y we are offering X% of our company.

This is the layman's approach to an equity deal, and it is conceptually accurate. But in practical terms, it is misleading. The current founders do not sell some of their own shares to the new investors. Rather, new shares are created and sold by the startup, resulting in more overall shares as well as a cash infusion into the company.

Figure: New preferred shares created for VCs

The founders will own a smaller percentage of a larger pie as a result of the pool being *diluted* by the new shares. The founders' 100% ownership pre-investment will be diluted by the creation of new shares, not by selling off some of their pre-existing shares.

Dilution is a scary thing, and many entrepreneurs struggle with losing a certain percentage of their baby. VCs will say, *it's better to have a slice of watermelon than a whole grape.*

> *Dilution is the lowering of overall percent ownership caused by issuing new shares.*

To facilitate the issuance of shares of stock, the startup must be incorporated. VCs cannot invest in an LLC or other entity for this reason. Startups pursuing venture capital must incorporate at some point before the investment.

While the founders' *percentage of ownership* in the startup has been diluted, the *overall value* of the founders' stock has not changed during this transaction. Rather, the valuation of the startup has increased by the exact amount of cash it received. In other words, if a founder owned 100% of a $1M startup and was diluted to 75%, that 75% would still be worth $1M and the startup would now be worth $1.33M, having received a $330K investment. (We'll cover the math soon!)

Option Pools

There is one more important variable that complicates this algebra: the *option pool*. These are new shares that are created and put in reserve to be used for incentives for key employees, most commonly to help recruit new C-level management: chief marketing officer, chief technology officer, perhaps even a new chief executive officer.

Figure: New shares created for option pool

The size of the option pool will vary depending on the needs of the startup. If we have a seasoned team of serial entrepreneurs, the option pool could be below 5%, recognizing that the key players are in place. On the other hand, with a couple of first-time entrepreneurs right out of college, we may need a large option pool, say 20%, to attract important new team members.

> *By convention, option pools are added pre-investment, diluting early shareholders, not the current investors.*

I do not want to get too complicated with the algebra yet, but these new shares, just like the new shares created for the VCs, further dilute the founders. The VCs in this round are *not* diluted by the option pool.

This is by convention, not by arithmetic. Theoretically, a strong founding team could negotiate that the dilution of the option pool be shared by the VCs, but industry standard has been that the founders take this hit entirely.

Pre-Money and Post-Money Valuation

The overall value of the startup just prior to the investment is called the *pre-money valuation*. Just after the investment, it is called *post-money*. The investment is wired directly into the startup's bank account and is the exact difference between the pre-money and post-money valuations.

Figure: Pre-money + Investment = Post-Money

What we agree the   The cash the startup   What the startup will
startup is now worth   will soon have in its   be worth directly after
                         bank account   the investment

VCs don't offer deals like Sharks do, offering to buy *X% for $Y*. We are not buying a percentage of the pre-existing startup; we are expanding the company's value by a specific amount (the investment), for which we will receive a specific number of (preferred) shares of new stock, thereby owning a percentage of the new, bigger entity.

For example, a VC would not offer *$1M for half of the company*. Rather, we would offer *a $1M investment on a $1M pre-money valuation*. The investment goes into the bank account of the startup to be used to create more value (by hitting milestones). The investors do end up owning half of the company, which is worth twice as much because it has $1M in the bank.[19]

Figure: "1 on 1" deal, $2M post

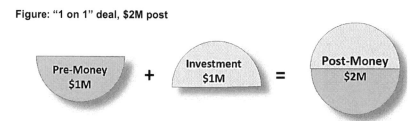

Cap Table

Between founders, investors and options, the allocation of the equity can get complicated fast. The *capitalization table* is the spreadsheet that indicates who owns what. Again, we don't want to delve too deeply into the mathematics yet, but I want you to see an example of a cap table for a Series A (below).

	Common		Series A (Preferred)		Total Post A		
	Shares	Valuation	Shares	Investment	Shares	%	Value
PREFERRED							
Vernon Capital			6,000,000	$ 3,000,000	6,000,000	37.5%	$ 3,000,000
VCIC Ventures			2,000,000	$ 1,000,000	2,000,000	12.5%	1,000,000
COMMON							
Founder #1	2,500,000	$1,250,000			2,500,000	15.6%	$ 1,250,000
Founder #2	1,500,000	$750,000			1,500,000	9.4%	750,000
Founder #3	1,500,000	$750,000			1,500,000	9.4%	750,000
Options Added Pre-A	2,500,000	$1,250,000			2,500,000	15.6%	1,250,000
Total	8,000,000	$4,000,000	8,000,000	$4,000,000	16,000,000	100%	$8,000,000
		Pre-Money ↑		Investment ↑			Post Money ↑

Pre-Money ÷ Shares = Share Price → $0.5

---

[19] These days I often hear "$1M on a $2M post-money valuation." As we see below, I wonder if they got this idea from the popularity of *Shark Tank*.

B. VC Job Cycle

This cap table above represents a *4 on 4* deal: a negotiated pre-money valuation of $4M and a negotiated total Series A round of $4M, resulting in an $8M post money valuation. There was also a negotiated option pool just over 15%. You can see in this cap chart that the option pool was created by adding shares "Pre-A," thus diluting the common shareholders and not the new preferred shareholders. You can also see that the round was syndicated, with two VC firms in the deal.[20]

We'll dive more deeply into a cap table in Part III when we walk through an exit analysis.

Investment Size: Startup Perspective

The most basic terms on the term sheet are the investment size and the pre-money valuation, often stated as an $X investment on a Y pre-money. But where do these numbers come from? Traditionally, it is the VCs who *put down a term sheet*. Does that mean the VCs choose these numbers?

The answer is that both numbers are negotiated and are influenced by a variety of factors, some driven by the startup and its needs, and some the VCs and their needs.

Let's start with the investment size, as it is the startup's need for capital that has initiated this whole process. Earlier, we discussed that VC firms begin fundraising by developing a fund strategy, including the fund size. Then they go on a roadshow, pitching their fundraising goal. "We're raising a $250M fund to invest in early stage startups, leveraging our expertise in…"

The same is true with startups. Founders must put together a growth strategy for their startup to include the amount of funding they are currently seeking to facilitate that growth. This may seem counterintuitive. Why not just raise as much as possible, let the market decide how much it'll give you?

> *Founders should attempt to raise a specific amount to hit specific milestones.*

---

[20] To see a Google sheet of this cap table, go to bit.ly/vcic-cap-table.

There is a very compelling reason founders should *not* raise more than needed. One word, dilution. Founders should want to hit milestones as quickly as possible because doing so will raise the valuation of the startup. The higher the valuation, the less the dilution. So founders should only raise enough (with some cushion) to hit some milestones.

Of course, everyone knows that entrepreneurs have numerous backup plans. In addition to the strategy being pitched, founders should have plans for different levels of funding, including a backup plan for bootstrapping in case fundraising is a flop. But the pitch to VCs needs to be the optimistic, *go big or go home* strategy that VCs need to hear: a moonshot strategy that could *return the fund* for whoever is receiving the pitch.

Here's what not to pitch: *With this investment, we will be able to reach profitability this year and never need any more funding.*

Red flag! This would demonstrate that you *don't have a clue*. This is a bank pitch. They'd love for you to hit profitability right away and pay them back. They don't care if you go to the moon because they will see none of that upside.

> *Founders should pitch maximum return for investors, not quickest path to profitability!*

But VCs want a moonshot. Unlike banks, VCs don't care about near-term profitability. In fact, they may *never* care about profitability in your startup. They care about value creation.

Isn't that the same thing, you ask? Not necessarily, particularly in early stage tech companies. VCs need the highest valuation at exit regardless of the current profitability of the company. Sometimes these are related, but more often in *early or growth stage* they are not. The valuation is based on future earnings potential, not on current profitability.

An extreme example is Amazon.com, which went public in 1997. Twenty years later, in 2017, Amazon had hardly reported any profit, having poured all operating cash flow back into growth. However,

Amazon's revenue numbers have consistently and impressively continued to rise, resulting in a market cap that is nearing $1 trillion in 2018. True, Amazon *could* be profitable if it chose to slow down its growth. Perhaps the most impressive part of this story is that Amazon is still in fast growth mode over 20 years after going public!

For VCs, growth is our goal over profitability. This is why we might walk away from a founder pitching that they'll hit break-even this year. We don't want to break even; we want supercharged growth! Growth is expensive. Profitability takes a hit when your goal is growth. Rather than tying a VC investment to profitability, we need to identify the *milestones* we'll have to hit on our way to hockey stick growth.

Milestones

Founders of tech startups need to make sure they are not in bootstrap mode when they start thinking about venture capital. You should <u>not</u> need the cash to keep the doors open or make payroll. Those are not value creating milestones. VCs invest in growth.

The goal of VC funding should be to hit a series of ever-increasingly important milestones on the way to a big *exit*. As a founder, your job is to create that list of milestones as part of your strategic plan to get to the moon (used to be called a business plan).

With that plan in the pitch deck, you should only try to raise enough cash this round to hit a big milestone or two. Then you should be planning for future rounds for future milestones.

A milestone can be any number of things depending on your industry: a prototype, a technical proof of concept, a beta launch, your first customer, your first Fortune 500 customer, your 1,000th customer, a new product launch, a new feature set launched, a patent secured, etc. (see table of example milestones on p. 227).

> *Milestone hit =*
> *risk reduced =*
> *valuation increased.*

All of these things reduce risk. They help prove that you are onto something. They corroborate the intuition that your startup has value. That validation adds value, which translates into increased valuation.

Startups: More or Less Money Now?

As a rule, founders should not want to take any more money than is necessary to hit a significant milestone because hitting that milestone will increase valuation. When valuation goes up, the share price goes up, meaning you can sell fewer shares for the same amount of money, minimizing dilution. The plan should be for a Series A to hit certain milestones, followed by a Series B at a higher valuation once the milestones are hit.

Of course, it is not certain that a founder will hit the milestones nor be able to raise another round. Those are big *ifs*, and most entrepreneurs are survivalists. So there is an incentive to get as much cash as possible when you can get it. More cash now means more wiggle room to recover from any potential problems down the road.

Fundraising can also take time and energy away from growing the business. It is distracting for a CEO to have to be on the road fundraising all the time rather than running the company. This is a powerful incentive to raise more money now, even though it is more expensive, i.e., results in more dilution, to do so.

> *Founders have to balance the temptation of extra funding with selling too much too soon.*

So there is an internal conflict on the founders' side: get as much funding as possible versus waiting until milestones are hit and dilution won't be as big an issue.

Investment Size: VC Perspective

We just spent a lot of time looking at investment size as a function of the startup's strategy. Here's a shocker: from the VC's perspective, the startup's strategy is not the main factor. It is but one of many variables in determining how much to invest in a given startup. Just as important to a VC is the amount of capital we need to *put to work* so that we can provide a return to our LPs.

Before a VC considers investing in a startup, there are some pre-determined parameters based on the fund that was raised. The typical investment size for a new investment, for example, will have been determined by our fund size and strategy. If we told LPs that we were investing an average of $15M in early stage biotech startups, we'll have some explaining to do if we are now looking at a $500,000 investment in a tech startup.

We can certainly make some exceptions when we find exceptional startups. Our LPs trust that we will be opportunistic, but within reason. Out of the gate, our fund norms are going to be very influential as we look at new investments. We'll want new investments to fit our *fund profile*.

VCs: More or Less Money Now?

VCs also have an internal conflict when it comes to the investment size of a given round. If we are bullish on a startup, we may want to *put more money to work*, thereby getting more equity for lower dollars and increasing the potential return on this round's investment.

Contrarily, VCs have an incentive to limit our exposure by only risking a little bit of capital now, knowing we'll have the opportunity to invest again if things go well. Yes, it will be more expensive, but it will be worth it because it will be less risky.

Another variable for the VCs is our fund size. We need the total investment into a startup to be enough to *move the needle* on our fund size. As we've pointed out, if your fund size is $500M, it doesn't help to

> *VCs have to balance the need to put capital to work with mitigating risk.*

have a 20X return on a $100K investment, or $2M, grossing a measly 1% of your fund.

Investment Size Summary

As you can see above, there are a number of potential conflicts regarding investment size that can arise when founders and VCs come together. It is not as simple as a founder pitching a specific funding need and an investor deciding whether to fill that need. VCs are aware of the numerous variables that founders are considering when raising capital. Founders similarly should understand the complex system through which VCs operate. Without VCs there to make tough decisions, LPs would never have made this capital available to startups.

To think like a VC, you need to see and hear opportunities as they are presented to you, but you must also put them into the context of your complicated life, with your metaphorical portfolio of opportunities and LPs breathing down your neck. Don't be afraid to assert a change in the terms of an opportunity to make it fit into your portfolio and make your LPs happy.

Valuations

Above we discussed some of the considerations when negotiating the investment size. It is a very important meeting of the minds. Founders and investors need to be on the same page about the specific "use of funds." They need to agree about how they will work together, on the same side of the table, to create value.

However, before they are on the same side of the table, they have to reach a deal. They have to agree on a *price*, which comes in the form of a *valuation.* It is the valuation that determines how much of the startup the VCs will have purchased with our investment.

Figure: Determining VC ownership

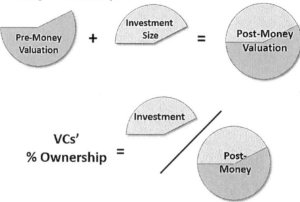

B. VC Job Cycle

VCs like to say that coming up with a valuation is more art than science. True, there is no algebraic formula to determine valuation. But the process VCs use to determine the price they are willing to pay is pretty scientific: based on "systemic knowledge of the physical or material world gained through observations and experimentation."[21]

Perhaps what VCs really mean to say is that determining valuations is more science than math. In other words, you can't rely solely on spreadsheet calculations to determine a valuation, much to the chagrin of many a business school student.

> *Valuations are based on science, not art or math.*

In his book *Zero to One*, Peter Thiel defines valuation as the current value of the summation of all the money a company will make in the future. This is probably the least flawed conceptual framework in which to think about valuation, but it is also not that helpful given all of the unknowns. Said differently, what is the present value of all the value a startup can expect to create?

Thiel is using a derivative of a Finance 101 concept called *discounted cash-flow*, or *DCF*. The theory is that tomorrow's cash is worth less than it would be if you already had it today. Hence, tomorrow's cash needs to be *discounted* to give it a value today. A more practical way to say it:

ONE *bird in the hand is worth* **TWO** *in the bush*

The two future birds in the bush have been discounted by one-half to give the present value of one bird. Why the steep discount? Risk. There is a relatively high risk that you will fail to catch both birds.

Similarly, there is high risk that a startup will not reach the millions of dollars in revenues projected by its founders. Hence, those forecasts can be *discounted* to give us a present value, via DCF. Here's the rub, the amount by which we discount the future revenues is basically arbitrary. Like the one-half we used to discount two birds to one bird, we will similarly pick some number, called the *discount rate*, which we will find difficult to explain.

---

[21] http://www.dictionary.com/browse/science

DCF is case in point why valuations are science, not math, based on observations, not formulae. The moment you stick arbitrary numbers into a spreadsheet, very smart people have a tendency to fool themselves into believing their own misconceptions. Valuations should be somewhat fuzzy. When we see too much precision, we can't trust it.

Work Backwards from the Exit

VC's start with the same *discounted future value* framework but have a more practical bent. They ask, what do we think we can sell this company for in 5 years? Or, what do we project the valuation to be at exit?

The exit valuation is the proxy for Thiel's summation of future earnings. That will be the number from which we can reverse engineer through several rounds of investments back to today's round. It is this reverse algebra that will get us to an offer for a pre-money valuation.

From the VC's perspective, the current valuation does not live in a vacuum. It cannot be considered without thinking through the future. It is intrinsically tied to the next rounds of financing and the exit. So we, too, must move forward to understand the rest of the VC Job Cycle before we can fully understand the science of valuation.

Invest Summary

This has been a busy chapter! We've sourced deals, performed due diligence, built syndicates and put down term sheets. We've explored the complexities of the investment size, and we've lifted up the covers (ever so slightly) on valuations, to be revisited after we understand the rest of the VC Job Cycle. We've also looked briefly at deal algebra, which we will revisit in the Return Analysis chapter to come.

WHAT WE COVERED

Invest

- Deal Flow
- Syndicate Partners
- Accelerators
- Due Diligence
- Term Sheet
- Investment Size
- Option Pools
- Pre- and Post-Money
- Cap Table
- Milestones
- Valuations

Chapter Questions

1. What are the benefits of syndication?
2. Why do VCs work backwards from the exit?
3. Why might a founder have mixed feelings about how much money to raise?
4. Why might a venture capitalist be conflicted about how much money to invest?
5. What factors determine the size of a venture capital round?
6. Why are milestones important?
7. What is the mathematical formula to determine the percent ownership of a startup by VCs after a round of investing?
8. What is a "3 on 6" deal?
9. Why might you need a large option pool after a round of venture financing?
10. What is a capitalization table?
11. Why isn't the term sheet the end of the VC investment process?
12. What is deal flow and what are some things that VCs do to create it?
13. Explain why VCs use a watermelon/grape metaphor to explain to founders how dilution is not entirely a bad thing.
14. How much equity would VCs have in a startup after a 5 on 10 round? How about with a 20% option pool?

Case Study: VCIC Ventures Series A

Jeff and Mark are nearing the end of their third year of their first fund, *VCIC I*, a $50M micro-fund. Things are going very well, maybe a little too well. They had targeted 10-12 portfolio companies with a total of $4M for each. They have already invested in 8 seed rounds averaging $500,000. Two of those startup have gone on to raise Series A rounds at $3M and $4M.

VCIC I was the lead investor in both Series A rounds, with $1M and $2M investments, respectively. So far, they've had capital calls totaling $7M. Another $25M is reserved as *dry powder* for *follow-on rounds* for these 8 portfolio companies.

Today, they are really excited about a ninth company, brought to them by one of their syndicate partners on another deal. This one is a little unusual in that it is a Series A for a startup for which they did not participate in the seed round. The other firm will lead the Series A. *VCIC I* is being invited to piggyback on the round as a *follower*.

Having already invested in 8 seed rounds, Jeff and Mark are feeling the burn of juggling so many early stage companies at once. It seems that everybody needs help at the same time. Coming in as a follower for this Series A may be a good way to deploy some capital without depleting more of their human resources.

Meanwhile, they are nearly out of available funds for new investments. All 8 investments are ongoing, and all are (knock on wood) still very promising. This is great news, but it also means that all of the funds reserved for those investments needs to remain reserved. That leaves room for only two more investments. Should this Series A opportunity be one of those last two?

It is becoming increasingly clear that they need to raise a new fund, but it's early. Being only the third year of their fund, they have no exits to tout. The Series A rounds indicate a little increase in valuation for two of the early investments, but those are unrealized gains. They have executed their plan to the tee, but it is still unknown whether the plan was a good one. LPs have received no proceeds to date, and there are none on the horizon.

TO PONDER: If you were an LP, what would you want to hear from Jeff and Mark so that you would be comfortable allocating a portion of your portfolio to their new fund?

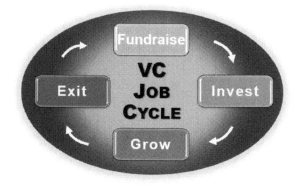

5. Grow

Contents

This aspect of the VC's job, helping startups grow, is perhaps least appreciated and yet most important. Most VCs I've worked with consider themselves company builders, not simply investors. They don't just create a portfolio and kick up their heels. For many, this is their favorite part of the job, rolling up their sleeves to help a startup succeed.

A startup is a unique type of investment going through a remarkable metamorphosis. The months following a venture capital investment are tumultuous for a startup and everyone who works there. Hopefully, it is a constructive tumult, a controlled mayhem, a chaotic but value-creating process.

There are many parallels here again with the music business. Our early startup is like a talented young band. Handing them $1M without any supervision is not a recipe for success. They need the guidance of industry pros who have been there, done that.

Record labels don't create a roster and walk away from it. They must *work the roster*. True, they need to attract top talent *to* the roster, but it is what they do with that talent that separates the top labels (and VC firms).

This flies in the face of the mythology of the *discovered artist*. In reality, thousands of artists are discovered and never become famous. When one does become famous, the myth is that the talent was retrospectively obvious and pre-determined. It was not.

Working the Portfolio

Labels and VC firms have entire bullpens full of potential. They constantly work the bullpen, keeping an eye on everyone's performance, looking for clues, any little hint that could indicate who might be the next breakout performer.

> A VC firm's portfolio, just like a record label's roster, is full of talent and potential.

Back in the day, when a new band started getting some regional radio airplay, the label would pour resources toward making a bigger success out of that small win. All of a sudden, that band would be booked on talk shows, the song would be placed in movies and promoters around the country would be hired to advocate for more radio play. A life-size full-color display would be set up at, I'm going to say it, *record* stores. Display ads would appear online. The band would go on tour as the opening act for a big national band.[22]

All of these things are very expensive. Record labels cannot commit these resources to every act on the roster. They have to work the bullpen and make tough decisions about the next act to get the benefit of the machine that is a major record label. You and I cannot call Steven

---

[22] Apologies for my Stone Age references to a record industry that no longer exists.

Spielberg and ask him to put our hot new band in his next movie. David Geffen can.

VCs similarly cannot commit all of their resources to every startup in their portfolio. They work the roster in their own way, similarly looking for *traction*, and similarly looking to push the gas pedal when something starts to take off.

I would argue that the true core competency of venture capitalists is the craft of working the portfolio, choosing when to pour on resources and when to withhold. It is the competency of grooming portfolio companies so that they may be in the position to become unicorns.

One key competency of VCs is developing, not just picking, unicorns.

Early stage investments are called "seed funding" for good reason. VCs plant a lot of seeds to see which ones will flourish. The seedlings that sprout get a whole lot of attention. The process is more like unicorn farming than hunting.

Just as record labels make stars out of raw talent, VCs know how to make unicorns out of startups. Nobody knows more about what it is like to grow a venture from 3 to 300 employees than the VCs, who have done it time and time again. Not many humans have experienced the roller coaster ride of growing startups.

Through this process, VCs and record labels share a moral hazard that individuals may not want to emulate. The bullpen model requires that some of the talent in the bullpen will inevitably be neglected. This *should* be the result of underperformance, but it is often a product of circumstance.

Think like a VC...

Only take on projects for which you are prepared to follow through, reserving 2-3X of your initial investment (energy, time, cash, creativity, etc.) for *follow-on rounds*.

Hence, my "Think like a VC" blurb in this section is <u>not</u> to create a portfolio of opportunities with the plan to bail on the ones that do not blossom. Rather, make sure only to take on projects for which you are prepared to follow through. As individuals, we'll be better served by choosing more carefully.

Follow-On Rounds

How do VCs create unicorns from portfolio companies? VCs can help in a variety of ways. Our expertise and vast networks are invaluable for connecting startups with potential partners and customers. Just as a record label can place a new artist in a big movie, VCs can make significant connections for startups.

Similarly, the deal itself is a form of credibility. A top VC firm backing a startup sends a significant signal to the industry indicating that the experts believe in the potential of that startup.

However, VCs have one main tool for growing companies: more capital. The first round of financing is just the beginning. If a startup gains traction, much more capital will be needed to reach unicorn-like growth levels.

As we've discussed, VCs are planning on several rounds of investing before exit. The *first institutional round*, when VCs enter the picture, is the *Series A*, and the plan is to have one or more follow-on rounds, called Series B, Series C, etc., on the way to a successful (big) exit.

Figure: Example follow-on rounds for unicorns

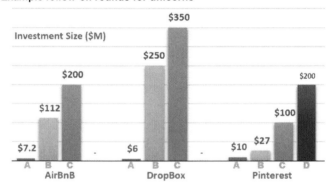

Let's recall that this happens within the framework of a 10-year fund, in which VCs can only make new investments for the first few years:

Figure: 10-Year fund life

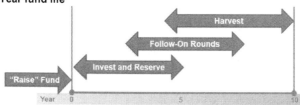

Below is an example of a startup that received two rounds of VC financing before reaching an exit. In this case, it was about 5 years from the Series A to exit, year 3 to year 8.

Figure: Example of a successful exit

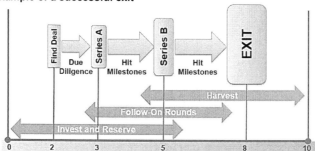

This pattern repeats itself throughout the fund's portfolio. For example, a typical mid-size fund might invest in somewhere between 15-25 startups, perhaps averaging 2-3 rounds of financing each. That's potentially 75 deals that have to be negotiated! You start to get the idea about why VCs have severe time constraints.

Figure: Portfolio of 10-20 investments

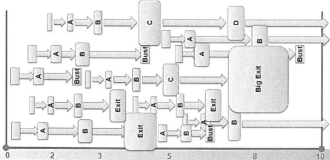

Reserve Capital

Every time our VC fund invests in a Series A, we make a note to save a certain amount of funding, called *reserve capital* or *dry powder,* to participate in *follow-on rounds* in that same startup. That is the plan. Several rounds. The reserved funding is somewhat conceptual. There is no real money put aside. There is no capital call today. However, everyone at our firm is on notice that some of our fund is reserved for this startup and cannot be used to invest in another Series A.

"Dry powder" is capital reserved for future rounds.

VCs often have a baseline plan to reserve 1-3X of the Series A investment for follow-on rounds. You might ask, why not just write a bigger check up front when the valuation is lower? Splitting the investment across multiple rounds is helpful in two ways: risk mitigation and opportunism.

We've already discussed how we can mitigate capital risk by investing less up front, giving us the ability to cut bait if the startup doesn't gain traction after a Series A. "Cut bait" in this case means to free up the funds that had been reserved for follow-on rounds. Those newly available funds can be redeployed into our winners.

We are hunting unicorns. When one of our startups starts looking like a unicorn, we'll want to pump as much capital as possible into its growth. This is exactly what record labels do with hot acts. As soon as one starts to take off, resources are reallocated from not-so-hot acts over to the hot act in an attempt to push the hit into mega-hit status.

As we discussed, one could argue that this was the core competency of the major record labels: identifying potential megahits within their roster and redeploying the resources necessary to fully capitalize on the opportunity.

In other words, it wasn't so much finding the early talent (signing new acts) as it was recognizing which artist on the roster was starting to take off, then jumping on the opportunity. In the music business, it is no accident that when a song starts to become a hit, you hear it *everywhere*. That's the label's diligence, getting the song out there and milking it for all it is worth.

The same thing can be said about VCs. While it is very important to find new talent (startups), it is just as important, perhaps even more so, to recognize when a portfolio company is starting to take off so that resources can be redeployed to accelerate that growth.

Similarly, VCs need to make quick tough decisions about failing startups so that they may redeploy much needed resources (time and capital).

To abuse the metaphor, we are no longer hunting unicorns or just farming them. Now we are transplanting the ones with the highest potential into our super expensive fancy greenhouse, giving them every unfair advantage we can muster in hopes of extraordinary returns.

> *Think like a VC...*
>
> Be on the lookout for opportunities to "double down" on an investment that is going well. Conversely, know when to cut bait so that you'll have extra resources to redeploy.

But where do we get extra resources? Our fund profile has dictated an average of X dollars into a portfolio of approximately Y startup. Perhaps if this were near the beginning of our 10-year fund cycle, we could convince our LPs to let us shift strategies to lower the overall number of startups targeted for our portfolio. However, LPs don't usually like changing strategies midstream.

Also, by the time we notice we have a potential unicorn, i.e., one of our startups has started to gain significant traction, we are likely well into our 10-year period with most of our fund committed. Remember, we are only making new investments for the first few years, perhaps to year five.

Here is where our strategy to spread investments across several rounds comes to our aid. By the time we have a startup taking off, we also have some that have tanked. Those that tanked no longer need the dry powder we had reserved for them, and we can reallocate those funds to our baby unicorn.

Figure: Funds from TWO busts have been reallocated Series C

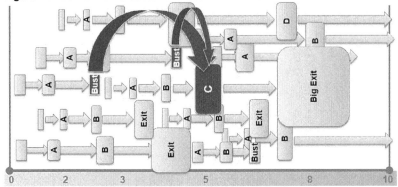

We might even want to add a Series D on the way to an even bigger exit. Having the ability to reallocate funds allows us to double down on potential winners. It also helps us mitigate one of our biggest risks: *dilution*, specifically that we will run out of cash before our unicorn is ready to exit.

Figure: Funds from THREE busts have been reallocated Series D

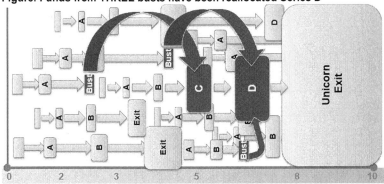

In addition to the benefits that VCs receive, founders also gain a significant advantage from breaking investments across several rounds: they are able to retain more equity. If entrepreneurs had to take all the funding they'd ever need in one lump sum at the beginning of their venture, they would lose an enormous amount of ownership.

For example, let's estimate that a startup needs $20M to get to exit. If the founders accepted a term sheet to receive all $20M in a Series A with on a pre-money valuation of, say, $5M, it would result in founders being diluted from 100% ownership to 20% (founder ownership = pre/post = $5M/$25M = 20%).

However, in the same scenario, if only $3M is raised on the $5M pre-money valuation, founders are only diluted to 62.5% (5/8). If the next two rounds were a "6 on 16" and an "11 on 30," founders would end up with about 33% ownership rather than the 20% above.[23]

Figure: Founder dilution example with total $20M needed to exit: one round (20%) vs. three rounds (33%)

Round	Inv.			Pre	Post	Founder Ownershp
A	20	on	5		25	**20%**
						=Pre/Post

Round	Inv.			Pre	Post	Founder Ownershp	Cumul-ative
A	3	on	5		8	63%	63%
B	6	on	16		22	73%	45%
C	11	on	30		41	73%	**33%**

This has proven to be a pretty good trade-off: VCs spread out their capital risk and entrepreneurs retain a little more equity. However, guess what can happen if the markets are down and startups are having a very hard time getting funding? In those situations, VCs sit in the driver seat, and norms begin to shift to favor the investors. Such was the case in the mid-2000s when *tranching* came into vogue.

Tranching

A tranche is simply a division of something larger, and "to tranche" in VC lingo is to divide a round so that only a portion of the round is given to the startup at one time. Some of the round is withheld, to be distributed when specific goals are met. In the example above, the VCs would price the round ($5M pre-money), and commit to a $20M investment, but only distribute some portion of that, the rest being contingent on hitting milestones.

If that sounds like VCs getting the benefit of lower capital risk without founders getting the benefit of retaining more equity, bingo! That is exactly what it was. Tranching is not founder friendly, and was only common for a handful of years. Since 2010, the VC market has been much more competitive, meaning that VC firms have had to compete

---

[23] We will walk through the math for several examples in the Return Analysis chapter, p. 218.

with each other to get deals. In a competitive environment, founder friendly terms become the norm, and tranching is a non-starter.

Tranching also suffers because it does not accurately reflect the underlying economic realities. If milestones are hit, valuations *should* increase. Tranching a round implies that we have the ability to pre-price those future valuation increases *today* into a fair market pre-money valuation for the current round.

Most agree that it makes more sense to fund a startup to hit some milestones, and then let the market decide what that should be worth. "Let the market decide" is VC lingo for raising a round and let other VCs price it. Early investors will be rewarded with good returns in an up round, and perhaps more importantly, they'll have a guaranteed seat at the table for the next round. In VC investing, one of the biggest challenges is getting in on the hot deals.

Dilution

Just as founders get diluted when new shares are created and sold, so do early investors. Each new round of funding dilutes all pre-existing equity shareholders. As new shares are issued and sold, the percent ownership of the earlier equity owners goes down.

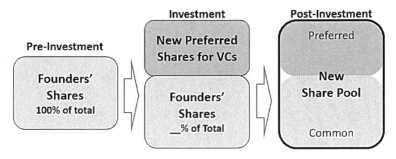

Conceptually, you can think of it as:

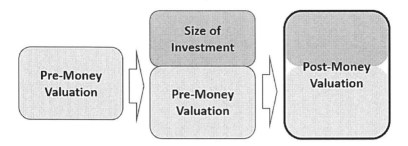

Founders, for example, start with 100% ownership of their startup. After receiving an angel investment, they might be down to something like 80%. Then a Series A could bring them down to 60%; then after a Series B, say 45%, and so on.

All along, if things go well and milestones are hit, the valuation will rise. The smaller percentage of equity will be worth more because of the new higher valuation. Another way to think of this is that the share price increases.

Dilution results in a smaller percentage ownership of a higher valued company.

You may recall the grape and watermelon metaphor in the last chapter.

Founders are hopeful that they're on the way to a unicorn exit, of which they may still own 10-20%.[24] Google and Facebook founders, for example, still held a very impressive 25-30% of the equity at the IPO. Not bad considering they were valued at exit at $26B and $104B, respectively, making Larry and Sergey nearly $4B and Zuckerberg over $25B.

Pro Rata

Early investors are in exactly the same boat, with a significant difference. They have a mechanism to minimize dilution: participation in future rounds. Typically, early stage VCs will attempt to maintain a *pro rata* stake in the startup. That is, they plan to maintain roughly the same equity position (% ownership) that they received in the Series A through future rounds, all the way to exit, if possible.

---

[24] Fred Wilson has a nice blog post about founder dilution. bit.ly/fred-dilution.

If you think of the end of Series A as a pie, then going into the deal, the founders' portion is represented by the pre-money valuation, and the portion purchased by the VCs is worth the exact value of the investment, which now sits in the startup's bank account.

Figure: Equity pie with two big slices

When it is time for the Series B, a new round of shares is issued, enlarging the pie if you will.

Figure: Adding Series B

In the above graphic at the end of Series B, both the founders and Series A investors own a smaller percentage of the total, which now also includes the Series B investment.

Let's look at an example with a Series A investment of $4M on a $6M pre-money valuation. That results in 40% ownership for the Series A investors and 60% for founders, with a post-money valuation of $10M.

Figure: Series A "4 on 6" deal

Now let's add a Series B of $10M. If this $10M is added to the $10M post-money from the Series A, then the earlier shareholders are diluted by 50%. This would look like:

Bonus question: did you catch the presumptive mistake we just made? Go back and think about it. What is the pre-money valuation of the Series B? How did we get that? How does it compare to the post-money of the Series A?

Figure: Flat round

We made a bad assumption. The Series A post-money valuation should <u>not</u> be equal to the Series B pre-money valuation. That implies no value was created between the rounds, and it would be called a *flat round*.

Up Rounds

Remember, we are making projections right now, and we should not be predicting a flat round. The Series A investment should be used to *hit milestones*, thereby increasing the valuation of the startup, leading to an *up round*.

Figure: Up round

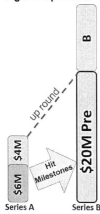

Let's assume our startup hit a big milestone, resulting in a doubling in valuation. The pre-money for Series B would then be $20M (after the Series A post-money valuation of $10M). Infusing $10M on a $20M pre would dilute by 1/3.

As Series A investors, we would be diluted from 40% to about 27%, and the Series B investors would own 33%. Since our plan is to maintain pro rata ownership, we should be planning to invest in the Series B to maintain our 40%.

Figure: Series B "10 on 20" after a Series A "4 on 6"

We'll delve more deeply into the algebra in the Return Analysis chapter. For now, let's note that we, the Series A investors, have been diluted down to 27%. We started with 40%, and had planned to maintain pro rata. Hence, we'd need to invest about 1/3 of the Series B, about $3.5M, to purchase 1/3 of that 33%, or 11%. This money comes from the dry powder we had reserved for follow-on rounds for this startup.

Our exposure for this deal would now be a total of $7.5M across two rounds ($4M in Series A and $3.5M in Series B). Our total ownership after Series B would be just under 40% of the total equity. We would own two classes of preferred shares, Series A and Series B.

This situation begs the question: if we are only putting in 1/3 of the Series B, who puts in the other 2/3? The answer is our syndicate partners. Since our plan all along was to maintain a pro rata position, we would have already been courting syndicate partners to be ready to take 2/3 of the Series B.

In fact, we may have already brought a key syndicate partner into the Series A, particularly if we think this startup will have a lot of potential and need a lot of funding and other help to get there.

> *Syndicate partners fill in future rounds, as our ability to participate is limited.*

We will attempt to follow this pattern through future follow-on rounds, Series C, Series D, etc., all the way to exit.

Down Rounds

Each time shares are issued, i.e., each round, the *new* investors are motivated to negotiate the lowest possible share price, i.e., the lowest possible pre-money valuation, for that round. Their return will be based on the increase in valuation after that round. So the lower the pre-money valuation, the higher the potential return. Buy low, sell high.

The founders and early investors are motivated to negotiate the highest possible pre-money valuation to minimize the dilutive effect of the round.

In our earlier example, with a $4M Series A investment on a $6M pre-money, we saw the difference in dilution between a flat round vs. an up round. With the up-round, the pre-money for Series B was 2X the post-money of Series A (increased from $10M to $20M). Series A investors were diluted from 40% to 27%.

In the flat-round scenario, the pre-money valuation remained the same as the post-money from the Series A, at $10M. Series A investors went from 40% to 20% ownership.

Imagine a down round. Dilution becomes a very serious risk when things go awry. Let's say we dropped from $10M post-money Series A to $5M pre-money Series B. If the Series B investment remains $10M, Series A and founders will be diluted 67%.

Figure: Dilution effects of up, flat and down rounds

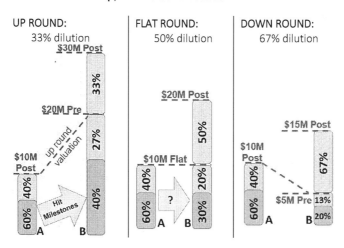

In this down round scenario, our original $4M investment decreased in value by 50%, to $2M, commensurate with the change in valuation from

Series A post and Series B pre. At the end of Series B, we own 13.33% of a $15M post-money, again, $2M.

A scary thought for Series A investors: down rounds can happen even when a startup is performing well. Macro events can move the whole market downward at the most inopportune times, such as after the great recession of 2008.

It is difficult to overstate how destructive down rounds are to the VC investment process, but Series A investors do have a couple of protections. First, they have the ability to participate in the Series B, taking advantage of the lower share prices to purchase more equity.

Series A investors will also usually insist on an "anti-dilution" clause as a special right that comes with *preferred* shares. In the event of a down round, an anti-dilution clause protects the Series A investors by issuing extra shares in the Series B to minimize dilution.

VCs get protection from down rounds with an anti-dilution clause.

Option Pools

The biggest potential losers in the down round are the founders and other common shareholders, who have little to no ability to participate in the Series B and no anti-dilution protections. It can be a sincere challenge to reorganize the cap table to make sure there is enough equity to incentivize management.

Enter options pools again. With each round of financing, the option pool may get *reset*, meaning new shares can be created and allocated to the option pool. This can be a particularly useful tool if there are cofounders on the cap table who are no longer contributing to the startup. They will be diluted with no opportunity to earn new options.

Current and future management, who will be responsible for our success, will get new options. It may not make up for all of the dilution suffered from a down round, but it could be enough to keep the wheels from coming off.

For example, according to Re/Code Magazine, Jawbone had a down round in January of 2016, with its valuation dropping by half from $3B to $1.5B. Re/Code called it "a restructuring of the cap table, diluting investors not participating in the new round." In an attempt to hang onto talent, "a larger pool of equity for employees has apparently eliminated losses in value of their shares." [25]

Grow Summary

We learned in this chapter that a venture capitalist must do much more than find and invest in startups. Many VCs' favorite part of the job is rolling up their sleeves to help startups succeed. It is how a VC firm manages its portfolio that separates the top quartile from the rest.

When VCs negotiate a Series A, we are already thinking about the Series B, C...all the way to exit. We reserve 2X of our Series A investment to participate in follow-on rounds in an attempt to thwart dilution and maintain pro rata.

> **WHAT WE COVERED**
>
> **Grow**
>
> - Working the Portfolio
> - Follow-On Rounds
> - Reserve Capital
> - Tranching
> - Dilution
> - Pro Rata
> - Up and Down Rounds
> - Options Pools

Chapter Questions

1. Why do VCs plan on several rounds of investing before an exit?
2. What is the role of milestones in the growth of a startup?
3. How are rounds of investing related to milestones?
4. What can happen when a startup misses key milestones?
5. What causes down rounds?
6. Why are down rounds such a potential problem for early stage investors?
7. How do Series A investors mitigate dilution?
8. How is a VC fund's portfolio similar to a record company's roster in terms of developing and investing in talent?
9. If a 2 on 4 round is followed by a 3 on 4 round, is the second round an up, down or flat round?

---

[25] "Jawbone gets $165M in Down Round," Jan. 2016, Recode, on.recode.net/2hwskMb

Case Study: VCIC Fund II

Jeff and Mark began testing the waters for their second fund, *VCIC II*, at the end of the third year of *VCIC I*, right as they were exploring joining a Series A lead by another VC firm. Timing was good. LPs seemed eager to put more money into this asset class, and their LPs appreciated that *VCIC I* was performing surprisingly close to its original strategy. It looked like a winning formula. True, there were no exits yet, but Jeff and Mark were able to demonstrate value creation through milestones that the startups had hit, including the two Series A rounds.

The LPs were particularly happy about the syndicate partners Jeff and Mark were working with, some very well-known VC firms with great track records. This enthusiasm for syndicates helped Jeff and Mark quickly pull the trigger and join the Series A they had been deliberating.

Because of the hot fundraising environment, Jeff and Mark decided to move quickly on fund II. To keep it simple, they pitched a profile very similar to *VCIC I*, with a relatively slight increase in size from $50M to $60M. This allowed them to close on *VCIC II* in weeks rather than months, with most of their LPs re-upping.

Part of the reason they kept the fund small was because their current strategy seemed to be working, getting in at the seed stage and helping early companies position for a Series A. They liked that sweet spot and did not want to increase the amount of funding per company.

Another reason to keep the fund small was that they had not found an individual that they might bring in as a third partner on *VCIC II*. They were not actively searching, but it was always in the back of their minds as a potential growth strategy for the firm. If they didn't want to invest more per startup, they'd need to invest in more startups. To invest in more startups, they'd need help.

The two of them were already nearing their limit in terms of how many portfolio companies they could manage. Thanks to the influx of management fees for the new fund (2% of $60M is $1.2M/year), they could afford to invest in infrastructure and get some help, including hiring an analyst and an administrative assistant. The new help would increase their bandwidth so that they would be able to handle the increased workload of a second fund on top of the first fund.

Their fund strategy was to focus on early stage. They still had a lot of work to do to get six of their *VCIC I* portfolio companies positioned for a Series A. After that, the strategy was not to lead future rounds and to focus their energies on new investments in *VCIC II*.

   TO PONDER: What can you imagine Fund III might look like? Should Jeff and Mark start looking for another partner with more expertise in later-stage investing?

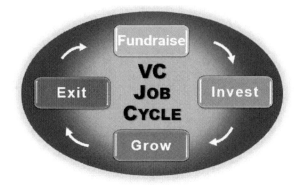

6. Exit

Contents

Ah, the exit. Such a terrible word for such an important part of the process. Exit refers to "exiting" the investment, but VCs would be well-served to figure out a better way to communicate this to founders. It doesn't seem like such a fun date if one partner is always looking at the exit, right?

But VCs must exit. It is a simple fact of life, built into the structure of the investment vehicle, and founders must understand the deal they are seeking when they solicit venture capital. VCs are but a cog in this entire machine, taking cash from LPs, delivering it to startups, and ultimately returning more cash to the LPs.

A *liquidity event* is an opportunity to convert an illiquid asset, like equity in a startup, into a liquid asset, like cash or publicly traded stocks, valued by LPs. Ultimately, for VCs this means our investments must be sold, and there are effectively only two options for a successful exit:

1. Be acquired by another company for cash and/or publicly traded stock; or
2. Go public via IPO, initial public offering, thus turning illiquid private stock into a publicly traded stock.

Acquisitions

Companies merge and acquire one another all the time. This is known as the *M&A market* (mergers and acquisitions). Business schools have classes devoted to M&A, and many business school graduates go into M&A careers. It is a popular field for students interested in venture capital, as there are some similarities. Both fields involve complex transactions that include valuing companies and negotiating equity deals. There are similarities in the rhythms of *doing deals*, and some people self-identify as *deal junkies*.

Sidebar about VC vs. M&A

In addition to the transactional nature of both jobs, they also both deal with organizations going through disruptive changes, relying on human beings to thrive in chaos. VC-backed startups are growing incredibly fast, often doubling their workforce every few months. Integrating all the new people hired and evolving the company culture are competencies that VCs often bring to the table. M&A professionals similarly must ensure that the cultures of the two merging companies can integrate.

While M&A professionals and VCs might both be deal junkies who rely on human capital, there are differences that create a gulf between the two, even though those differences may seem academically minor. Perhaps it can be summed up as *mindset*. VCs consider themselves *value creators*. Their holy grail is making something out of nothing.

M&A professionals, on the other hand, are kings of synergies. Like many business school students, their holy grail is an *arbitrage* situation, in which they can purchase and sell something simultaneously, making money without creating value. In the VC world, there is no arbitrage. You have to create real value to make real money.

Another key difference is *structure*. Both thrive in disruption, but the VC world is fraught with ambiguities. M&A professionals have the luxury of things that already exist! Their spreadsheets, for example, have real numbers in them, not just projections. The people who work at the merging companies are real people already in place, not imagined new hires, and they already have real customers paying certain prices for existing products.

VCs build companies from scratch, from a few founders and no customers to a few hundred employees and millions of customers. There is a lot more uncertainty where VCs thrive, as well as much higher highs and lower lows, in terms of business outcomes.

> *M&A and VC are both transaction driven, but each has its own culture.*

Back to Acquisitions

Historically, exit via acquisition is the more common but less unicorn-like route. It is the faster, cheaper option versus going public. In being bought, a startup has to give up the bigger vision of growing into its own large, public company. That said, there are some acquirers out there that are big enough to buy unicorns.

When VCs first begin considering a Series A investment in a startup, we are already doing mental calculations on that startup's attractiveness to potential acquirers. Each buyer has its own set of needs. Perhaps they are trying to break into a new market or looking for a rebranding opportunity. Buyers may want to add new products to offer to their current customer base, or find new customers for their current product base.

VCs will have some ideas about potential acquirers from day one. They may even begin checking in with acquirers as part of the due diligence process for the Series A. This is the VC equivalent to being *Lean*: test

> *VCs are thinking about the exit strategy from the beginning.*

the MVP (minimum viable product) with customers.

If an acquisition is considered the likely exit, the VCs will want to groom the startup while courting potential acquirers. The goal is to make the startup the most valuable asset it could possibly be for the most likely acquirer, resulting in the highest purchase price (and highest return for the VCs).

This can, of course, be a source of conflict between VCs and founders, who will have their own vision for the company. VCs may begin imposing strategic direction toward becoming the perfect acquisition target while founders are focused on creating the most sustainable company.

IPO

An IPO, initial public offering, as an exit strategy provides the largest return potential for the rare startup that has the potential to mature into an industry leader, generating steadily growing revenues north of $50-100M a year. An IPO is not a good choice if future earnings are unpredictable. Public markets reward predictability.

This makes sense if you think about the nature of these liquid assets. Lots of people are buying and selling shares of public stocks all the time, just as you and I buy groceries regularly. Imagine how confusing it would be if the price of groceries was highly volatile. How would we budget for that?

> *IPO is only a viable option with predictable revenues north of $50M.*

There is value in predictability, which means we should not be seeking an IPO as an exit strategy unless we are confident we can reach a stable stage, no easy feat for a startup.

An IPO is another round of financing much like any Series A, B or C that preceded it: new shares are issued at a certain price and the overall valuation of our startup grows by the amount raised by the offering. However, there is one big difference: the new shares are being offered to the *public*, and all of the fancy preferred shares that VCs received will be converted to common stock.

After an IPO, there is now a public market for the company's stock, and the share price can fluctuate minute by minute. There is now a specific value at any given moment for the VCs' investment. The stock is liquid.

However, VCs cannot sell right away. There is usually a lock-up period ranging from 90 to 180 days post-IPO during which the VCs cannot sell our shares. This is to prevent a steep decline in stock price if a large number of the shares were dumped on the market at once.

The VCs will usually be divesting as quickly as we can, as our business model is not in holding public stock. We'll want to get liquidity as quickly as possible, thereby creating a higher IRR for our LPs.[26]

Return the Fund

Whichever exit strategy we pursue, we have the same goal in this hit-driven business. Just as record labels need multi-platinum records to drive their business model, we need startups that can *return the fund*. In other words, upon exit, there is a possibility that the proceeds from this one investment will be equal to or larger than the entire fund size.

For example, let's say we raised a micro-fund of $50M. As an early stage investor, we may own something like 20% of a startup upon exit. To return the fund on this investment, owning 20% at exit, the valuation would need to be $250M ($50M/20%=$250M).

If we were in the same situation, owning 20% of a startup, and our fund size were a mega-fund of $500M, we'd need an exit valuation at $2.5B to return the fund.

A rule of thumb in the venture business used to be that startups needed to have a *10-20X return potential*. Since VC funds routinely have portfolios of 15-25 startups, the 10-20X goal gets you to nearly the same place as *returning the fund*.

10-20X potential return is a common rule of thumb, roughly equivalent to one deal "returning the fund."

---

[26] There are exceptions to this rule, of course, and some firms may choose to hold onto public stock beyond the lock-up period. IRR-internal rate of return, a function of money and time.

For example, let's look at a $100M VC Fund. From the top, we can take out 10 years of 2% management fees, leaving $80M to invest. If we are planning a portfolio of 12 startups, that would imply an average around $6-7M in each startup ($80M/12). At that rate, one of them would have to hit 15X to return the fund.

These days, I don't hear a lot about the 10-20X rule, likely due to two trends: 1) startups need less cash and 2) VC fund sizes got bigger. If a startup only needs $100K, then the 20X rule is pretty irrelevant even to a micro fund of $50M. The $2M return barely moves the needle, nowhere near returning the fund.

Backwards VC Math (again)

For VCs, the exit strategy comes first. Learning to think like a VC includes having a vision of the endgame, even in this startup world of ambiguities. VCs may not know exactly which acquirer or when the IPO might be held, but we will be aiming for a vision for success, which we define as financial return.

The math of VC funding, whether it is a Series A or Series F, is dictated by the end game. As VCs, we start by making a rough estimation of an *exit valuation*. Based on our experience as VCs, we try to guess what this startup may be able to get upon exit. We then estimate what percentage of the startup our firm will need to own to return the fund.

For example, let's imagine we're looking at a very exciting startup that

we think could be a unicorn, with an exit valuation of $1B. How much of the equity we need to own at exit depends on our fund size, as our default goal is usually to return the fund. If we have a $500M fund, we need to own half so that our proceeds would be $500M from the $1B exit.

Note that returning the fund is not necessarily *always* the goal. For example, our firm may be in a more conservative region, such as the southeastern U.S., characterized by fewer home runs and more doubles and triples. Another example, we might perceive lower risk with a certain startup and be willing to get lower returns.

If we have a $100M fund, owning 10% would return the fund. Of course, with a much smaller fund, we have much less capital available for any one startup. With a $100M fund, we would not have enough cash to own a large percentage of a startup on the way to a $1B exit.

The next question we need to ask, *how much are we willing to spend for that particular exit scenario?* The answer to that question will be an important factor as we negotiate the terms of all rounds, including the Series A.

Earlier we discussed the investment size and the valuation as the two fundamental terms of the term sheet, determining the ownership structure. Intuitively, the investment size *should* be dictated by the needs of the startup. How much cash will it take to hit milestones and get to an exit?

Now we see that there is another force from the VC perspective. How much cash do we want to put to work? We arrive at this number based on backwards math from an estimated exit. We must then make our needs fit the situation or conclude that this investment is not a fit for our fund.

Back to our unicorn example, let's go with the $100M fund scenario in which we need 10% at exit. Let's assume we are building a portfolio of 12 startups. Taking out our management fees, we have $80M to invest, thereby averaging $6-7M per startup.

Do we offer a Series A term sheet with an investment size of $6M? No! Recall that VC-backed startups generally go through several rounds of VC financing before exit. We will want to participate in those future rounds and must therefore reserve some capital to be able to do so. We might, for example, invest $1.5M in the Series A and reserve another $4.5 for later rounds, like this:

Figure: $1.5M Series A, $4.5M reserved for later rounds

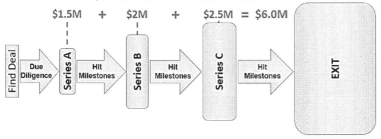

Walking Dead

Unfortunately, follow-on investment decisions are often not black and white. Here's a startup with a great concept and wonderful team that customers just haven't jumped on yet. Can we get there with some more capital? Here's a team that has gangbuster traction but has had a cofounder become disgruntled and obstructive.

> *Walking dead ironically describes sustainable businesses.*

Of all the scenarios, perhaps the most frustrating is the startup that is doing great by conventional standards. They delivered a product, found a customer base and have solid, recurring revenues. However, the company has plateaued with no clear path for superfast growth.

Normal people would call this an impressive accomplishment, to create a sustainable business out of nothing, to employ dozens of talented people, to consistently meet payroll, to serve hundreds of customers, to pay rent and utilities...to be an upstanding member of the local business community.

What most people would call an accomplishment, VCs call the *walking dead*.[27] Their lips might curl into a sneer as they define this formerly promising startup as a "lifestyle business." These abominations have the gall to create a good *lifestyle* for their founders, while promising little in the way of return potential for investors.

---

[27] The phrase is also used for VC firms that are unable to raise a new fund and are slowly wrapping up their old fund(s). Turnabout is fair play.

While the potential appears to be diminished, the workload may not be. In fact, it could be a higher workload as the investors work overtime trying to figure out how to get this thing to grow. Board meetings, strategy meetings, partner meetings—these good-but-not-great startups have the potential to be a real time-suck.

It is also difficult to reallocate the reserved capital from these companies. At any moment, something in the market might shift, and one of these walking dead might have a new opportunity worth jumping on. If that happens, we'll want to have cash in reserve so that we can participate in the next round. But we have little confidence it will happen.

Ironically, these perfectly sustainable businesses are a bigger problem for VCs than startups that have the good grace to blow up in a blaze of glory. No more meetings, no more payroll, no serving customers, no reserve capital. The nerve of some of these companies to become, ugh, *sustainable*! (See Hits and Everything Else, pp. 31 and 43.)

> *Think like a VC...*
> Clear your "portfolio" of investments that no longer have potential and are draining your resources.

Exit Summary

We now understand that VCs are always planning on multiple rounds of investments on the way to a successful exit, and that those multiple rounds will be split across a syndicate of VC firms. In a Series A, VCs will reserve *dry powder* to be invested in *follow-on rounds* to maintain *pro rata* ownership.

To estimate the return potential for VCs, we have to start at the end, at an estimated distribution of proceeds at the exit. This means we must pre-suppose an exit valuation as well as the percent ownership of the VCs.

> WHAT WE COVERED
>
> **Exit**
>
> - Acquisitions
> - VC & M&A
> - IPO
> - Return the Fund
> - Backwards VC Math
> - Walking Dead

It sounds (and is) quite complicated to do the math correctly. But there is good news. The assumptions we are making are so broad that there is no point in doing highly precise math. Broad strokes suffice.

For example, suppose we have a VC fund and there is a startup in front of us seeking $2M in funding at a pre-money valuation of $6M. Off the top of our heads, we can determine this would imply 25% ownership for us (2 on 6, post of 8). We'd typically reserve another 2-3X for follow-on rounds to maintain pro rata. So we might plan on a total of $8M invested for around 25% at exit.

Then we must figure out what the exit needs to look like. If we plan to invest $8M in something, and we know we want to return the fund, i.e., 10-20X return, we'd need $80-160M at exit. If we own 25%, the exit valuation would need to be $320-$640M.

> **Think like a VC...**
>
> Any investment you make (time, energy, cash) should be tied to short-term goals (milestones) and a long-term goal (exit). You should attempt to estimate the total needed over the life of the investment.

The question becomes, do we believe that this startup can become a half billion-dollar company from this starting point? If we have a vision for how to make that happen, and we think the chances of getting there are reasonable, it's a go.

Maybe we think the exit will be closer to $200M. In that case, we'd need to own 40-80% to get our $80-160M. Perhaps we offer $2M investment at a pre-money of $3M. Notice the current pre-money valuation changed based on our assessment of the startup's exit potential. Valuations of startups is all about potential, and that means we have to have a vision for the finish line.

As Foundry Group's Brad Feld wrote in an excellent blog entry about deal algebra:

> For early-stage companies, venture investors are normally interested in owning a particular fraction of the company for an appropriate investment. The valuation is actually a derived

number and does not really mean anything about what the business is "worth." [28]

Perhaps we think it could become a $500M company, but we believe it needs to go faster and bring in new senior level talent. We might offer to lead a bigger round of $5M on a $10M pre with a larger option pool to help attract a new chief marketing officer.

Notice that the pre-money valuation of this startup nearly doubled, but not as a function of its current inherent "worth." Rather, it was an outcome of identifying the optimum exit scenario and funding strategy to get there.

Thus concludes our exploration into the *context* of venture capital. Understanding the industry in which they operate and the key job functions they perform, we now have a strong foundation from which we can further dive into one of the aspects of a VC's job: making investment decisions.

You might think of the first part of this book as a macro lens through which VCs look at investment opportunities. In Part II, we will explore a micro perspective, drilling down into the VC Razor framework to assess the viability of investing in a given startup.

Chapter Questions

1. How is "returning the fund" nearly the same goal as reaching a 10-20X return on a startup?
2. How could a sustainable company be a negative thing for a VC firm to have in its portfolio?
3. Working from the exit, assuming you found comps to justify a $150M acquisition, how much of the startup would your fund need to own to return a $100M fund?

---

[28] bit.ly/vcrazorfeld

Case Study: VCIC Fund III

Jeff and Mark are killing it. Funds I and II are both up and running. Fund I is in year 7. Fund II, year 4. Fund III is in the works.

They had raised $50M for *VCIC I* and invested in 12 startups, just as targeted. Problem is, they are victims of their own success and are running out of cash.

Particularly pressing at the moment is a $20M Series C being raised by their most promising portfolio company, *eStart*. Jeff and Mark discovered and nurtured this startup, and they would love to participate in the Series C. However, after a $500,000 seed round, they invested $1M of the Series A and another $3M of the Series B. Having $4.5M of exposure is about all that they can justify for *VCIC I*, even though the eStart team loves having them as investors, and it looks like a potential unicorn.

Mark and Jeff cannot justify using *VCIC II* funds for eStart because the investment thesis of fund II, like fund I, is to invest at the seed stage and follow on. It would not make sense to jump into a Series C from that fund, and it could create conflicts between LPs who may be in one fund but not the other.

One potential solution is to raise a fund III that includes the strategy to follow-on from the other funds, but this again can create conflicts from the very people (LPs) you never want conflicted. Also, they missed last year's white-hot fundraising climate, and this year the public markets have dipped a little bit. That means the LPs are sitting tight to rebalance their portfolios. No way to quickly raise a new fund, particularly one with a new strategy.

Another potential solution is to invite an LP to invest directly. Jeff and Mark have an excellent relationship with the eStart team, and they also have a great relationship with an LP who has expressed interest in direct investing. This would not have provided *VCIC Ventures* with a financial return, but it could create a lot of value for partners, which often pays off in the long run.

Lastly, they could bite the bullet and over-expose *VCIC I* in this one startup, perhaps taking a very small amount of the Series C just to stay in the game. However, for eStart to hit unicorn status, it will likely need to raise a Series D. Perhaps by then, VCIC Ventures will have another fund from which they could invest in later stage.

TO PONDER: What would you do?

Part II: Practice

VC RAZOR DUE DILIGENCE

Product/Market Fit	1. Value Proposition 2. Market Size 3. Traction
Founder/Industry Fit	4. Team 5. Secret Sauce 6. Business Model
Fund Fit	7. Growth Milestones 8. Exit Strategy 9. Return Analysis

Contents

INTRO TO VC RAZOR

The Razor is a tool for assessing new opportunities derived from the discussions of venture capitalists as they assessed startups at scores of VCIC events. From these discussions, I noticed several themes emerging in the way VCs look at "deals" (startups). What I've attempted to do is distill the disparate perspectives of many VCs into some universal lessons, creating a framework to aid in Go/No-Go decisions in the face of sometimes debilitating complexity and uncertainty.

With the Razor, we have a system of categorization and prioritization that will ultimately lead to better decisions, moving from 100% intuition to a blend of intuition and analysis, integrating narrative and data.

Truth be told, the move from intuition to analysis is only a partial one. We'll never have enough certainty nor access to enough data to get all our questions answered. We will necessarily make many decisions with too little information.

Balancing intuition and analysis is a fascinating area of study, popularized in part by journalist and author Malcolm Gladwell. In his 2005 best-selling book *Blink,* he proposes that when it comes to complex decisions, gut decisions (intuition) have a bad rap. The main thesis of *Blink* is that our "gut" is actually our subconscious being far more thoughtful and processing far more information than we ever realized. The subtitle of the book is *Thinking Without Thinking.*

Interestingly and contrarily, Gladwell wrote a different perspective a few years later. In *Outliers* (2008), he examines a specific secret to success for people like Bill Gates and the Beatles: the *10,000-Hour Rule.* Many of the world's most successful people (outliers) coincidentally immersed in their craft to build an exceptionally deep competency. The "aha" moment in *Outliers* is the realization that good old hard work, and *lots* of it, 10,000 hours, is perhaps the most consistent building block for success.

So, which is it, Malcolm? Can we just make stuff up, trusting our gut? Or do we need to work full-time for five years on a single mission before we can expect any chance of success? Of course, the answer is both. Intuition is meaningless without expertise. We wouldn't trust a nine-year-old when it comes to pharmaceutical innovations, for example.

> *Trust your gut, especially if you have 10,000 hours of domain expertise!*

The *VC Razor* framework is a tool for balancing intuition and analysis. The name *VC Razor* is in homage to *Occam's Razor*, also known as the "law of parsimony." In the 14th century, philosopher William of Ockham posited that when problem-solving, the simplest solution is probably the best one. VC Razor is intended to help slice away some of the complexities of analyzing startups by focusing on specific key issues. You will be able to make decisions with considerably more depth than a blink and much less investment than 10,000 hours.

However, the Razor is not a shortcut. The less you already know about the variables that surround your decisions (your industry, customers, technology, team, trends, etc.), the more time you will need to become an expert so that your intuition will indeed provide an advantage.

Frameworks

The Razor is a framework that leverages the expertise of professional decision makers: venture capitalists. However, any framework is only as good as the information plugged into it. Fundamentally, a framework is simply an outline, a *frame* that needs filling in. Like the basic structure we all learned for writing essays on our college applications, the Razor offers the structure onto which we can hang our narrative. However, we still need to come up with the narrative and choose the data that support it.

> *The Razor, like any framework, is an outline for a narrative.*

The same is true of other favorite business school frameworks, such as SWOT analysis and Porter's Five Forces. The depth and usefulness of the conclusions produced from such examinations are a function of the users' expertise and ability to create a narrative.

If we simply invent assumptions to fill boxes, frameworks are useless, or even worse, destructive, as they can give the appearance of logic in the face of a faulty foundation.

In other words, garbage in, garbage out.

On the other hand, if we are experts in our domain, or even part of our domain, frameworks can help us focus in the face of an overwhelming multitude of variables and potential rabbit holes. Frameworks help us prioritize our efforts and refine our narratives.

As VCs, the most basic decision we face daily is whether to invest in a startup. Will this be a good investment? A high risk/high return investment? A long- or short-term investment? The Razor does not answer any of these questions. It provides a vehicle for organizing our energies so that we can find the data and create a narrative that answers the questions.

Narrative

I think of VCs as *data driven storytellers*. When they find a promising startup, they create an entire movie around that central character, just as movie producers will often know the actors they plan to hire, the locations they want to shoot, the caterers and set designers they plan to use, and perhaps most importantly, how everything will wrap up with an incredibly happy Hollywood ending!

> *VCs are data-driven storytellers.*

VCs similarly create a vision of the future, imagining future customers, key hires, strategic partners, milestones, future financing, and, most importantly, a unicorn exit, their version of the Hollywood ending. VCs also know the same thing film producers know, that no matter what vision they intend to create, things will certainly go differently, often worse than expected. But with a little luck and a lot of hard work, things can turn out a lot better than anyone might imagine.

In listening to all sorts of VCs talk about how they would invest in different types of startups, it became clear that they were using a relatively simplified script. This struck me as similar to other creative endeavors, such as making a movie.

Filmmakers juggle countless daily creative decisions about actors, locations, camera angles, sound design, shooting schedule, music, writers, etc. These endless choices are juxtaposed against a relatively consistent process to which nearly every filmmaker conforms. Certain things are done before you start shooting the film, followed by the actual filming process and concluding with activities required to finish the film and get it into theaters. Pre-production, production and post-production. There is a consistent structure onto which the creative endeavor is super-imposed, like a body hung onto a skeleton.

In this metaphor, the VCs are the film producers and the founders are the directors. Producers supply financing and high-level control. Directors make the day-to-day decisions. VCs and movie producers are both types of financiers, having more in common than with other types of financiers, like bankers or money market managers.

> *VCs have more in common with movie producers than bankers.*

It is curious then that the field of venture capital is often taught as a finance topic driven by numbers and spreadsheets. Traditional financiers are taught to be risk averse. They create very fancy spreadsheets to assess risk, and they get into all sorts of trouble when those assessments turn out to be wrong.

VCs, on the other hand, are funding directors to shoot movies. We've seen their scripts and their schedules, but we know that the film we have visualized in our heads will not perfectly match the final product. We expect things to "go wrong." In fact, we don't call it "going wrong." We call it a part of the creative process, one that would likely give bankers heart attacks!

Still, despite the uncertainties in the filmmaking process, we have a vision for success for the movie. This lesson of having vision in the face of uncertainty, including embracing failure, may be the most valuable entrepreneurial lesson for business school students learning to think like VCs, particularly in today's fast-changing, uncertain world.

Business schools are fantastic at conventional planning. Our students are terrific strategic thinkers. I am consistently impressed with their skills in teamwork, financial projections and presentations. However, conventional strategic planning can backfire in the context of doing something truly novel, when much is unknown, and we have to make a series of assumptions just to get started. I've seen startup students crestfallen after learning that their "plan" was flawed because one of their assumptions was wrong. They'd been trained in conventional planning, which dictated that things should *go as planned*.

Don't you lose points on the test if you are *wrong*? The answer is no, not if you are thinking like a VC. You already knew that things would go wrong. That *was* the plan. The question becomes, how quickly and coherently can we react to new knowledge? The purpose of the Razor is to provide a framework to quickly assimilate new information into a refined narrative so that we can iterate quickly.

> *Think like a VC...*
>
> Have a vision of the future even though you know it will likely be inaccurate. Plan on things not going as planned.

Journalism Skills Needed

As I mentioned, business school students are great strategic thinkers. They can take a dataset, often provided in a written case study, find the patterns, come up with a new strategy and effectively communicate that new plan. These are critical VC skills.

However, we do not train business students in the art and science of *discovery*. The narratives that b-school students are trained to create are based on pre-existing information, on givens, rather than on incomplete datasets that are ever-changing based in current reality.

Meanwhile, across campus in the journalism school, future reporters are being trained to hypothesize a storyline, go out into the field and gather data (interview people) to support (or refute) the hypothesis, iterate the story based on what they find in the field, and finally create a compelling narrative supported by the newly collected data. The final story may or may not look much like the original story idea. These are also critical VC skills!

I'm not surprised that some tech journalists have become venture capitalists. Journalist Michael Carney talks about it in a 2015 *Pando* article just before he left journalism to become a VC. He points out that journalists and VCs share some key skills: [29]

1. Pattern matching
2. High volume filtering
3. Building relationships
4. BS detecting

This is a great list, but he left out a big one: the ability to assemble a coherent narrative in the face of an abundance of semi-relevant, often conflicting, data. A journalist going after a story is much like a VC going after an investment. A director going after a movie has a similar iterative process:

> ➢ Here's what we're going for;
> ➢ Here's what we're finding as we go for it;
> ➢ Here's how we react to the difference.

A journalist going after a story is like a VC going after an investment.

It is a constantly iterating narrative.

I bring this up as a challenge to my business school readers: you will need to tap into your creative side and find your voice. There are no right and wrong answers as we move forward with thinking like a VC. Investing in startups results in creating new realities. We'll need to develop skills for envisioning the future as well as a voice to communicate those visions.

---

[29] "What's it take for a tech journalist to become a successful venture capitalist?" Pando, 2015, http://bit.ly/vcr005.

The Value Network

Now, how do we take these philosophies of discovery, failure, iteration and storytelling and create a framework for analyzing startups? The first step is to set the stage, or context, of the startup.

Figure: A million dollar idea, floating.

Let's start with the proverbial "million dollar idea." There is a mythology in our culture that these amazing ideas are out there floating around like balloons in a ballroom. The reality is that ideas do not thrive by themselves. They are tethered to the people who dreamed them up, and those people are just as important as the ideas themselves, often more so.

Many VCs value the founders *over* the idea. They say they'd rather back the jockey than the horse. That is because it is the people who must translate the idea into a product and then navigate the *value network*, the complex web of customers (market) and the competitors (industry).

The value network is usually stacked against startups. Pre-existing businesses *should* be able to take care of all customers. They have the expertise and the economies of scale. The need for startups *should* only arise in the rare cases in which current systems and structures are somehow failing.

A startup enters the value network with a product designed to address a market need. How well it does that is called *product/market fit,* a phrase often attributed to noted venture capitalist Marc Andreessen of

Andreessen Horowitz.[30] *Product/market fit* addresses such questions such as, exactly who is the customer? What specific pain points do we address? How is our product better/faster/cheaper? How big is the market? Can we prove that customers really want this?

Customers are a very important part of the value network, but VCs are also well aware that the startup will be entering into a potentially treacherous competitive landscape. Even if the founders are able to satisfy a market need, their business may fail if they are unable to thwart copycats and protect their turf.

While product/market fit deals with creating value for customers, *founder/industry fit* focuses on the business side. Do we have the right team in place to grow this business? What is our secret sauce? How will the competition react? Can we stop copycats?

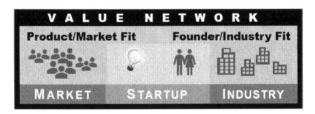

Do you notice a glaring omission from this value network of market, startup and industry? What about venture capitalists? What about the investors' perspective? In addition to product/market fit and founder/industry fit, this third point of view must be taken into consideration if the startup wants to raise venture capital. Actually, these three perspectives can be useful for assessing the viability of any project.

Question #1, from the market perspective: does the project create value? Is someone going to benefit from the endeavor? Question #2, from the industry perspective: is the project sustainable? After we

---

[30] Andreessen delves further into product/market fit starting on p. 25 of his excellent blog cum e-book, circa 2007, http://bit.ly/vcr007. He gives credit to Andy Rachleff, lecturer at Stanford Grad. School of Business and cofounder of Benchmark Capital.

create some value, will we be able to build an organization to continue creating value?

The third question is one of happiness, really: is it worth our investment? Can it achieve a vision for success? For VCs, this is required to be financial return since VCs have a fiduciary duty to maximize returns for their LPs. However, for the rest of us, including the founders, it is a much more complicated question.

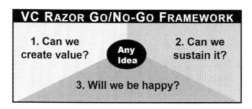

Put these three together and you have a framework for making Go/No-Go decisions about most any risky endeavor.

PV Music Career Digression

For example, one of the major reasons I gave up on a music career was an ever-souring vision for success. When I started, frankly, I never really defined success. I was writing songs, and I wanted someone to hear them. Beyond that, it got pretty fuzzy. If I finished a song, success! If I got a gig, success!

By the time I hit 32-years-old, I had released four independent CDs and performed over 500 shows in 13 states. I had the opportunity to quit my day job to perform music full-time. Was that success? I had a Go/No-Go decision to make about music: should I quit my day job?

The problem was, success kinda sucked. Being a full-time touring musician is really, really hard. Even as a part-time musician, I had already missed many of my friends' weddings, baby showers and even family memorial services. Two nights into our first west coast tour, my guitarist's grandfather passed away. We were in the middle of nowhere in Oregon at a dive motel between gigs to basically nobody. The guitarist had to decide: kill the tour or skip the service? The show must go on, and she stayed on tour with us.

At that moment I realized that "success" was going to be tough. We were making hard decisions even though we really had no fans. Imagine if we had an arena full of fans waiting for us, and we had a family emergency. Imagine we were booked on a late-night national TV show, and my child got into an accident that day. I realized very early that success came with some significant baggage, particularly in the form of lack of control. It was ironic, being a touring musician *looked* like it would be a lot of creativity, freedom and fun. In reality, it was grueling and regimented. (We will talk about the "be your own boss" myth in the team chapter.)

By the time I was 32, I had validated the market perspective (created value) and the industry perspective (built a sustainable organization). However, I no longer had a viable vision for success. My needs had changed, and I had learned more about the realities of what life as a successful musician would entail.

My decision was a No-Go, and rather than move to Portland, Oregon, to pursue music full-time, I moved to Chapel Hill, North Carolina, and enrolled in graduate school.

Back to VCs and Success

Since VCs have only one type of success, financial, they have a phrase that sums up this quest for success: "the math has to work." A startup could be addressing a compelling market need, have the right team in place in an attractive industry, yet still the math might not work.

As investors, we need to be able to buy low and sell high. With our hit-driven thesis, our startups must grow quickly and large. We need to be able to identify specific milestones that will create equity value. And there must be a vision for success: a path to exit. These are all issues arising from the investor's perspective of the value network, what we'll call *Fund Fit*.

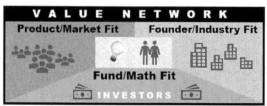

Put them all together and we have the basis for our VC Razor Due Diligence Framework:

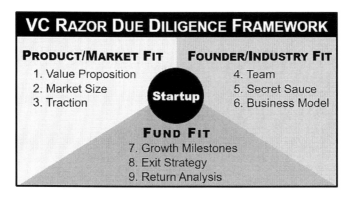

Note that the outcome of due diligence is an investment decision. This is a binary outcome, a Go/No-Go choice. In this book, we will focus specifically on venture capital and how to make a Go/No-Go investment decision, but there are broader implications to this type of approach for decision making for any project. Question 1: Can we create value? Question 2: Can we build a business? Question 3: Is it worth doing?

Chapter Questions

1. What are the primary components of the Razor framework?
2. Why is it important to combine numbers and narrative?
3. Discuss some similarities between creating a movie and investing in startups.
4. How can traditional strategic planning backfire when working on truly "new" things?
5. Why might you argue that VCs are more like movie producers than bankers?
6. How can frameworks be misleading if we lack expertise?

VC RAZOR DUE DILIGENCE

Product/Market Fit	1. Value Proposition 2. Market Size 3. Traction
Founder/Industry Fit	4. Team 5. Secret Sauce 6. Business Model
Fund Fit	7. Growth Milestones 8. Exit Strategy 9. Return Analysis

A. PRODUCT/MARKET FIT

In his now famous 2007 blog post, Marc Andreessen made a bold statement, which he credited as Rachleff's Corollary of Startup Success:

The only thing that matters is getting to product/market fit.

He went on to define product/market fit as:

Being in a good market with a product that can satisfy that market.

In the decade since, product/market fit has stuck as *the* descriptive phrase explaining one of the most important early goals of a startup: creating value for customers. Like any overused catch phrase, there are proponents and detractors. A catch phrase, like a framework, attempts to simplify the complicated, which is a risky endeavor.

To explore product/market fit, we are going to deconstruct Marc's definition into three key questions about a startup:

1. How are we solving customers' problems?   VALUE PROPOSITION
2. Are there enough customers out there?   MARKET SIZE
3. Can we prove that customers really want it?   TRACTION

1. Value Proposition

How are we solving customers' problems?

Value Proposition Contents

From Idea to Value Creation

In the late 1800s, Ralph Waldo Emerson made a statement that evolved into the well-known adage: "Build a better mousetrap, and the world will beat a path to your door."

Turns out, it's a lie.

Far too many entrepreneurs have holed away in their garages perfecting mousetraps, thinking that the world would indeed beat a path to their doors, only to discover that the current mousetraps were good enough. VCs have seen many "better" mousetraps that went nowhere. They know how hard it is to get the world's attention.

> *Value Proposition, Definition #1: statement explaining how a startup makes the world a better place.*

For an idea, like a better mousetrap, to become a startup opportunity, we need to translate that idea or innovation into "value creation," which we articulate in a statement we call the "value proposition." It is not good enough to be clever or novel. An idea must somehow make the world a better place. It must change the world for the better. However, this needs to occur in the context of a world that hates change.

Special note to college students: I need you to take a leap of faith with me here. Your world is so full of profound changes, you may find it difficult to fully comprehend the rest of the world's aversion to anything that rocks the boat. Every few months, you are changing schedules, housing, cities, friends, activities, jobs… But you will soon find permanent employment and begin falling into comfortable routines like the rest of us. Despite your current ability to adapt quickly, be aware that most people are doing everything they can to keep an even keel.

And *groups* of people are worse! Organizations are notoriously resistant to change, even in the face of obvious need. Institutional inertia is perhaps a stronger force than gravity (I'll check with Newton on this one). As a small example, students, have you ever been a leader in a student club? How many of the things your club did were the result of "that's how they did it last year"?

Understanding this resistance to change is a first step toward articulating value. Build a better mousetrap, and the world will not beat a path to your door! The world is busy, and the old mousetrap has been working fine. How then can we make the world a better place in a world that is unwilling to change?

The key is to identify something that is making the world uncomfortable, so much so that the world is already looking for a change. VCs have a handy metaphor for this phenomenon: *customer pain.*

Customer Pain

This phrase implies that the customer has a problem, one that is so pronounced that it hurts. Customers who are in pain need a solution. The clever turnaround here is taking an innovation (a better mousetrap) and articulating the value it will create from the customer's perspective, by alleviating *pain points.*

> *Customer pain is the level to which customers perceive a problem and desire a solution.*

A mousetrap is a pretty good way to demonstrate this shift from *idea* to *value creation*. What exactly does it mean to have a *better* mousetrap? Many readers may agree with me that we peaked in 1894 with a mousetrap design that to my eye seems to do everything necessary. It attracts and humanely kills mice. Simple, elegant, cheap.

Figure: Best mousetrap ever?

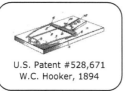

U.S. Patent #528,671
W.C. Hooker, 1894

However, some customers have pain points associated with this solution. Some people would rather not deal with a mouse carcass, for example. Others might not like the potential for personal injury in the form of getting a finger snapped in the trap (can you recall your level of anxiety the last time you tried to set a trap?). Still others may want a way to remove mice without killing them.

Segmentation

Better will be perceived differently depending on the customer, as each has a different pain point. This will allow us to *segment* our customers based on their preferences. Startups are on a quest to find the customers with the most pain. Those customers are the most likely to be our early adapters, at whom we will target our limited resources.

> *Customer segmentation is the grouping of customers based on their pain points.*

A quick Amazon search will yield scores of mouse eradication solutions: traps, repellents, poisons, even electrifiers. The zapper touts reducing the "yuck factor" with a "no touch, no view" solution.

In each case, *better* is not necessarily found in the descriptors for the product, technology, science or innovation, per se. Rather, *better* describes the superior *solution* as perceived by the customer. For

> *Value Proposition, Definition #2: statement explaining how a startup addresses specific customer pain points.*

example, the zapper is not better than that 1894 mousetrap because it employs a newer technology (electricity). It is better because it offers a "no touch, no view" experience for the user.

Let's look at a couple more examples. Imagine we have invented a new battery with very interesting and innovative underlying properties. We could explain that we have "a proprietary photo-voltaic technology that creates a positive ionic charge within silicon that enables diodes and ions to inversely affect one another, thus extending longevity for very low-voltage batteries."

That might be a fantastic statement for an academic paper or trade conference, but not for VCs. To understand the value potentially created, we need to know how the technology can be applied. What pain points might be addressed?

A better way to articulate value creation for our invention would be to explain a situation in which the technology would be used, often called a *use case*. For example, we might say, "CalTrans has sensors on the top of the Golden Gate bridge that monitor the safety of the bridge, and we have a battery that will last so long that nobody from CalTrans will ever have to climb up there again." *Aha!* That sounds like a better solution!

> *A "use case" is an example of how a customer segment might use the solution.*

In class, I occasionally do an exercise in which we brainstorm startup ideas. Generally, they are pretty goofy ideas, as we've only had 10 minutes or so to come up with them. We get a list together and then take some time to discuss how some of the ideas might be used to create value.

One semester, a student came up with the idea of a self-cleaning shoe. The idea came from his irritation (customer pain) of having dirty shoes. It's a silly idea, but then we discussed other potential applications. It doesn't necessarily matter where an idea came from as much as what can be done with it.

We eventually came up with the setting of an operating room in a hospital. If the shoe were truly self-cleaning (and we assume anything can work in this exercise), it could potentially help save lives by reducing germs in the OR. It is a stretch, but it is a good example of how to take an idea (self-cleaning shoes) and begin to describe its potential value (lowering infections in an OR).

> *Think like a VC...*
> Think outside of the box in search of bigger problems to solve with your solution.

Identifying customer pain is a very important step in translating an idea into value creation. However, there is an equally important factor: the existence of other solutions. For our idea to create value, we need to address pain points with a *superior solution*. If the problem is already being solved, what value is there in another "me, too" solution?

Once again, VCs to the rescue with a rather simple mantra to describe a startup's differentiation: *better/faster/cheaper.*

Better/Faster/Cheaper

This phrase is slightly outdated, a throwback to origin of the venture capital industry and early investments in silicon chips. In that space, value was (and continues to be) defined by size, speed and cost of materials (see Moore's Law, p.13). To be differentiated, a chip must be better, faster and/or cheaper.

The same cannot be said for other innovations. A faster mousetrap? Let's say the traditional spring-loaded-neck-breaker takes 500 milliseconds to do the job. Is there any value in an electric model that takes only 400 milliseconds?

Though a bit outdated, better/faster/cheaper is still used as a shorthand way of asking, "How is our offering superior to the alternatives when it comes to addressing specific pain points?" In other words, how are we differentiated from the status quo, understanding that the world already gets along without us and is averse to change?

This takes us to our final iteration of the definition of a value proposition statement: addressing specific pain points for a customer segment with a better/faster/cheaper solution. Remember it is the *solution* that must be perceived as superior, not necessarily the technology (as in the electric mouse zapper).

> *Value Proposition, Final Definition: how a startup addresses specific customer pain points with a better/faster/cheaper solution.*

I want to stress that better/faster/cheaper is a code phrase for differentiation. It does not require that a solution be all three: better, faster *and* cheaper. Rather, it alludes to some superiority. Also, on the cheaper front, we are not talking about simply charging less for doing the same thing the competition does. For "cheaper" to be our differentiation, we must have a cost advantage.

If we are claiming to be better/faster/cheaper, it begs the question, *than what?* It is a question that is so important, we have a chapter devoted to competition in the Industry Fit section of this book. However, we really cannot proceed with a narrative about the value we are creating without stopping for a moment to consider competition.

(Early Look at) Competition

My students are often surprised at the level of debate that can occur when analyzing a startup's competitive landscape. It turns out that "competition" can be a rather esoteric topic for a startup. We are doing something new, and as such, it can be argued that we don't have competition. Nobody else does what we do!

Using the mouse zapper as an example, if we choose to define the competition as electric mouse traps, we may be the only one on the market. Yay, no competition!

This may seem like a simple trap to avoid, but a surprising number of founders firmly believe they have no competition. And in a way, they are not wrong. They *are* the only ones doing *exactly* what they are doing in the *exact* way that they are doing it. This is not inaccurate, but it is misleading and dangerously insufficient.

The main issue is not how a startup is doing something. It is how customers perceive the solution. If people don't want to live with mice, electric mouse traps will compete with other mouse traps. They'll also compete with poisons, professional rodent control companies and cat adoption agencies. True, the underlying technology is vastly different, but from the customer's perspective, they all serve the same function: to get rid of mice. Hence, they are competitors.

Within the broader "get rid of mice" market, we can segment by pain points, as we have discussed. Our zapper is addressing the "no touch, no view" segment. Note that poisons and cats also address this segment (depends on the cat!). We would be deceiving ourselves to think that these customers have no other solution available to them, even if we are the only "mouse trap" that serves them.

There is no shortcut to avoid a thorough exploration of customer pain points and competition. We must think it through and consider all the options. A value proposition statement that has not considered the competitive landscape is largely meaningless, because *there is always competition*! Starting with business as usual and the inertia of the earth spinning just fine without our startup.

> A startup's competition includes ALL the customers' alternatives, including doing nothing.

We will circle back to discuss competition in more detail in a later chapter. For now, let's assume we can make a better/faster/cheaper value proposition. We then have the question of scale. Is the improvement enough to compel customers to change behavior? This leads us to a third step in defining a value proposition: after identifying customer pain points being addressed by our better/faster/cheaper solution, we need to quantify the value that we are creating.

Incremental vs. Disruptive

In the 100-millisecond faster mousetrap above, it is rather easy to deduce that from a user's perspective, the improvement is *incremental* (if even perceptible). We might not expect this small improvement to drive large numbers of customers to change behavior. VCs are looking for profoundly better/faster/cheaper solutions, on the scale of 10X, not 10%.

On the other end of the spectrum from incremental changes are *disruptive technologies,* a phrase popularized by Clayton Christensen in his groundbreaking 1997 book, *The Innovator's Dilemma. Disruptive technologies* are so revolutionary that they *disrupt* the value network.

Electricity disrupted whale oil. Automobiles disrupted horses. Cable TV disrupted broadcast. Cell phones disrupted landlines. Closer to home, Uber is disrupting the taxi industry; AirBnb is disrupting hospitality.[31]

Recall the hits-driven model of the venture capitalist. We are looking for super-fast growth. This cannot be achieved by incremental improvements. To justify the millions of dollars we will invest in a startup, we require a better/faster/cheaper solution that is an order of magnitude superior to current offerings.

> VCs are looking for solutions that are 10X superior, not 10%.

Let's be clear, an incremental improvement is a good thing that can be the basis for a successful business. However, the growth associated with incremental changes is likely to be incremental and will need to be funded by traditional methods (retained earnings, credit cards and bank loans). For example, none of the previously mentioned mousetrap innovations would meet the disruptive requirement. Not surprisingly, none of those innovations was funded by venture capital.

Platform vs. Focus

An innovation from which many solutions may be created, perhaps in entirely different industries, is called a *platform technology*. It is

---

[31] Ironically, while most people view Uber as disruptive, Christensen actually argues that Uber does not technically fit his definition for a disruptive innovation. Harvard Business Review, 2015: https://hbr.org/2015/12/what-is-disruptive-innovation.

sometimes a requirement of VCs who do not want to invest in a *one-trick pony*, unless the one-trick is a very, very good trick in a very big market!

Whenever possible, it is preferable to have multiple future markets to be able to move into, made possible by a technology that can be adapted into multiple solutions addressing various pain points. This can ensure that we'll have a large enough market size down the road to justify an investment today.

Figure: VCs love to see disruptive + platform solutions

For example, we may have a match-making algorithm designed to connect startup founders with tech talent. The same technology could be adapted to create a product that connects high-end caterers with the best local service staff, or car sellers with car buyers. We may have numerous applications built off the same match-making platform.

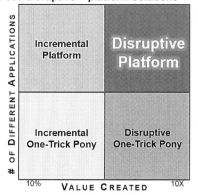

Note that a platform technology could serve numerous customer segments, each with its own set of pain points to address as well as peculiarities in culture and business models. In the example above, startup founders and caterers may have some commonalities, but they also have disparate needs and conventions. For a startup with limited resources, it is challenging enough to figure out how to serve the specific pain points of one segment.

A platform innovation is a terrific asset, but it comes with a terrific challenge: *focus*. With numerous potential markets, startups can quickly get stretched to the point of poor execution. This is one reason experienced leadership (founder fit) is so important.

As investors, we hope that our founders have done their homework and identified the best initial target market, characterized by having the most profound customer pain in which our solution is clearly superior. We want a team with hyper-focus and stellar execution.

However, we often work with first-time entrepreneurs. Helping them figure out the best initial market can be an opportunity for us to leverage our expertise and network, increasing our financial returns with our strategic input.

> Early stage startups need to focus exclusively on an initial target market to prove the concept before moving into other markets.

A classic example is one we've mentioned before, a founding team over-focused on solving the original problem that inspired the solution. In our above example, perhaps our founders originally created their algorithm for other founders. They may be blind to the reality that caterers need the solution more and represent a better market opportunity. VCs can provide that broader context.

In my VC and Startups class, this is often a challenging aspect of the job of a VC analyst: pushing back on the founders' ideas about which customer segments to target. A surprising number of early stage startups are not sure (yet) which market they should go after. In fact, this can be the source of great conflict. Agreeing on which markets to pursue can be an important part of the negotiation when VCs and founders explore the possibility of doing a deal together.

Push vs. Pull

Let's recap this chapter so far. We have translated ideas into value creation by identifying customer pain points to be addressed by our better/faster/cheaper solution. There are two sides to this equation: the pain side and the solution side. The pain side is driven by customers' needs. The solution side is driven by the startups' ability to innovate.

As we analyze a startup, something to consider is which side of that equation is driving the agenda. Is the startup driven by the technology and an attempt to push it out there? Or did the founders identify a problem that they then developed a solution for? There really is not a right or wrong answer to these questions. To some extent, we want both, i.e., some balance.

> Technology push is a solution in search of a problem.

It does us little good to identify a serious customer pain and not be able to address it with a better/faster/cheaper solution. Similarly, having the most amazing technology is useless if nobody wants it.

Think like a VC...

Look for a balance between technology push and market pull.

VCs are going to want to see product and market balance in any startup, including on the management team, which we'll discuss more in the founder fit chapter. For example, there may be a chief technology officer (CTO) who is hyper focused on perfecting the underlying technology. Meanwhile, we'll need a CEO or perhaps chief marketing officer (CMO) to provide the customer perspective as an integral part of the startup's culture.

In this chapter, as we focus on value creation, part of our narrative will be the balance of technology push and market pull. If the startup is leaning too far one way or another, it is something for us to note and attempt to correct, if possible.

B2B Value Creation

So far in this chapter, we have implied that our customers are individual consumers making personal purchasing decisions. This model is called business-to-consumer, or B2C. We have largely looked at better/faster/cheaper in the context of how an individual might perceive the value of our offerings.

However, many startups serve other businesses in a business-to-business, or B2B, model. Businesses behave differently than consumers. Whereas consumers (aka, humans) have numerous and complex priorities that can be maddingly difficult to decipher, businesses often have one relatively simple bottom line.

This may make our job in defining and quantifying value a little easier (or at least more focused) when it comes to B2B startups. We need to identify how our offerings will affect the profitability of our customers (other businesses).

There are only two ways to increase the bottom line. The most compelling is to increase income. Whether in the form of more customers or more income per customer, higher income equals growth, and growth defines opportunity. For our B2B startup, the best way to articulate and quantify value is to translate our "idea" into the amount of growth it could produce for customers.

The second way to articulate value for B2B startups is through cost savings. Assuming revenue is stable, we can achieve higher profits with a reduction in expenditures. This does not directly affect growth, though it may enable a company to grow by reinvesting the savings.

B2B –value is defined as increased net income, either in the form of higher revenue or lower costs. Let's look at a simple example of a B2B software-as-service (SaaS) startup. Our product is a productivity tool for dental offices. (Side note: this could be a platform for other types of businesses, but we have identified dental offices as our go-to-market.) Let's say our software can save dental office support staff 20% of their time.

The first question we need to address is whether our offering is incremental or disruptive. On the surface, it seems rather incremental. If the dental office has two support staff, for example, the improvement may actually have no effect on the bottom line. It is not helpful to have staff who are idle 20% of the time. The practice cannot lay off 20% of its staff of two. Cutting hours by 20% could put morale at risk, causing other problems.

We might conclude that this productivity tool would only be useful for larger dental offices with at least 5 support staff, but even then, it is questionable that they would want to lay off one person (20% of staff) to achieve cost savings. It could be too disruptive for too little benefit.

However, what if we knew from our market research that most dental offices suffer from patient attrition caused in large part by forgetful customers. Further, studies show that phone calls are extremely effective in bringing those patients back into regular rotation. Let's take it one step further and point out that 20% of a support staff person's time could be applied to making those phone calls, thus increasing the revenue for a dental practice by as much as 30%.

Increase my practice by 30%! Now we're turning some dentists' heads. I want to point out a couple of takeaways from this example. One is that it is much more compelling to figure out a way for our offerings to induce revenue growth. As VCs, part of our job is to help founders understand this (if they don't already).

Secondly, I want to take a moment to note what I did with the numbers in this example. I made them up. I prefer to say, I hypothesized. This may seem trivial, but it demonstrates the comfort VCs have with hypothetical numbers. In early stage startups, we need to make up numbers all the time. Then we need to test them. One of the main jobs of early-stage startups is to validate hypotheses.

In this case, we'd need to test and prove: a) specifically how much time is saved using our tools; b) the efficacy of making phone calls to increase revenue; and c) the resulting revenue growth that could be expected. In other words, we need to prove and quantify our value prop.

> *Think like a VC...*
>
> Get comfortable with hypothetical numbers, knowing that they are guesses that need to be validated.

High Concept Pitch

The last topic I'd like to cover as we explore how to articulate value is the *high concept pitch*, a technique stolen from the film industry. Founders who are pitching to VCs are in many ways like screenwriters pitching to movie producers. A relatively complicated and creative subject matter (startup/movie) is being communicated by creators (entrepreneurs/screenwriters) through words (the pitch) to potential funders (VCs/producers) who will play a key role in the execution of the ultimate project.

The high concept pitch is a tool for simplification, or more accurately and dangerously, over-simplification. It boils the entire pitch down to a

> *High concept pitches:*
> *"Star Wars meets The Muppets" or "Uber for pets."*

simple phrase or sentence, such as "Star Wars meets the Muppets" or "the AirBnb of camping."

The high concept pitch has one purpose: speed dating between founders and funders with a binary outcome: "pass" or "learn more." This helps save founders from wasting time pitching to investors who are not going to be interested, and it helps VCs pre-filter an inundating number of prospective startup ideas. It is in nobody's interest to have a long conversation about a project that is a no-go from the get-go (note to self, potential band name, "No-Go from the Get-Go").

With a high concept pitch, each party can make a quick assessment about whether the other might be a good match. This reminds me of my old band days. People would often ask what kind of music we played or who we sounded like. They were inadvertently asking us for our high concept pitch. Frankly, we hated the question (as do many startup founders), but we realized it was not going away. Eventually, we made a pact on a seven-hour van ride to decide on an answer.

Figure: The Zookeepers' "Obi-Van Kenobi"

Our high concept ended up being *folkadelic party rock: sorta like Van Morrison meets Dave Matthews.* Was it an accurate depiction of our music? I don't know, but it certainly made it clear to any grunge, punk or ska fans (hot at the time) that they could move along to the next show, and it allowed us to engage in a deeper conversation with anyone who liked the comparison and wanted to know more.

I realize now that our high concept pitch was a clear indicator to major labels that they should steer clear. Van Morrison had peaked more than two decades prior. Comparing ourselves to him was a clear signal that we were not even trying to be mainstream, that we didn't understand the record label "hits-driven" model.

It should be noted that a high concept pitch is not always a helpful tool. It can be distracting and cliché. For example, it would be impossible to count all of the "AirBnb of {fill in the blank}" comparisons out there.

Nonetheless, there are occasions when this simple device can help founders and VCs pre-screen their audience and focus their energies.

Getting Granular

One thing I've noticed through the years of teaching my VC and Startups class is that founders and students alike are happy to be a bit vague about value propositions. In the earlier example about productivity software for dental offices, many are happy to leave the value prop at a 20% reduction in staff time. It checks the "faster" box for better/faster/cheaper; so, we're done, right?

I tell my students that the 20% value statement is not inaccurate, but it is not enough. We've got to dig deeper to get to our customer's perception of value. In this case, since it is a B2B offering, that'll mean connecting the dots all the way to the bottom line.

True, staying at 20,000 feet keeps more options open, but it also keeps all options obscured. As VCs, part of our job is to explore every option. This is one of the more challenging aspects of being a VC, as there are not enough hours in the day to pursue all possible options for every startup we meet. However, that is where the jewel in the rough may lie. If we can find the better go-to-market and/or growth strategy, we may have an opportunity that others do not recognize.

It is understandable why students (and founders) are comfortable with rather broad terms when it comes to value creation. Being specific is risky. There is a much higher chance of being "wrong" when being specific. Vagueness allows some wiggle room during interpretation.

VCs have to get deep in the weeds. We cannot let vague statements slip by. We must investigate every possible use case, and we must be headstrong about the best go-to-market and growth strategies. After all, it will be our money that funds these activities.

> ### Think like a VC...
> Get granular with specific pain points and "use cases" when exploring value creation. Staying at 20,000 feet keeps all options open, but it also keeps all options obscured.

Value Proposition Summary

There may have been a time when having the best technology (mousetrap) would automatically result in garnering the largest market share (path beaten to door). But times have changed! Now we look for a balance between technology push and market pull. We need to identify a customer segment that has a problem (pain) for which they are searching for a solution, and we want our solution to be dramatically superior (better/faster/cheaper) to the status quo.

Often the best way to describe a startup's value proposition is to include all of the following:

1) The problem (customer segments, pain points, use cases);
2) The solution (technology, product attributes);
3) The differentiation (better/faster/cheaper).

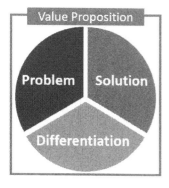

Value Proposition

Problem | Solution

Differentiation

WHAT WE COVERED

Value Proposition

- Idea to Value Creation
- Customer Pain
- Segmentation
- Better/Faster/Cheaper
- (Early) Competition
- Incremental vs. Disruptive
- Platform vs. Focus
- Push vs. Pull
- B2B Value Creation
- High Concept Pitch
- Getting Granular

Chapter Questions

1. What is a platform technology and why is it preferred by VCs?
2. Give an example of a high concept pitch.
3. What is at the other end of the spectrum from *incremental* change?
4. Is "better/faster/cheaper" referring to the technology itself or the customer's perception of the technology as a solution? What is the difference?
5. Come up with two use cases, one B2C and one B2B, with specific pain points being addressed for each of the following:
   a. A drone with a high definition camera.
   b. A self-driving lawn mower.
   c. A ride-sharing app for teenagers.
6. Explain a situation in which a "me, too" idea could create value.
7. Is cheaper always better? Why or why not?
8. Is faster always better? Why or why not?

Due Diligence Advice for Students: **Value Proposition**

Do not take the founders' word for it! Push back on assertions of value creation. Find your own words to describe the value proposition. Be very granular in your search for specific pain points tied to specific target customer segments. Prioritize customer segments. You may need a separate value prop statement for each segment. Be prepared to revisit value prop after an in-depth investigation of the competition in chapter 5.

2. Market Size

Are we in a big enough pond?

Market Size Contents

We've already talked about the market from the customer perspective, specifically their pain points being addressed. Our next investigation into the market fit has a singular focus: to size the market. How big could this thing get?

Market sizing is tricky business. A *market size* is an abstraction onto which we assign misleadingly specific numbers. Years ago, a founder speaking to my class said, "Market size is just some BS number you have to make up because VCs want to hear something." He went on to raise over $25M in venture capital funding.

I believe he was expressing frustration with assigning too much meaning to something that is highly speculative. However, I think he was misunderstanding the point and context of market size, and would have benefited from thinking like a VC. True, in the abstract, the number itself has very little meaning. "We have a $1B market!" What does that mean exactly? It needs context. Most people think market size is a number. It is really a *story* about a number.

> Market size is not just a number; it's a story about a number.

My favorite market size anecdote of late comes from a VC whose firm passed on AirBnb. "We didn't see a big enough market there. We thought it was only going to be dudes crashing on friends' couches."

This anecdote demonstrates the importance of *vision* when defining a market size. One venture capitalist may envision a small niche market adopting an innovation, whereas another may have an insight for world domination. Dudes on couches vs. what we all now know AirBnb to be.

Because market size is often given as a number, founders often over-emphasize the number at the expense of the explanation of the number. The meaning of market size emerges as we weave it into the narrative that was begun in the last chapter. We began with a value proposition statement. If we did our jobs well, we identified specific pain points for specific customers. Now it is time to count those customers to determine if the startup has the potential to grow as large as our investment would require.

In theory, market size is the summation of all the conceivable future transactions in our value network.

Figure: Market size, all transactions in the value network

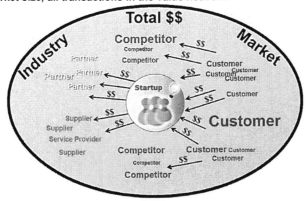

That's the concept, but in practice, the data for all those transactions are unobtainable. Most of the data doesn't even exist, and the data that does exist, like sales data for competitors, is closely guarded information. We won't have any luck calling our competitors and asking them to share their financial statements with us!

Again, we'll be looking for a narrative to tell a story of how big this could be. We will find all the data we can and speculate about the data we can't find. It must all then be put in the context of our value network.

> *Market size is like the pond in which our fish (startup) can grow.*

A helpful metaphor here is *pond size*. We are metaphorically trying to quantify the size of the pond (the market) in which our fish (the startup) will be growing.

When VCs are assessing a market, we want to make sure that the pond is big enough for the startup to grow exponentially. An old rule of thumb is that there needs to be the potential for a $1B market to warrant a VC investment.

I have found it to be particularly challenging for some business school students, immersed primarily in quantitative lessons, to reframe

> *VCs are (usually) looking for at least a $1B market size.*

market size as a creative endeavor rather than a numerical calculation. At this point, I often think of the concept of the soccer mom as an example. Somebody created that phrase to identify a group of people.

Sizing a market is both creative and quantitative, and again uses data and narrative to paint a picture. Below are some of the approaches we can take as we create our story about market size.

Total Addressable Market (TAM)

As we've mentioned before, one thing we would like to see from startup founders is an intimate understanding of their customers. In the last chapter, we wanted the founders to find effective solutions for specific problems. Now we'd like the founders to count all the potential customers that share those problems.

This is called a "bottom up" approach to calculating the market size. Founders should quantify the customers and multiply that number by a price, assuming customers would buy the maximum amount. This formula, # customers x price x maximum quantity, yields the *total addressable market*, or TAM.

> $TAM = \# customers$
> $x\ price$
> $x\ maximum\ quantity.$

Again, think pond size. We're not saying we expect revenues to be anywhere near the number calculated for TAM. Because we are using customers x price, many of my students get confused about this point. We are not saying the startup has the potential to be this size. We are estimating that the *market* is this size.

Realistically, very few companies garner more than 10-20% of market share of any given industry. So later, when we forecast our startup's potential revenues, and in particular when we estimate the revenue we would need to achieve for a successful exit, we had better find that it is

> *A startup's projected revenues at exit should be no higher than 10-20% of the TAM.*

well under the TAM. If we have estimated the TAM at $100M, and we need revenues of $50M to reach our exit, we've got a problem!

At this point, as we are quantifying the opportunity, it is adequate to make generous assumptions about the number of customers and the price they may be willing to pay for our offering(s). Later, when we are looking more closely at the business model, we will challenge these assumptions and test different revenue models.

The most basic usefulness of TAM is to ensure that the number is large enough to warrant an investment. In this way, TAM often serves as a quick, back-of-the-napkin *Go/No-Go* decision factor.

> *TAM serves as a quick Go/No-Go decision factor.*

For example, let's assume we have a new product for medical school students. After a quick Internet search we find that about 20,000 students enter medical school each year in the U.S. If our product were priced at $100, our TAM would be $2,000,000 a year, as we are assuming every student purchases our products at the asking price. This is probably not a very compelling number for a VC firm looking to return the fund.

It is common (and not very useful) for TAM to be ridiculously generalized and overestimated, particularly for any startup that has an online presence. Put up a website and we have a worldwide potential market, right?

Well, maybe. It depends on the narrative that was begun with the value proposition. The 'A' in TAM stands for *addressable*. We should not be counting customers who are not realistically in our market, whom we would never really plan to serve.

Meanwhile, it is also common for entrepreneurs not to think big enough about market size, particularly when they are pursuing venture capital. VCs are a think big or go home audience. Founders who have been bootstrapping sometimes forget that venture capital will bring many new resources aimed at exponential growth, often translating into *bigger markets*. When considering VC funding, founders are challenged to ponder, "What would I do if I were not constrained by capital?"

Founders need to think big when pursuing venture capital.

Founder Credibility

Who is to say that a TAM is over- or under-estimated? This is an aspect of the founder/investor courtship. It starts with the entrepreneur's job to communicate the vision of the startup, including the size of the market being addressed.

However, many founders don't quite understand the context, like my guest above who thought all he needed to do was invent some very large number to satisfy VCs. He ultimately learned to empathize with investors, but it was six years later before he closed a $25M VC round. I noticed in the press release that they were going after a second, bigger market after having worked for years in a niche market.

Defining the TAM is an opportunity for founders to demonstrate their understanding of their customers and of the VC investment process. TAM is also a point of potential conflict. Agreeing on a TAM and on a roadmap for the growth made possible by that TAM is a key element of VC/founder negotiations.

Here are some takeaways about TAM and a bottom up approach to market size:

- Reported as a dollar amount, though there should be a story behind the number.
- Called *bottom up* because it utilizes *unit economics* to build up to a number for market size, as opposed to *top down*, which describes market size as a percentage of a larger pre-existing market.
- Provides an opportunity for founders to demonstrate a deep understanding of their customers.
- Creates a roadmap for future markets, which may be needed to make the numbers work (Fund Fit).

Competitors' Sales

I confess I have misled you so far in this chapter. I have stated that market size is a story about a number (singular), but the best stories have more than one plot line, and market sizing should have more than one number. TAM is a very important starting point, and I believe all startups should take the time to calculate their own TAM, including creating a narrative around the number. However, there are other numbers that can help the market size story along.

> *A market size narrative should include more than one approach to getting numbers.*

The existence and quantity of competitors' sales can be an important part of the plotline. Once again, we are broaching the topic of competitors well ahead of its own chapter because once again we need to understand our value network to help quantify our opportunity.

Prior to our startup's offerings, the world is getting by somehow. Perhaps they are using inferior solutions to the problems we are helping solve. If we were able to, we'd add up all of the money being spent on these other solutions, that is, we'd add up all of our competitors' revenues.

This sounds like a quantitative exercise, but again, it is really much more creative and qualitative than it appears, especially when our founders are convinced they are doing something that is so new that there is no competition. This creates the creative challenge of identifying and quantifying the competition. Again, we are dealing more with story than numbers.

Don't get me wrong, we want numbers! But we have to explain the context of any number we share. The numbers simply will not tell the story on their own.

> *Market sizing is just as much qualitative as quantitative.*

Cost Savings

Another number than can help with our market size narrative is cost savings. Sometimes it is possible to estimate the cost of the problem and use that as the implied value of our solution.

For example, a highly reputed trade journal reported that inefficiencies in bookkeeping in dental offices cost the industry $500M per year. If our aforementioned productivity software could address this problem, we could argue that we have a market size of $500M. Remember we're talking pond size. We are not projecting that we could achieve $500M in sales. Rather, we are saying that there is a $500M problem out there into which our startup has room to grow.

We could complement the $500M market size estimate with a bottom up approach, looking up the number of dental offices in the US, which is approximately 150,000 according to IBISWorld. If we could charge $500/month, or $6,000 annually, we'd have a TAM of $900M. Now we are beginning to have a market size narrative: a top down approach that indicates $500M in cost savings, and a bottom up TAM calculation at $900M.

Pop quiz, what is illogical about the scenario above? What is wrong with that particular story about numbers, assuming we trust the source for the $500M problem?

{Please pause and think about it before reading the answer in the next paragraph.}

The disconnect in our logic is that we've estimated a TAM larger than the overall potential cost savings. There are two possible fixes for this narrative. We could make the case that that our startup creates more value than simply the cost savings cited in the article. We used an earlier example in which we could redirect staff time toward revenue producing activity. Hence, that increased revenue could be an additional benefit, and our TAM would include this additional value creation.

The second way we could make our narrative consistent would be to lower our TAM by reconsidering our pricing strategy. We need a lower price so that we are not claiming to be extracting more value than can possibility be created. In this case, our $6,000 annual per customer price would need to be more like $3,500. Multiplied by 150,000 offices of dentists, the newly calculated TAM would be $550M.

Remember, we are not saying we can capture $550M in revenue. We are describing the pond in which our fish can grow. If it is a $500M'ish pond, we have some idea about the limitations of our growth. For example, we know we will not have a unicorn on our hands, as unicorns by definition have valuations above $1B. It would be unusual to have a company worth more twice the entire market!

Pre-Existing Macro Market Size

Unfortunately, the worst kind of market size data is also the most commonly used in startup pitches: pre-existing, big picture market reports. The culprit here is convenience. With a few keystrokes, founders (and VC analysts) can search the web and find industry overviews from 50,000 feet that include generalized market sizes. Think, "biotech industry" or "productivity software."

Big picture industry reports are the most available yet least helpful sources for market size.

The problem is that the numbers are usually too general to be relevant or helpful. The business plan highway is littered with phrases like, "We only need to capture 0.001% of the $30B wearables industry."[32] We might as well compare ourselves to the US GDP. Heck, if we only capture one millionth of the $13.84 trillion GDP, we still have revenues of nearly $14M! Of course we can capture one millionth, right?

For our dental office productivity tool, it is not particularly helpful to point out that enterprise software is nearly a $300B market. Perhaps it's slightly more relevant to note that productivity software is predicted to be an $80B market by 2018.[33] Actually, no.

> *Never say, "We just need to capture 1% of this billion-dollar market."*

These are the kinds of numbers that had my aforementioned guest-speaker shaking his head at the stupidity of market sizing.

After a little creative web searching, I found a report with the headline, "Medical Practice Management System Market worth $247.1 Million by 2018."[34] Given that dental practices would be a subset of this market, I may have discovered a piece of evidence that this startup should not pursue California-style venture capital. There doesn't appear to be a $1B pond for our fish to grow in.

Market Trends

Because VCs are investing in the latest technologies, often in the newest markets, trends can be more important than current market size. There was no sharing economy, for example, just a few years ago, and a few years before that, there was no social networking.

> **Think like a VC...**
>
> Balance your portfolio to be able to "ride the waves" of potentially hot spaces.

In fact, a fast-growing sector could be a compelling reason for a venture capitalist to make an investment. I've heard VCs talk about a startup as an opportunity to gain exposure into a particularly hot space, with the

---

[32] TechCrunch, Global Wearables Market, April 2017, http://bit.ly/global-wearables.

[33] Statista, Oct. 2017, http://bit.ly/prodsoftware.

[34] Markets and Markets, May 2014, http://bit.ly/MPMSM.

startup's specific offerings seemingly a secondary consideration for the investment. I sometimes call this a "me, too" investment, and it can be an effective strategy when there is room for more than one winner in a new space.

As of this writing, for example, our VC firm might want to have some exposure in our portfolio to the sharing economy, the Internet-of-things, social networking, software-as-a-service and healthcare IT, to name a few hot spaces. (Note that some firms specialize in a specific sector and would not want to diversify in this way.)

By the way, we are also on the lookout for downward trends, which could indicate the potential for disruption in a lackluster industry. Remember, we are optimistic contrarians. True, we'll want exposure to hot sectors so as not to miss the boat, but we also need to find exceptional opportunities that are not along the beaten path.

Niche, Platform and Future Markets

When I was the faculty advisor for UNC's startup competition, Carolina Challenge, I was often asked by students, "Which is better: having a really big idea, or one that you could reasonably accomplish?" Of course, the answer is both. The best idea includes a path of accomplishable milestones on the way to making a major impact in the world.

Which is better: a really big idea or a realistic one? Answer #1: both.

We are really talking about two separate goals. First is *nailing the niche*, addressing the needs of a small market. Second is identifying and moving into larger markets.

Nailing the niche implies hyper-focus to satisfy core customers who share similar pain points. As we discussed in the previous chapter, we need to identify a customer segment that has the most to gain from our offerings, and we further need to iterate and refine our value proposition based on their feedback.

To attract venture capital, nailing the niche is not enough. VCs don't generally invest in niche markets (remember the $1B rule of thumb). In fact, the infusion of venture capital into a startup often facilitates the jump from a niche to a larger market.

As a rule of thumb, startups raise friends and family rounds, as well as perhaps angel investors, to nail the niche. It is not until said niche is nailed that VCs are approached.

Answer #2: nail the niche, then go big. Back to my Carolina Challenge inquirers, the shorthand answer could have been: Step 1) nail the niche. Step 2) go big.

Not only are these two separate goals, they also require different skill sets, as we'll discuss in the Founder Fit chapter. It is very common for a startup to need new talent as it moves into phase two.

I mention this now because in this chapter we are attempting to size the "go big" market. However, we often have founders who frankly are not that great at it. They've been focused on addressing the needs of the niche market. It often falls on the VC analyst to assess the size of future potential markets.

VCs often must do their own market analysis because founders have focused on nailing the niche.

This can be cumbersome when there are several possibilities. There are no shortcuts. We need to size all potential markets into which our startup may grow. We will necessarily run into a breadth vs. depth dilemma when it comes to allocating the limited resource of our time. How deep should we go into the most compelling markets vs. how broad should we explore many markets?

Once again, we will use the tool of narrative, and once again, the market size is more a story than a number. We must assert a vision for the future, and we must articulate that vision in a narrative.

Note we will have the same challenge when analyzing startups with platform technologies, which by definition have many prospective future markets. To fully size the market potential, we must quantify all promising markets. That means creating a narrative around TAM, competitors' sales, cost savings, market date and/or trends *for each market* (see "there are no shortcuts" above!).

Market Size Summary

In the value proposition chapter, we began thinking about startup ideas as VCs do, by focusing on value creation, often articulated by solving a problem in a better/faster/cheaper way. Now, with Market Size, we've attempted to quantify our opportunity. How big could this thing get? The challenge is that numbers imply specificity, which is not realistic given the broad assumptions we must make to calculate these numbers. Using a variety of approaches (TAM, cost savings, macro market trends), our goal is to build a compelling narrative to determine whether our metaphorical fish is swimming in a big enough pond.

WHAT WE COVERED

Market Size

- Total Addressable Market (TAM)
- Founder Credibility
- Competitors' Sales
- Cost Savings
- Pre-Existing Macro Market Size
- Market Trends
- Niche, Platform and Future Markets

Chapter Questions

1. What is TAM and how do you calculate it?
2. Why is a bottom up approach preferable to a top down approach when sizing a market?
3. With pre-existing markets, which is more important: size or trends? Why?
4. Why is it important to combine numbers and narrative for market size?
5. What is a handy shortcut for calculating market size for startups with platform technologies?
6. Why must VCs often perform their own market size analysis?
7. Name a variety of types of market size data that one might use.

Due Diligence Advice for Students: **Market Size**

Do not take the founders' word for it! Calculate several TAMs of your own, **using *your* assumptions and *your* research**, not the founders'. For each segment, create a narrative with multiple data points: TAMs, current market trends, competitors' sales. Tie it all together. Be sure to size any customer segment identified in the value prop statement(s).

Product/Market Fit

3. Traction

Can we prove customers really want it?

Traction Contents

Imagine a startup pitching on a Monday morning at our VC firm's partner meeting (for some reason, all VC firms have partner meetings on Monday mornings). Their big idea is an amazing new dogfood. They talk at length about a proprietary synthetic ingredient, how the processing plant is a green facility and that the packaging is state of the art. They even mention their product's great mouthfeel.

Meanwhile, we (the VCs) just want to know one thing: *will the dogs eat the dogfood?* This was a popular VC catch phrase a decade ago. It's outdated now, but the metaphor is still vividly effective: a bunch of humans sitting around a boardroom discussing whether dogs are going to like something. This happens all the time: a bunch of _{fill in the blank}_ sitting around a boardroom discussing how _{fill in the blank}_ will behave.

Before the founders say another word, the VCs want to see a video of a big group of dogs running away from Purina toward this new dogfood. The VCs are looking for validation that the theory being asserted about a value proposition has some basis in reality. It sounds good, but what *proof* do we have that this new product really is better/faster/cheaper?

At this point, we are looking for evidence, not reasoning. Plenty of logical ideas turn out to be wrong. The world is too complex for us to be confident with a purely logical approach. Customer behavior is almost impossible to predict with logic alone. We need proof that our value proposition has merit. We need empirical data.

Let me emphasize the word *empirical*, which means, "based on, concerned with, or verifiable by observation or experience rather than theory or pure logic."[35]

> Traction: *empirical validation of the value prop.*

Just as VCs have a simple phrase for the concept of a differentiated superior solution (better/faster/cheaper), they also have a word for empirical evidence that validates the value proposition: *traction*.

The music industry used to call this *buzz*. They wanted to sign bands that already had a *buzz*. I had a wall of rejection letters from major labels. None of them said anything disparaging about our music (i.e., our value prop). Most rejection letters encouraged us to go out and create some buzz.

Years later, I better understand what they were saying, just as VCs say, "Go out there and get some empirical evidence that your music/product could take off. If you can show us that people will like what you are doing, we can take you to the next level."

From the Market Size chapter, this may sound a little bit familiar. Nail the niche, then go big.

> For traction just like market size, nail the niche, then go big.

There used to be a prevailing mythology that A&R guys sat up in ivory towers and cherry picked great talent, plucked from obscurity and thrust into the limelight. "She was discovered in a coffee shop!"

---

[35]https://en.oxforddictionaries.com/definition/empirical

The myth has some basis in reality but is still steeped in plenty of mythology. Yes, it has happened. But no, it doesn't usually go like that. The normal process includes years of "paying dues" while trying to create buzz/traction, i.e., iterating and validating the value proposition.

VCs are like A&R scouts: not really looking for "raw" talent, but for talent that has some buzz or traction.

What is much more common in the myth above is the move from obscurity to the limelight. That rings true, as even a band with tons of buzz is relatively unknown. They may have a great following in a geographic region or within a certain circle. Major record labels know how to take that limited success (relative obscurity) and go big with it (limelight). There is still significant risk in making that transition, but it is a far cry from the "discovered randomly while walking down the street" myth.

Same with VCs and startups. Even with significant traction, startups are largely unknown to bigger markets, and often it requires an influx of venture capital to break through to the next level. But first a startup needs empirical evidence that it is ready to go to the next level.

VCs are often willing to take a leap of faith on traction when working with serial entrepreneurs.

There is an exception to this rule: serial entrepreneurs, which we'll discuss in the Founder Fit chapter. If the founding team had previous successful exits, VCs are often willing to take a leap of faith on traction.

For everyone else, we want empirical evidence, which can come in many forms. To the right is an upside-down pyramid that represents, in priority order, some of the more common types of validation venture capitalists are looking for.

It should be noted that nearly every one of the data points on the pyramid can be represented with numbers. Once again, the numbers

will only tell part of the story. We'll want numerous sources as we weave a narrative about traction. For example, note the "everything we can learn about them" under Paying Customers. Sales figures are important, but the story behind them is equally relevant. Once again, we have a story about numbers.

Paying Customers

The absolute, by far #1, hard data validation of market fit is paying customers. Simply stated, customers who are willing to give us money in exchange for our offerings erase skepticism (and reduce risk). The theory is the value proposition. The proof is the paying customers.

> *Paying customers are the #1 (by far!) source of validation of market fit.*

Investors should never say, "That's a stupid idea" (i.e., weak value prop) until after they have asked, "How many customers do you have?" If a startup has no customers, then perhaps the stupid-idea-intuition has merit.

However, I have seen many, *many* crazy sounding startups for whom I simply was not the target market nor an expert in the space. My intuition about adoption was irrelevant. The data they had about their customers was the story.

The existence of paying customers is a great start, but we also need to know everything about those customers. *Everything!* This is perhaps the most important and time-consuming element of due diligence, learning everything we can about what the customers think about the startup.

Exactly how many customers are there? Do they all share the same pain points? How enthusiastic are they? How much are they spending? Are they repeating? How often? Why? Are they telling their friends? What are their biggest complaints? Why have some customers left? Can we fix the problems?

> *Getting to know customers (past, present, future) can be the most important and time-consuming part of due diligence.*

VCs spend a lot of time talking to past, current and future customers to answer the questions above. For B2B startups, VCs will even make connections to potential corporate customers and ride along on big sales calls.

Why is so much energy devoted getting into the weeds with traction? The answer is the first sentence in this section: the absolute, by far #1, hard data validation of market fit is paying customers. Our best indicator for successful adoption of our value proposition is... wait for it... past adoption of our value proposition.

This may seem painfully obvious, but it is that important. The theory is the value proposition, and the proof is the traction. All the customer information we can gather goes into a narrative that helps us determine whether the market fit is compelling enough to warrant a venture capital investment.

> **Think like a VC...**
>
> VCs are constantly balancing breadth and depth (50,000 ft vs. into the weeds). Getting to know customers is a place to go deep.

Has the startup nailed the niche so that it is ready to go big?

Going big implies moving into new markets, and that could mean markets in which the startup has no current traction. Again, we need vision and narrative to explain how this startup's solution for one set of customers will be adopted by another group of customers, who may have different pain points.

I want to stress the need for narrative here, not just data. Too often startups will report this year's sales data as if that data point alone tells the story. We need to know the context around that number. One data point does not a narrative make. Tell the story!

Let me repeat that information from paying customers is by far our #1 objective validation of market fit. That said, not every customer pays, and not every startup needs to have a revenue model (as we'll explore in the Business Model chapter).

Early stage VCs do make investments in pre-revenue startups, in which case they need other tools for assessing traction. Whether or not a startup has paying customers, some tools have emerged to assess engagement.

Engagement Metrics

These days, startups interact with their customers in very complex ways, well beyond the old transaction model. Back in the day, a customer would pay for a product, take it home, and the company that made the product would have little idea exactly what that customer was doing with it. If we bought a bottle of milk, we could take it home and drink it at our leisure.

The Internet and the ubiquity of connectivity changed all that. Many startups can now monitor customer behavior in a very granular manner, unimaginable just a few years ago. Data can now be collected that can paint a picture of *engagement*, a description of how often customers are *engaging* with their products.

> *Ubiquitous connectivity brought the ability to measure engagement.*

At one extreme was our milk company, which knows very little about our milk-drinking habits. At the other extreme are online companies with which we interact numerous times a day: social media, email, browsing, word processing, searching, etc. It is staggering to think of the level of detail these companies have about their customers.

To be honest, I think VCs have gotten a little spoiled with this ubiquity of data, and subsequently get carried away sometimes with the *engagement metrics* that have sprung up as a result. I could imagine some VCs asking a startup dairy about its "daily active users," also known as people who drink milk every day.

The chart below explains some of the most common engagement metrics. Remember, we are in the context of creating a narrative around *traction*. We are trying to validate a startup's market fit. Also, note that these metrics are not mutually exclusive with paying customers. Rather, they are a complement to that narrative. A startup may or may not have paying customers to be tracking some of the metrics below.

> *Engagement metrics complement the narrative we began with paying customers.*

Table: Engagement Metrics

Daily Active Users (DAU) / Monthly Active Users (MAU)	This metric has evolved into the gold standard of engagement for many types of startups. It is represented as a raw number of users or a percentage of overall users who interact daily or monthly.
Month-over-Month Growth (MoM or m/m)	Sometimes called month-*on*-month growth, this can be used when measuring revenues, logins, users, downloads, hits, etc. This is analogous to the more traditional financial measure CAGR (compounded annual growth rate), which is specifically a revenue trend metric. Something in the double digits (above 10%) is generally considered a healthy MoM.
Retention/Churn	Retention is the opposite of churn. Some types of businesses focus more on one or the other. Retention often comes as renewals; churn is cancellation of services or lack of renewal. Both are usually presented as percentages and can be representing active users or MRR (monthly recurring revenues).
Net Promoter Score (NPS)	A tool measuring customer loyalty based on the single question, "How likely is it that you would recommend our product/service to a friend or colleague." There is much debate about its effectiveness, but it continued to grow in popularity since its introduction in 2003 by Fred Reichheld of Bain and Co.
Downloads	This simple count is considerably less compelling than the metrics above, but some very early startups won't have enough data for DAU or m/m metrics. A very large number of downloads does validate customer pain, but it does not necessarily indicate that the startup's solutions are getting used. We'll also need numbers from above. Still, this metric can be a part of the traction narrative.
Followers	As you can probably tell, this list is in order of priority, and social media followers as a metric is near the bottom of the list. Nonetheless, a very large number can be an interesting part of our traction narrative.
Survey Data	At the very bottom of the list is results from surveys. This is really only applicable to a startup in the "idea stage." Survey data can be a key driving point for a seed stage startup, but by the time VCs are getting into the picture, we'll usually need something more compelling from the metrics above.
Customer Acquisition Cost (CAC)	The cost associated with attracting one new customer, include promotions, advertising and compensation for salespeople. (Discussed further in Chapter 6, Business Model.)
Lifetime Value of a Customer (LTV)	The summation of all income to be generated over the lifetime of one customer. LTV minus CAC gives us some indication of growth potential. (Discussed further in Chapter 6, Business Model.)

Letters of Intent (LOIs)

So far, to answer the question, "Will the dogs eat the dogfood," we've looked at paying customers and engagement metrics as validation of market fit. "Look," we can say. "Some dogs are eating it. With our venture capital investment, even more dogs will get on board!"

As our inverted traction pyramid suggests, the items in this chapter are presented in priority order. Customer data and engagement metrics are extremely compelling if we can get them. However, some startups are not in a position to do so. For example, if we have a high-ticket item in a specialized market, we may not have the luxury of testing beta products to build an early customer base.

In these cases, letters of intent (LOIs) can be an effective way to demonstrate interest in a startup's offerings, i.e., validate the market fit. An LOI is a non-binding document written by a potential customer who is excited enough to put on paper their intent to become a customer. This is a letter, not a contract, written on the customer's company letterhead, basically saying, "We'll buy this if..."

> LOI: non-binding contracting expressing intent to buy.

The "if" is usually in reference to something that the startup needs to accomplish, often with a venture capital investment. "We'll buy this product if you can deliver xx thousand units..." "We'll become a customer if you can build a system that will..."

For example, a startup might have a solution to help universities save on energy costs. The cost is $1,000,000 and will require the installation of $100,000s worth of equipment. The startup claims that a university will save over $1,000,000 per year after installation.

Sounds like a no-brainer to me, but I am not the facilities coordinator or chief sustainability officer of a university. I need to know how they are reacting to this value proposition. The best medium for this would be a letter of intent indicating a profound interest in purchasing the product once it becomes available.

You might think of LOIs as non-binding pre-orders. I have not included pre-orders or purchase orders in our discussion about traction because I lump them in with a type of paying customers, discussed above.

Inferior Direct Competition

There are some occasions when the most compelling evidence we can use to validate our market fit is the existence of competitors, specifically in the form of inferior solutions already on the market. Competition is not always a bad thing! In fact, it can be a terrific thing when it comes to validating the need for a solution.

In this case, I confess, we are not really talking about traction of our startup. We are talking about validation of the market fit and our startup's *potential* traction. In other words, we can use the competition's customer adoption success as an indicator of our startup's potential acceptance in the marketplace.

In this circumstance, we need to have a very compelling differentiation. In other words, we need a strong argument that we are significantly better/faster/cheaper so that customers will leave the competition and come to us. If we are not distinctly superior, the existence of competition is nothing but bad news!

Assuming they are inferior, existing competitors not only validate our market fit, they can lower our go-to-market cost. This is because the first-to-market competitors have

> *Inferior competition is both validation and an opportunity.*

already educated the customers about this new type of solution. They may have also made mistakes from which we can learn and avoid.

In this situation, you might say the competition had a first mover *disadvantage*. We'd be a "fast follower" or "smart successor," which we'll discuss in more detail in the Industry Fit chapter. For now, with our focus on market fit, we can include direct competition to help validate our market fit narrative.

Seed Investors

There is a bit of a catch-22 with startups and traction. By definition, a startup is just getting started, right? How can venture capitalists expect traction right out of the gate?

The answer is complicated and again reminds me of my life as an artistic entrepreneur (the new phrase I like to use rather than "guy who couldn't get a record deal"). The major labels that rejected my band never said that our music was great or terrible. Rather, they suggested we get out there and create some buzz. Prove that somebody likes it. Gig a lot, build a mailing list, get more and more people coming to the shows, perhaps get some limited indie radio play. These were all things that were within our power.

Before a major record label was interested in signing our band to a record deal that could put us in front of an exponentially broader audience, they wanted to see that we could at least fill the local clubs. In retrospect, we should have known that and not pitched to the majors in the first place. It was a waste of their time and ours. We were naïve in thinking that A&R reps were finding nobody bands and making them into stars. They were finding "somebody already really likes them" bands.

For VCs looking at startups, deciding *how much somebody is enough* is the $1M question. How much traction do we need, given the stage of the startup? The lack of traction is not necessarily a refutation of a startup's market fit. Rather, it is indicative of its early stage.

Investing in a startup before it has traction is called *seed investing*. There has been a trend in the last decade of more and more VC firms participating in seed financing. Sometimes this is with a fund dedicated to seed investing. Other firms may carve a portion of a larger fund to use for seed rounds.

Seed stage investments are higher risk, largely due to the lack of traction. That translates into lower pre-money valuation. The more traction a startup has, the more

> *Investing in a startup before it has traction is called seed investing.*

expensive it will be for investors, and the more competition a VC firm will see from other VCs interested in the deal.

When answering *how much somebody is enough*, it's a delicate balance. Ideally, we'd like to see enough traction so that <u>we</u> see the potential, but perhaps not enough to attract every other VC in town.

Recall our rounds of equity financing from Part I of this book. In many ways, financing rounds are beholden to traction. There is usually no *Series A* without traction after the seed round. There is no *Series B* if the *A round* produced no traction. Other factors can affect the timing and size of rounds, such as technical achievements or macro market conditions. However, it us usually milestones based on traction that dictate when and why money is raised.

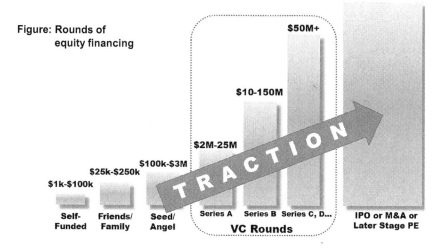

Figure: Rounds of equity financing

Industry Validation

Because seed stage startups have little to no market traction, we may need to look elsewhere for early validation that a startup has a compelling value proposition. Note that we are now at the bottom of our traction pyramid. These sources are not nearly as compelling as paying customers. In fact, if we have paying customers, we probably don't even mention these any more. However, in the earliest stages of a startup, this may be all we have.

Early Funding

Early funding from grants, angel investors or accelerators indicates that someone who has performed due diligence on the startup has chosen to back it. This can be a very positive sign depending on the source of the funding and how much their investment criteria align with ours.

> *Other Sources of Validation:*
> - *Early funding*
> - *Awards*
> - *Publication*
> - *Industry experts*

Grants, for example, may be awarded for a variety of reasons that may be unrelated to our hyper-growth criteria. Some grants are awarded to facilitate scientific achievement, economic growth or environmental impact. All of these could be related to our market fit, but they are also potentially distracting. (Our favorite part about grants is a Fund Fit issue in that they are a non-dilutive source of funding. They can help the founders achieve milestones without having to give up a percentage of their startup.)

Angel investors and accelerators are generally more aligned with VCs. However, VCs are professional money managers with a fiduciary duty to create returns for our limited partners. That is why our first investment in a startup, i.e., the first institutional round, carries more validating weight. Still, we like to see that others are on board.

Awards

Awards are like grants in that they can be bestowed for any number of reasons which may or may not help validate a startup's market fit. We would like to see awards that indicate our startup is indeed creating value for a market segment. Other awards are irrelevant.

Industry Experts

One last hope for validation is the presence of industry experts who are willing to be associated with the startup. This is often in the form of an advisory role. If a startup is working on a new kind of search engine, having the likes of Sergey Brin (co-founder of Google) as a listed advisor will go far in giving the startup credibility.

Traction Summary

In this chapter, we've looked at a variety of ways to "prove" that a startup has truly identified a market fit. Value proposition is the theory; traction is the proof. We've shown some ways a startup can answer the question, "Will the dogs eat the dogfood."

> WHAT WE COVERED
>
> **Traction**
>
> - Paying Customers
> - Engagement Metrics
> - Letters of Intent (LOIs)
> - Inferior Competition
> - Seed Investors
> - Industry Validation

The Holy Grail for validation is the existence of paying customers. There is simply no better way to prove that a startup creates value than to have customers paying for the solution. However, the existence of customers is not enough information for VCs to create a narrative around growth. We need to know everything about how customers perceive our startup.

Of course, not every startup is in a position to have paying customers before they seek funding from venture capitalists. We explored a variety of other tools that can validate market fit. Engagement metrics such as daily active users (DAUs) and month-over-month growth (MoM) are examples of data sources around which we can build a traction narrative.

For earlier stage B2B startups, we might seek letters of intent (LOIs) if we have high-priced offerings for large institutions. B2C startups could offer survey data as empirical evidence that customers like what they're hearing. Lastly, we might look for outside validation in the form of previous investors, grants, awards and/or industry experts.

As we learned in the Market Size chapter, we'll need to create a story around numbers to explain a startup's traction. Top line revenue does not clarify the trajectory of our traction, nor does a grant for *x* dollars. We need to know everything about those paying customers or the grant funding criteria to fully understand whether they validate our startup's market fit.

Chapter Questions

1. What is the #1 way to prove a startup has a market fit?
2. True or false: humans in a boardroom can determine whether dogs will like dogfood?
3. In the absence of customers, what are some ways an early startup can show traction?
4. Think of your favorite technology business. What do you think are the most important engagement metrics for that company?
5. Think of a traditional (non-tech) company. What kind of traction metrics would you like to see for a startup in that sector?
6. When are LOIs effective indicators of potential traction?
7. In what scenario might low traction <u>not</u> be a bad sign, i.e., not necessarily a refutation of the value proposition? When would low traction definitely be a bad sign?
8. Why is it important to combine numbers and narrative when describing traction?

A. Product/Market Fit

Traction is where many VCs spend the most time in due diligence, specifically talking to current, past and potential future customers. This is where the rubber meets the road for product/market fit. Get granular! We need a very robust story around any numbers. If the startup has customers, we want to know *everything we can* about them.

Students should similarly focus their due diligence efforts here. Unfortunately, students performing due diligence as part of an exercise are somewhat hampered because we do not want to disrupt a startup's business by contacting their customers, particularly if the startup is B2B. One exception is if you already know people in your network whose behavior would not be disrupted by your questions.

Since we cannot rely on customer interviews, we must get creative with online research. Google the startup name along with adjectives that might highlight successes or failures. Some examples: startup name + reviews / my favorite new company / problems / made me sick / saved my life / happy customers.

Note that the founders may be our only source of information about current customers. Take advantage of any Q&A you have with founders to find out everything you can about customers. You need to be assertive in these Q&A sessions, as founders will tend to gloss over some important details if they don't reflect well on the startup's offerings. Dig, dig, dig. In later chapters, you'll find that the founders are probably not our best authority on the competition or growth milestones, for example. However, for their own current customers, they may be the best source.

VC RAZOR DUE DILIGENCE

Product/Market Fit	1. Value Proposition 2. Market Size 3. Traction
Founder/Industry Fit	4. Team 5. Secret Sauce 6. Business Model
Fund Fit	7. Growth Milestones 8. Exit Strategy 9. Return Analysis

B. FOUNDER/INDUSTRY FIT

"Product/market fit" is a well-known and often used phrase amongst venture capitalists. It is also the place to start when assessing the viability of a startup. Question #1: can we create value?

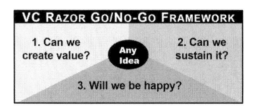

It is not surprising the VCs often focus on this first point, as there is little reason to proceed unless we have product/market fit. I have also heard VCs use the phrase "founder/market fit" in reference to the team having what it takes to succeed with a particular set of customers. However, the phrase "founder/industry fit" is a new one, which I believe gives us a more holistic view of the enterprise and how it fits into the value network.

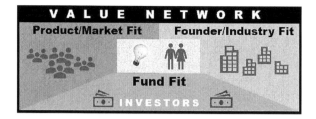

We can agree that market fit comes first, but even if we are able to identify customers who are in need of our offerings, we also need to have the right management and be in an industry in which the startup can thrive. We'll break down our investigation of the founder/industry fit into three sub-chapters: team, secret sauce and business model, answering three fundamental questions:

- Do we have the right people in place? TEAM
- How will we stop copycats? SECRET SAUCE
- How quickly and perhaps profitably can we grow? BUSINESS MODEL

4. Team

Do we have the right people in place?

Team Contents

In his book *The Startup Game*, VC pioneer William H. Draper III asserts that one of the key ingredients for a successful startup is having founders who are "...smart enough to understand how the world works today and are able to envision a range of better outcomes for the future." He's talking about the ability to understand the industry and create value by disrupting it.

Most VCs agree that there is one factor that is most important when deciding to invest in a startup, one thing that predicts success better than anything else: talented management. The people are paramount.

To my ear, when I hear VCs say this, I interpret it as a risk reduction strategy. I would say it this way: the #1 way to mitigate risk in any new venture is to have the right people—ideally, seasoned entrepreneurs who are experts in their industry. One of the biggest misconceptions about entrepreneurship is that the idea is paramount. Many people believe that the key to success in a startup is the great idea. VCs disagree. It's the people who are most important; ideas cannot *do* anything.

VCs would rather back an *A team* with a *B idea*, or an *A jockey* with a *B horse*. It takes people to get things done, and not just any people, the *right* people.

> Most VC's prefer an A team with a B idea.

For example, imagine you are just meeting me on an elevator, and I begin telling you about my idea for a new sharing economy startup. You may be in the middle of a yawn (who is this Vernon character thinking he knows about the sharing economy?) until you hear that my co-founder just quit her job as the chief marketing officer at Uber. Can you feel a large portion of the risk leave the room?

If we are looking to minimize risk with the best possible team, let's look at how VCs would define "the best."

Serial Entrepreneurs

Generically speaking, a *serial entrepreneur* is anyone who has started multiple companies. However, to VCs, the phrase has a more specific meaning: a *serial entrepreneur* (to a VC) is a founder who has raised venture capital with more than one startup and had successful exits.

> VC Definition of Serial Entrepreneur: a founder who has had successful exits for VCs.

This is quite different from individuals who have an entrepreneurial spirit and started their own lifestyle businesses in the past.

Having your own paper route as a kid followed by starting a lawn-mowing company demonstrates an entrepreneurial personality, but would not fall under the VC definition of a serial entrepreneur.

The experience of quickly growing a company from a couple of cofounders to 50 employees, or from 50 to 500, is an adventure like no other. Even across various industries, there are commonalities in this high growth, high stress, ever-changing, distinctly non-corporate atmosphere.

From a VC's perspective, much of the risk that we are identifying with the Razor Framework (market fit, industry fit…) diffuses when there is a tried and trusted team in place. We can trust experienced founders to know how to juggle the various priorities of taking care of customers, competition and business fundamentals.

The ideal scenario here is an entire founding team that has previously started a company, raised venture capital, gone through good times and bad and concluded with a successful exit that made a lot of money for themselves and investors. This proves to investors that the team can work together, build something from nothing, get along with investors and exit the company in a way that is beneficial to everyone.

> *A^+ team: an entire founding team who did it before, from idea to 10X exit.*

The second-best scenario is a serial entrepreneur CEO planning to build out a new team. Third best is a team that did amazing things, but perhaps due to macro market conditions did not achieve a high return for investors.

It may seem counterintuitive, but VCs would often rather see a team that failed at a previous startup (assuming there were good reasons for the failure) than a team with amazing corporate pedigree and no startup experience. I have also heard VCs express skepticism about founders who have only experienced success. The worry is that the team may not be able to rally when things get tough.

Industry Expertise

If the team lacks serial entrepreneurs, perhaps the next best recipe for success is a startup team of professionals who have identified a significant unaddressed problem in their industry and have quit their day jobs to start a company that will solve the problem.

These individuals are intimately familiar with the problem they are solving, pre-validating the market fit. They know the specific pain points that customers are experiencing. They also have a deep understanding into how those customers behave. Lastly, in the scenario I've painted, these founders have enough confidence in their concept to leave their jobs to pursue it.

In a word, they are dripping with *credibility*: in their industry expertise, in their intimate and granular familiarity with the customer, and in their belief in the opportunity.

I just did a word search of the word *expert* in this book. Over 30 mentions. Through that repetition, you probably already understand the importance of deep domain expertise on our team, including familiarity of the customers and competition. Industry experts come to the table fully versed in the value network.

Most industries have intricate cultures to navigate. For example, who makes purchasing decisions? What are expectations from suppliers? What are typical sales cycles? What are average margins? There are myriad issues embedded into the cultures of most industries, and without expertise on our team, we enter a minefield of risk.

> *Without industry expertise on the team to navigate the intricacies of the value network, we enter a minefield of risk.*

Vision, Coachability and Customer Passion

Let's be honest, there is something a little *special* about entrepreneurs. At the risk of painting with a broad brush, successful founders have a curious mix of strong personality traits, many that seem somewhat self-contradictory.

For example, great entrepreneurs need to be in control but also must serve numerous constituencies. For high growth startups, one of the great myths to dispel is the "be your own boss" myth. True, you will be the one to make big decisions. But also true, you are beholden to customers, cofounders, investors, strategic partners, competitors and external factors over which you have no control, like stock market crashes. Founders are in control like surfers are in control.

VCs are looking for a curious mix of character traits in a founder. We want confidence and optimism, but we also require coachability and collegiality. We want to know the founder has a headstrong vision, but we'll also need to be able sit down together to make tough decisions about future funding rounds and exit opportunities.

> *VCs are looking for founders who are headstrong but also coachable.*

Another key attribute that is critical to a founding team's ability to capitalize on a startup opportunity is a passion for learning about and taking care of customers. You might think of this as *market expertise* to complement the industry expertise above.

This depth of familiarity with customers is essential for a team to be able to recognize customers' problems, create solutions that will be desired by customers and develop a business model that will lower customer adoption risk. Venture capitalists want to see a team that is working closely with potential customers, getting their feedback and responding quickly to their needs.

> *A passion to serve customers is a key attribute for a startup team.*

This used to be described as a *sales-oriented* founding team but is now more commonly referred to as *customer focus*. By contrast, a *tech-oriented* team is more focused on the science or technology. In the Value Proposition chapter, we discussed the difference between push and pull. A tech-heavy team may push solutions that nobody really wants. A sales-only team may create demand (pull) by promising solutions that the team is not able to fulfill.

Not every founder needs to be a salesperson, per se, but we do want to see demonstrated competencies on the team in working with and responding to customers.

Origin Story

Venture capitalists create a narrative for founder fit just as they do for market fit. Why is this team doing this? Where are they coming from and where do they want to go? What motivates this team? One place to start this narrative is the origin story of the startup. What was the original idea and how did it come to fruition?

VCs are often in search of a reason not to invest, i.e., a *fatal flaw*. It is a time-saving technique. If we discover the airplane has no fuel, a fatal flaw, we do not have to investigate the integrity of the fuselage or the pedigree of the pilot.

Think like a VC...

Be on the lookout for a *fatal flaw* and be prepared to cut bait on a project if you find one.

By exploring the origin story, we are often looking for a fatal flaw or some other cautionary signal. Founders may be in business for the wrong reasons or be pursuing the wrong objectives (by our accounting).

A major pivot, for example, could be a red flag. If a startup was founded to serve one customer segment and has switched to another, we want to make sure we understand why. One questionable reason for a pivot would be zero traction in the first market and a speculative foray into a new space. In that case, we may be building off a track record of failure. That does not ensure a future of failure, but it is a cautionary tale.

Note that such a pivot can create an unfortunate conflict. The founders have been working long and hard on their startup and should be commended on pivoting to a more attractive market. However, that work may not have created much equity value. Venture capitalists can argue that the founders have little or no traction in the market they are pursuing, leading to a lower pre-money valuation than founders may be comfortable with.

Much more compelling for a right reason for a major pivot would be the accidental discovery of an eager market segment. "We intended to serve these folks when these other customers started coming out of the woodwork."[36] This is a situation much more comfortable for VCs. Generally, we are hoping to fuel growth with our investment, not test new markets.

I can practically hear early-stage VCs pulling their hair out in response to that last sentence. True, early-stage investors are, by definition, taking on more risk and may be interested in a startup in the middle of

---

[36] "Come out of the woodwork," to appear unexpectedly, www.thefreedictionary.com.

this kind of pivot. That said, one of the reasons they are interested is the lower pre-money valuation that is commensurate with the higher risk.

I want to stress that VCs are not necessarily averse to risk. Their business model is predicated on taking significant risk, particularly in comparison to other asset classes (see the definition of venture capital back in Part I). However, venture capitalists want risk to be priced appropriately.

My students often find a red flag in the origin story and think, "Aha, gotcha!" Good job identifying an issue, I tell them, but this is not a gotcha game. The question for the VC analyst is, can you find a way to make an investment work? If you find something that indicates an increase in risk, great, now figure out if there is a way to price that risk so that you can still do a deal.

> *Venture capital is not a "gotcha game." It is a "figure out if there is a way to make this work" game.*

In the above situation, with a startup pivoting, some VCs might state that the startup is "too early for us." That translates into more risk than they are willing to take (for the price). They want to see traction or other risk mitigating factors such as experienced management before they would be willing to invest. Of course, the future lower risk would imply a higher price (valuation). A common VC dilemma: get in early and cheap with more risk or later at a higher price with less risk?

So, if we find a cautionary tale in the origin story, aha, we have some work to do to figure out if we can price that into a deal we could do.

Skin in the Game

Another part of our Founder Fit narrative that often comes out of the origin story is the level of commitment of the founders. VCs are expert detectives in search of clues to indicate risk. One indicator is the level of confidence of the founders. This is by no means guaranteed, but with everything else being equal, we'd prefer to see entrepreneurs who are very confident about their ability to succeed with a startup, so much so that they have invested a significant percentage of their personal wealth in the project, giving them *skin in the game*.

> *Founders who have invested their own cash into the startup have "skin in the game."*

Why do we care about their confidence? Because they know more than anyone else about their startup. The founders are the only ones who have been there from the beginning making every decision, seeing every reaction, forging every relationship and interacting with nearly every customer.

We want the founders to be inside traders taking every advantage of their own opportunity, hoarding the equity. We want them to be ambivalent about selling shares to us. What? They don't even want us? Yes, as in dating, we find the most attractive founders are somewhat indifferent and never desperate.

Entrepreneurs have a time-worn and valid complaint about venture capitalists: you cannot raise money unless you don't need it. While there are plenty of exceptions,[37] this is very often true. Venture capitalists like to see a startup that could become profitable and grow all by itself, only needing an infusion of capital to take advantage of a bigger market opportunity.

What VCs *don't* like to see is a startup almost out of money raising capital simply to stay alive. I should correct that. VCs don't mind seeing desperate founders, but it implies a lower pre-money valuation and includes a red flag. As optimistic contrarians, VCs don't mind cautionary tales, but we do need to be able to build a story about how the cautionary tale is going to turn into a fairy tale, and we pay (a lot) less for a startup in a cautionary phase.

---

[37] Most fall into the category of capital-intensive startups with no quick path to revenue. A cure for cancer is a good example. That's going to cost a lot of money to develop and get through trials, and there will be no income for many years. Hence the startup will by nature be entirely dependent on outside cash.

STARTUP CASH NEEDS

On the verge of bankruptcy.	Most Startups	Already profitable. Need for growth.
Desperate		**Indifferent**

Most startups seeking venture capital are in a nuanced position somewhere in between desperation and indifference. In these cases, the founders' skin in the game is a risk indicator, and it can mean different things depending on the situation.

For example, risk is lower when we have founders who could self-fund but have chosen to seek venture capital to gain access to the other resources that VCs bring to the table, such as our vast network of potential strategic partners, access to more capital down the road and a path to a much bigger exit.

On the other hand, risk is higher when founders *could* self-fund but have chosen not to because they see the endeavor as too risky. They are looking to offload risk rather than to take advantage of a market opportunity.

A related example is the founder who still has a day job. This we cannot abide! If an entrepreneur does not have the confidence to commit all their time (let alone money), how can we have the confidence to invest?

> *Think like a VC...*
> Take cues from early partners in a project. Are they fully committed or are they hedging?

Picture our earlier team of professionals who had identified a problem in their industry, but this time they have yet to quit their day jobs to pursue it. Sounds risky. Now imagine that same team having foregone six figure jobs six months ago, so confident that the new startup was going to lead to something. Can you feel the difference?

Now imagine each has invested $100,000 of their own money into the startup. In addition to opportunity cost and confidence, these founders are also equity investors, lowering the risk further. This is one step toward ensuring venture capitalists and founders have harmonious interests, as one thing we want to avoid is conflict.

B. Founder/Industry Fit

Potential Founder/Investor Conflict

Back in Part I we discussed some of the characteristics of the equity partnership (p. 24). It is a long-term relationship between founders and investors that will persist until an exit. The partnership will have to survive a lot of stresses, and before we offer a term sheet to a founding team, we want to think long and hard about how well we can get along.

VCs will look for clues in the origin story and while going through the due diligence process, including talking with customers, strategic partners and even former employers. We will also spend time with the founders, including at the office and after work hours. It is a courtship. We have to make sure we'll be able to get along through this long process, the ups and the downs, all the way to a successful exit.

> *The equity partnership is a long-term relationship that must survive many ups and downs on the way to exit.*

One of the most common sources of conflict can arise from the venture capitalists' need for fast growth. Entrepreneurs who have been successfully bootstrapping may have a hard time shifting gears after receiving venture capital. We want to make sure they are ready to move into growth mode, changing their thinking from cash-conservation and survival to opportunity-seizing and growth. The latter is inherently cash inefficient, which can be difficult for bootstrappers.

Another potential cause for disharmony is a shared vision for success. Do investors and founders agree on an ideal exit scenario? VCs are going to want to maximize financial returns, but founders may have other concerns. Some founders signal early that they'll never want to lose control of their baby. This dedication can be an asset if the plan is to go to IPO. However, it could create serious problems if acquisition is the likely exit and we have persnickety founders.

Conflict may also arise in many other arenas: Do we agree on: the current target market? Future target markets? Technical milestones? The speed of growth? Key hiring needs? Strategic partners? Future funding needs? How to cope when we hit hiccups? VCs are not going to take part in day-to-day operations, but they will be active members of the board of directors where major strategic decisions will be made.

While we cannot predict the future, we will do our best to read the tea leaves to assess the potential for future conflict because *conflict is risk*. It is hard enough to succeed with a startup while firing on all cylinders. The moment any intellectual energy gets consumed by conflict, our chances of success plummet. Sometimes the writing is on the wall that we won't be able to get along with a founding team through thick and thin. In those cases, we have to pass.

Still, conflict will inevitably happen. Sometimes (hopefully rarely) it gets to the level where the board must take drastic measures, such as replacing the CEO.

Replacing the CEO

It has been said that VCs only do two things: 1) write big checks; and 2) hire and fire CEOs. We started this chapter noting that VCs would rather back an *A* team with a *B* idea. What we failed to mention was that sometimes VCs can help assemble that *A* team.

Remember how much VCs love serial entrepreneurs? We love them so much that we don't just wait around for startups that already have serial entrepreneurs on board. We proactively surround ourselves with successful founders who have exited their startups and are ready for their next projects.

There is a virtuous cycle with serial entrepreneurs and venture capitalists. A successful founder will likely have become independently wealthy after an exit. After a couple of trips around the world in a sailboat, they get restless to get back into the game but may not have their own new startup ideas.

VC firms will often put them on a token retainer, a modest salary to be advisors for the firm while looking for the next opportunity. Most firms have several serial entrepreneurs on staff with such titles as *venture partner* or *entrepreneur-in-residence*.

> ### *Think like a VC...*
> Surround yourself with talented people. If you don't have a specific project to work together now, come up with some excuse to stay connected.

That next opportunity will come in the form of a new startup with a fantastic opportunity but an inexperienced team. The founders may have done a terrific job getting the startup to the current phase, on the cusp of VC funding. However, a different set of talents will be needed once the startup moves beyond concept testing and into high growth. Enter the serial entrepreneur.

In these cases, it can be a delicate negotiation. Most founding CEOs are understandably protective of their company and proud of their successes to date. They are used to being in control. However, starting a company from scratch is quite a different thing than growing it. Different skills are required to manage a three-person founding team focused on a technical achievement, for example, as compared to hiring and managing a 100-person sales force to go to market. Coachable founding CEOs may be excited about and capable of acquiring those leadership skills, and VCs are in a great position to provide that support.

Alternatively, some founders realize that the CEO role may not be their best fit as the startup matures. Said differently, they agree that bringing in seasoned management might increase the chances of success. Replacing CEOs is a relatively common practice in VC-funded startups and is not necessarily a result of conflict nor an indictment of the founding CEO's skills. Rather, it can be an agreed upon strategy to reduce risk.

> *Replacing a young founding CEO with a serial entrepreneur might be part of the funding plan.*

Founders transitioning out of the CEO role often move into other leadership positions at the startup. Tech-focused founders may become chief technology officers. Customer-centric founders may head up sales efforts. Creative types may transition into idea guru positions.

Whether by distress or by plan, replacing the CEO is a common enough activity to be considered and discussed prior to any investment. We want everyone involved in the startup to be focused on success as the goal, and if new leadership increases the chances of success, we should all be in agreement.

Holes on the Team

While the CEO is the most important role in a company, there are other integral functions on a startup management team, particularly as it starts to grow. During the bootstrapping phase, all founders wear multiple hats. It's required, and for many, it's fun, perhaps the best part of working at a startup. Everybody rolls up their sleeves to do whatever needs to be done.

However, as a startup grows from a core group of founders to dozens of employees, job functions become more specialized. We can no longer expect the CEO also to be the head of sales or the technical co-founder to be CTO *and* CMO.

In the due diligence phase, VCs and founders need to agree on a plan to augment the management team. This will be an important part of the "use of funds" plan, i.e., how the VC investment will be spent. This is also an arena in which the VCs can add value beyond the cash they are investing. This helps differentiate VCs (from one another). If founders receive equal term sheets from two separate VC firms, the VCs with the best network are going to win the deal.

> *"Use of Funds" is the startup's strategy to expend the cash raised from VCs.*

Advisory Board

Lastly in this Founder Fit chapter, I want to talk about a way to bring credibility to a young founding team. This chapter started with what could well be a depressing note for first-time entrepreneurs: you need to be a *serial* entrepreneur! How can one become a serial entrepreneur if you cannot get funded as a first-time entrepreneur!?

Most importantly, you need to be executing your plan and creating a track record of success *within* the startup, since you won't have had previous startup successes to tout. First-timers should plan on bootstrapping a little longer than serial entrepreneurs would have to.

Another way to bring some credibility to a young team is by recruiting advisors, who bring several benefits. First, of course, is advice. Smart, well-connected people who understand the value network are tremendously valuable and signing them on as advisors is a cash-efficient way to improve the performance of a young team.

Secondly, the presence of advisors who are willing to lend their names to a project adds credibility, as we discussed briefly in the Traction chapter (p. 156). While that chapter focused on market validation, we are now exploring how a young founding team might gain some credibility by having experts vouch for them. With the advisors' permission, startups can include advisors' names in pitch decks and conversations with VCs, who will often reach out to advisors to get their input.

A third benefit of recruiting advisors is for young founders to demonstrate to VCs that they understand how important it is to build a team. It takes a village to raise a startup! The founders must develop the competencies of recruiting and encouraging *evangelists,* people who will sing the praises of the startup. Recruiting well-respected industry professionals to join the startup, even in the limited role of advisor, demonstrates to investors that the founding team is developing a core competency, one that will be used later to recruit investors, strategic partners, key hires and future acquirers.

But wait, there's more! Another benefit of recruiting advisors for a young team is access to angel investors. Raising money is a dating process. Never ask for money on the first date! Young founders need to cultivate relationships with numerous potential investors. One way to begin those relationships is by bringing on experts in a limited capacity as advisors. That limits their risk and the startup's. If the relationship blossoms, the founders may gain the benefit of an angel investor, or better yet, an angel investor with other angel investing friends.

Benefits of recruiting advisors:
1) Receive invaluable advice
2) Increase team credibility
3) Develop recruiting competency
4) Begin relationships with angel investors

It is difficult to overstate the value a strong advisory board can bring to a young startup. That said, even the best board of advisors only brings a limited amount of credibility to the team. The founders still must run the company. Advisors by definition have a limited role. Some may be more active than others, but they are not considered to be *on* the founding team.

Team Summary

The people are paramount! This was the lesson I learned at my first VCIC event, which ultimately led to this book, and it remains a constant in the industry today. Most VCs would rather have an *A* team with a *B* idea, because the process of growing a company from early stage to exit requires an uncommon set of skills. Like leading a platoon into battle, having commanders who have done it before reduces risk immensely.

Of course, most entrepreneurs are not serial entrepreneurs. First-time founders with a great product/market fit can present a challenge (read, risk) but also an opportunity (reads, lower pre-money valuation and coachability). Pre-money valuations for a serial founding team can be through the roof, for the same reasons stated above. With greener founders, VCs look for signs of industry expertise, vision, coachability, and a passion to learn about and serve customers.

VCs are often actively involved in the process of growing the team, particularly new c-level talent that will be hired using VC funding. VC firms often have serial entrepreneurs on retainer, called entrepreneurs-in-residence or venture partners, available to step in and help a young team. This might even include replacing the founding CEO, which can happen by plan or by distress.

Lastly, young teams can benefit from recruiting advisors. In addition to their expertise and guidance, advisors can add credibility and access to future investors.

> WHAT WE COVERED
>
> **Traction**
>
> - Serial Entrepreneurs
> - Industry Expertise
> - Vision, Coachability and Customer Passion
> - Origin Story
> - Skin in the Game
> - Founder/Investor Conflict
> - Replacing the CEO
> - Holes on the Team
> - Advisory Board

Chapter Questions

1. Why are serial entrepreneurs highly valued by venture capitalists?
2. What are some ways that founders can gain credibility?
3. What is "skin in the game" and why is it important?
4. What is one major benefit of an inexperienced team from a VC's perspective?
5. Why do VC firms hire entrepreneurs-in-residence?
6. List several benefits for young teams of recruiting advisors.
7. List several entrepreneurial attributes VCs are looking for in founders.
8. Would you invest in a startup team if you did not think they were coachable?

Due Diligence Advice for Students: *Team*

Normally, VCs would spend scores of hours with founders as well as talk to customers, employees, strategic partners and former employers as part of the due diligence process. Since none of these are possible, students will have to make some educated guesses based on limited time together. Ask questions that help you gauge what type of people you are working with. In a limited amount of time, you'll have to assess whether you could make good partners.

In your analysis, start with and focus on the CEO. The rest of the team is very important, but the CEO plays the most critical role. Check bios on the company website. Check everyone's LinkedIn profiles. Google individuals along with some keywords like "problems" or "complaints" to see if you can uncover any issues. Point out any holes on the team and *go the extra mile to see if you can find suitable candidates to fill those holes*. Remember, real VCs add value with their extensive networks. We are simulating that competency here. Bring solutions, not just observations.

5. Secret Sauce

How can we stop copycats?

Secret Sauce Contents

Competitive Advantage

When VCs talk about a "secret sauce," they are referring to a startup's ability to do something that nobody else can easily replicate, something that makes *this* startup special. Specifically, they want a unique ability that gives the startup an edge, a *competitive advantage*. In this book, the phrase "secret sauce" is synonymous with "competitive advantage." Both refer to barriers to entry that keep the competition out.

Before we dive into some of the elements of secret sauces, we need to agree on a definition of the oft-misunderstood phrase "competitive advantage." First, it is important to understand the difference between a competitive advantage and a differentiation.

Differentiation refers to how a startup's offerings are better/faster/cheaper than competitors. If that sounds familiar, it should. We're talking about value proposition, part of the product/market fit. Recall our definition for value proposition: how a startup addresses specific customer pain points with a better/faster/cheaper solution, i.e., a differentiated solution.

Here's the confusing thing: having a differentiation appears to give a company an advantage. However, for business strategy purposes, being superior is not considered an *advantage* unless you can protect it by preventing copycats. If you cannot protect it, everyone will copy your "advantage" and you'll have no advantage.

For example, Quizno's took the sandwich world by storm by toasting sandwiches. That was a differentiation. However, there was nothing to stop Subway from installing toasters at every location, which it did, thereby copying Quizno's idea and eliminating any advantage.

A competitive advantage, on the other hand, is a barrier to entry, something that will stop or slow down competitors who want to copy our differentiation. These are sometimes called "unfair advantages," though that phrase will probably never catch on since nobody wants to be associated with being "unfair." But let's be clear, creating unfair advantages is perfectly legal and ethical. In fact, it is written into our constitution:

> "The Congress shall have power…to promote the Progress of Science and useful Arts, by securing for limited Times to Authors and Inventors the exclusive Right to their respective Writings and Discoveries."

The "unfair advantages" of patents and copyrights are in the U.S. Constitution.

In one sentence, our founding fathers put copyrights and patents in the constitution, guaranteeing an unfair advantage for writers and inventors. They have the exclusive right to profit from their writings and discoveries "for limited times."

Quizno's would have had an unfair advantage had they invented and patented the innovation of toasting sandwiches. Then they would have had the exclusive right to their discovery. Unfortunately for Quizno's, toasting sandwiches was a differentiation, not a competitive advantage. Once Quizno's proved the market, copycats followed.

In conclusion, differentiation refers to value proposition, usually articulated as better/faster/cheaper. Competitive advantages, or unfair advantages or secret sauces, are barriers to entry, there to stop copycats.

> *Differentiation = better/faster/cheaper. Competitive advantage = stops copycats.*

Competition

Before we get into some of the elements of erecting barriers to entry, we need to take a deep dive into competition, the people we are hoping to keep out with our barriers. We have already alluded to competitors in the product/market fit chapter when we used the phrase better/faster/cheaper. The obvious follow up question is, *than what?* Exactly who do we see as the competition?

As VCs, we would hope that the founders would have already done this analysis. However, as we discussed in the last chapter, we are often working with young entrepreneurs who may not be the best experts in their industries. Further, and this continues to astound me, even many veteran founders address competition superficially or not at all in their pitch deck, as if their startup will grow in a vacuum. I cannot count the number of times I have heard a founder assert that they have *no* competition.

> *Many founders overlook or underestimate the competition.*

There are two ways to look at this failing. On the one hand, it may discredit the founders if they are naïve enough to believe there is no competition. This could be a red flag (reads, more risk), and we need to investigate why the founders are not fully versed in the competitive landscape. We also price in this risk (reads, lower pre-money valuation).

On the other hand, this is an opportunity for VCs to leverage our expertise and add value to the startup beyond our investment. With our vast networks of industry experts, we are in an excellent position to help founders understand their competition. We can even help build the management team to include industry expertise as the startup goes to market.

There are two levels of understanding of the competition that we need to achieve: 1) macro: the ability to give an overview of the landscape, including the biggest risks; and 2) micro: deep granular knowledge of all key competitors. We should be able to give

Founders and VCs need a competitive overview as well as depth about key players.

an overview of the dynamics of the industry as well as do a deep dive into the specifics of each key individual player.

Macro: Competitive Landscape

On the macro side, there are several helpful business-school tools that help summarize the competition. Business school is the place to go for 30,000-foot macro-level frameworks. Be warned though, this macro analysis is a start, not an end, and must be followed by a deep dive into specific competitors. Nonetheless, these frameworks are commonly used for a reason: they work. They can be very effective at boiling down complexity into a simple graphical summary.

Porter's Five Forces

If you tell a business school student that you want to assess the competitive dynamics in an industry, they are likely to recall Porter's Five Forces, a venerable framework for analyzing the power relationships between various groups in the value network.[38]

Porter's Five Forces examines how harshly current competitors are battling it out, how easily other companies might enter the market, whether there are other types of products that could

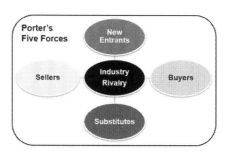

---

[38] "How Competitive Forces Shape Strategy," Michael E. Porter, Harvard Business Review, March 1979. http://bit.ly/vcr008.

solve this problem and the relative power of buyers and sellers.

Porter's Five Forces is a high-level framework that can be helpful as a mental screening tool, particularly for students. However, you would never see this in a startup pitch or any presentation shared by VCs, mostly because it lacks necessary granularity to explain the context for a specific startup. It also comes across as naïve, which is not an adjective that founders or VCs ever want to be associated with.

For students first learning about an industry, Porter's Five Forces is a helpful starting point. I encourage my student teams to use this framework as a place to begin your team discussion about competition. However, this framework should not be part of any presentation. It's a starting point, not an ending place. Below we will discuss better tools to demonstrate the competitive landscape.

2x2 or X/Y Matrix

This is a classic b-school framework in which we boil down a startup's value proposition into two main variables for which we are better/faster/cheaper. This exercise is not suitable for all startups and is too often used inappropriately. A 2x2 matrix only works if there are truly *two key attributes* of our value proposition, each of which will make up an axis. The often-insurmountable challenge here is identifying those axes.

However, on the occasions when we really are competing on two main points, the 2x2 matrix can be a very effective representation of our position as compared to the competition and as perceived by our customers. It gives very clear strategic inputs. We need to be looking out for some competitors to do one thing, and others to do another. Ideally, we can stop them from doing that.

In the example below, the X axis is "Pain Reduction." Clearly that axis is addressing customer pain (actual pain in this case). In this example, there is only one competitor as effective as we are at reducing pain.

Figure: Example of a 2x2 or X/Y matrix

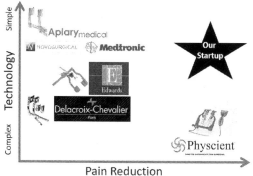

The Y axis is a little less clear. "Complex technology" reads like a description from the founder's perspective. I would prefer to see the axes labeled from the customer's perspective. In this case, "ease of use" might be a better reflection of the value created on this axis. The clear conclusion from the chart is that our startup is the only one that reduces a lot of pain with an easy to use solution.

But what if we spoke to some customers (hospitals) to discover that "ease of use" is not an issue for them? They already have trained employees involved in these processes using current solutions. They would have to restructure their org chart to implement our proposed solution. Their major concern is "ease of integration into current operations," not "ease of use."

Customer Perspective

Beware the founder who is pushing a 2x2 matrix using variables that are not relevant to the customer, and hence are not relevant to the product/market fit. Because the 2x2 is such a popular tool in business strategy, many entrepreneurs push a square peg into the round hole. In the above example, it may be true that this startup has the easiest solution to use. If the world were starting from scratch

> *The X and Y axes MUST be the main differentiators as perceived by the customers.*

today, with no pre-existing infrastructure, "ease of "use" may indeed be one of the two major indices. However, in the real world with the feedback above from hospitals, we now see that this startup is focusing on the wrong thing.

Founders often want to assign a semi-relevant attribute to an axis because they know they are better/faster/cheaper in that regard, and it can blind them to the fact that the customer does not care about that particular differentiation. This is a profound strategic quandary for a startup that will result in going back to iterate the value proposition in the product/market fit. Recall a value prop is to address customer pain points with a differentiated solution. Well, if our solution is differentiated in a way that is not addressing the pain points, we may not be creating value!

I'd like to pause for a moment to stress the iterative process for analyzing startups. This is not a linear procedure, where we've nailed down product/market fit and then moved on to founder/industry fit. More often in practice, we'll start with a quick once-over of the entire Razor. Then we'll drill into problem areas. Once we discover something, we have to incorporate that new finding into our understanding across all aspects of the Razor.

Iterating the Product/Market Fit

This chapter on competition is closely tied to value proposition. In fact, in an earlier version of this book, I had competition as a topic within the value proposition chapter. My argument was that we cannot assert to be better/faster/cheaper without a full explanation of the competitive landscape. I still believe this theoretically, but in practice I have found the world to work otherwise. Founders *do* assert their product/market fit with little to no regard for competition.

I adapted. I concluded that a deep investigation of the competition was not appropriate in the first chapter. Rather, we can take an early leap of faith. Later, as we perform due diligence and learn more about the space, we iterate. At this point in the due

> *The Razor is iterative, not linear. It's a process of discovery, and new information changes earlier analysis.*

diligence process with a deeper understanding of competition, a revisit of the value prop is often in order.

In the example above, we discovered that hospitals care more about ease-of-integration than ease-of-use. We have two options to revise our product/market fit: change the product or revise the target market. On the former, we could add features so that we are addressing our customers' true pain points. On the latter, we could change our target customer to newly constructed hospitals.

Either way, we would then need to revisit all our analysis to date. Is the market big enough? Do we have any traction with new hospitals? If we discover that most hospital construction is in developing countries, do we have the right team in place?

Venn Diagram

Back to macro-level competitive analysis, another venerable business school framework is the Venn diagram. It's a classic because, again, it works. It can be a very effective way to graphically represent complicated strategic concepts, in this case the commonalities between some groups, or what we called back in high school algebra, *sets*.

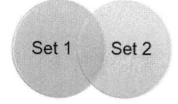 Venn diagrams can be used in a variety of strategic settings, really anywhere that concepts can be grouped into separate sets so that you can study the relationships between the sets. Venn diagrams are most commonly used by VCs to analyze the market (customers) or industry (competitors), particularly if a startup is creating a new space.

Often the headings of the sets are identical whether it is the market or industry. It is the descriptors in each group that changes. For the market, you'd identify market segments or attributes within each group. For the industry, each set would contain competitors.

Whereas the 2x2 matrix assumes a startup will be competing in a *pre-existing* space, the Venn diagram can be helpful for startups attempting to define a *new* sector. In the 2x2, a startup is represented as being superior by being represented in the upper righthand corner, asserting that it is differentiated from current competitors. In the Venn diagram, the startup is usually alone in the new space at the intersection.

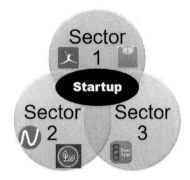

Blue Ocean Markets

There is a school of thought that startups should always create their own new markets, a concept explored in depth in the 2005 book *Blue Ocean Strategy*.[39] The metaphor here is that the ocean is blue out in unchartered waters where there are no sharks (competitors) bloodying the water. In other words, compete in a space where there are no other direct competitors (yet). This is often best represented by a Venn diagram, where the old competition is competing in the old spaces, and the startup is in the new space at the intersection of the old.

For example, Salesforce.com came into the world offering a new tool that was as powerful as enterprise software but performed a very specific productivity service, at the intersection of software and

services. They pioneered a new space that came to be known as Software-as-a-Service (SaaS).

Steve Blank, one of the thought leaders behind Lean methodology, calls this type of competitive analysis a "Petal Diagram" due to the resemblance of a flower when enough industry sectors are being included.

Micro: Key Players

So far, we have only looked at high-level strategic frameworks for competition: the 2x2 matrix and Venn diagram. While these can be effective as a macro snapshot of the competitive landscape, founders

---

[39] Chan Kim and Renée Mauborgne, Harvard Business Review, 2005, bit.ly/vcr009.

Macro: competitive
landscape.
Micro: each key player.
and VCs also need to be able to get deep into the weeds on the specific offerings in the market. Said differently, we need to know *everything* about the key players in the value network, including their current offerings *and* how they are likely to respond to our entering the market.

In the value proposition chapter, we discussed which was better: an idea that was clearly feasible or one that could truly change the world. The answer, of course, was both: a series of accomplishable milestones on the way to large impact. The world changing impact is the macro vision. The accomplishable goals are micro steps.

Similarly, the competitive landscape is the macro product of the relationships between all the micro players in the value network. We cannot know everything about everybody, but it is imperative that we identify the most important players and understand how we might compete or interact with them.

Interestingly, founders consistently fall short on this fundamental understanding. Playing armchair psychologist, I think they are worried that if they go looking for competition, they might learn something that could threaten their baby. Frankly, it's a valid concern, but it won't help to bury your head in the sand, particularly when approaching venture capitalists.

This oversight of founders is so prevalent that I'd like to take a moment to suggest a plan of action for young founders (and VC analysts).

> *Think like a VC...*
>
> When it comes to the competition, connect to your inner journalist and investigate with intellectual curiosity and integrity (don't fool yourself!).

It is a simple one. Google, Google, Google. If you are somewhat new to an industry, you might benefit from a *keyword suggestion tool*. (Google the phrase and you'll find many.) These tools take your keywords and suggest new ones based on what other people have searched. This is a great way to begin learning the lexicon of your industry, i.e., the language used by your customers and your competitors.

Googling is just the beginning, but it is an important start. I cannot count the number of times I've had a young founding team in my office pitching their idea as I start Googling some of the keywords in their presentation, and I uncover some competition they've never heard of!

Once you've identified key players in the industry, it's time to put on your Sherlock Holmes hat and learn *everything* you can about them. Check out every nook and cranny of their website. Google their company name along with keywords like "reviews" or "problems" or "I hate this company!" Conversely, add the phrase "I love" with your search to investigate what they are doing right.

Product Attribute Chart

One helpful tool to assimilate the information gathered on current competitors is a product attribute chart, which allows us to list numerous key features. Generally, our startup should be the only one with all ✓'s rather than X's, or all green lights rather than red lights.

Figure: Example of a product attribute chart

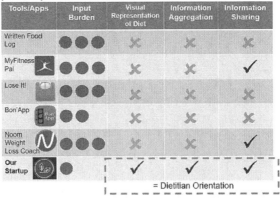

Whereas a 2x2 matrix specifies two axes, a product attribute chart may contain as many features as we think are important. We again have the challenge of identifying which key features are truly value-add for our customers, i.e., which features address specific customer pain points. Founders are unfortunately motivated to include any feature for which they are better/faster/cheaper, which can sometimes blind them to their customers' needs.

VCs have to bring our optimistic contrarianism to challenge the assumptions behind product attribute charts. For every feature listed, for example, what kind of traction does the startup have? Can they validate the value prop for each feature?

Barriers to Entry

So far in this chapter, we've discussed how to *investigate* the competition with a goal of a deep understanding of the industry side of our value network. Going forward, we'll address how to *deal with* competition, specifically, how to exploit a startup's pre-existing competitive advantages *and* how to create new barriers to entry.

> *A barrier to entry impedes competitors from entering into our market.*

Notice the duality: we must analyze a startup's current situation, and we also have the opportunity (with our venture capital investment) to do new things: go after bigger markets, add features...and, in this chapter, erect barriers to entry. Our goal is to protect our turf against competitors, to give our startup a competitive edge to maintain its differentiation.

The traditional gold standard in this department was to have *strong IP*, referring to intellectual property, specifically a patent. Back when most VC investments were in silicon chips, it was intellectual property law that gave innovators legal protection from others copying their technology. As the VC industry has shifted over the decades from hardware to software, the focus has shifted away from IP toward other ways to prevent copycats, things like network effects, trade secrets, sticky products and strategic partnerships.

First-Mover ~~Advantage~~ Opportunity

A second misunderstanding about competitive advantage that we need to address is the *first mover advantage*. There is an ongoing debate about which is better, being first or second to market. Is it better to be a first mover or a smart successor? Would you rather be the early bird or the second mouse?

We all know that the early bird gets the worm. That is a great metaphor for first-mover advantage. Arrive first and enjoy the spoils of victory!

But what about the eager mouse that is first to get to the mousetrap? Not such a good ending. Better to be the second mouse in that case.

Whether it's better to be a first mover or a fast follower depends on the situation. There are risks and benefits associated with both. Being first is fraught with risk: will the technology work? Will customers want it? Will the market grow? Being second allows us to learn the lessons from someone else's mistakes and take advantage of a newly educated market.

> *Being a "fast follower" is sometimes better than a first mover.*

On the other hand, being first might give us the opportunity to create advantages if we can lock in customers with contracts, create switching costs, learn some way of doing business that others can't figure out, get that one great location, sign exclusive partners, or, most commonly these days, hit critical mass to create a sustainable network effect.

The bottom line is that being first to market is not in-and-of-itself an advantage. Rather, it's an opportunity. Being first gives us the chance to raise barriers to entry. If we are going first, to have a competitive advantage, our strategy needs to include one or more barriers from the list below.

Network Effect

A *network effect* is a benefit that grows as the number of users (the network) grows. Hence, whoever has the biggest network is providing the most benefit, and thus has an advantage. Thanks to the feedback loop of the network improving as it gets bigger, the advantage should grow with time. When a network effect is possible, being the first-mover to get to critical mass does indeed create a sustainable advantage.

> *In a two-sided marketplace, being the first to critical mass is truly a first-mover advantage.*

Social networking and two-sided marketplaces are the most common examples of startups that benefit from network effects these days. More specifically, *sharing economy* startups like Uber, AirBnb, Etsy and (old school) eBay bring together some form of buyers and sellers.

Once the marketplace hits critical mass, it is very difficult for a competitor to come in and steal market share unless the first-mover makes a big mistake.

That said, it can happen. Just ask Friendster or Myspace. These companies had network advantages and still were not able to stop Facebook from taking over social networking.

As Fred Wilson, partner at Union Square Ventures, said in a 2011 blog, "...investing in web services is different than investing in chips, routers and enterprise software...Differentiation is more about user experience than proprietary technology. Defensibility is more about network effects than patents."[40]

Sticky Products

Another type of competitive advantage that we may pursue, particularly if we are first movers, is to create *sticky* products that help keep customers from switching to our competitors' offerings. Once a customer, whether a business or a consumer, has adopted a sticky solution, there are considerable costs associated with switching to a new solution, traditionally called *switching costs*.

> *Sticky products are defined by high switching costs so that customers will not want to leave us.*

Like network effects, this advantage is not available to all startups. We need to have offerings that either are inherently sticky or can be modified to help retain customers. Often, this comes in the form of some kind of investment in the product that the customer makes and does not want to have to repeat with a competitor. For example, once a customer has set up all their preferences in a music service like Spotify or Pandora, there are costs associated with switching to a new service and having to start over from scratch. Cloud storage services have a similar quality.

Many B2B SaaS (business-to-business software-as-a-service) offerings require an initial investment to get up and running, which can lock customers in to some degree. Accounting software, like TurboTax, is a

---

[40] *The Opportunity Fund*, blog post by Fred Wilson, January 15, 2011, https://www.usv.com/blog/the-opportunity-fund

great example. Once a customer has adopted TurboTax as their tax prep solution, they will invest hours entering information into the TurboTax system. When tax season rolls around next year, TurboTax has significant stickiness. A consumer would have to choose to re-enter the information into a new system.

Social networking websites have a similar stickiness. Once a customer establishes a network of friends, family and/or colleagues, it's a pain to recreate it elsewhere. Credit cards that allow you to accrue points are another example.

> *Stickiness can be an outcome of customers' investment in adopting and using a specific product.*

Retailers have gotten into the game lately, attempting to create stickiness through memberships. Once you pay your Costco or Sam's Club annual fee, you are somewhat locked into shopping at that outlet. Shopping elsewhere would create the perception that you wasted your membership fee. Amazon.com has invested very heavily in becoming a sticky product. One-click checkout, Prime membership, subscriptions and the dash button are all attempts to make Amazon stick as our go-to for online shopping.

If we have the chance to create significant switching costs, that is, create a very sticky product, then there is an incentive to raise a lot of capital as early as possible to get as many customers as possible. Just as Google invested in its tech lead to maintain a competitive advantage, investing in acquiring customers quickly can be a smart investment to create an advantage. Akin to a land grab, in a sticky market, whoever gets the customers first is going to come out on top.

Trade Secrets

Trade secrets refer to anything that we are doing as part of our business that others cannot easily figure out. This advantage is the source of the phrase "secret sauce," and was made famous by food producers like Coca Cola and Kentucky Fried Chicken, whose secret recipes supposedly made it impossible to recreate their amazing (differentiated) taste.

> *Trade secret: the original secret sauce.*

Today, Google is probably the most successful company whose advantage originally came from a trade secret: its search algorithm. Back when the Internet was still figuring itself out, there were many search engines: Excite, Alta Vista, Yahoo, Lycos and infoseek, to name just a few. Each had its own approach and shortcomings. Google launched with a splash in 1998 with a new algorithm developed by Stanford PhD computer science brainiacs, Larry Page and Sergey Brin.

Google started with a *technology lead* that others could not easily figure out. Then, to maintain that advantage, Google invested heavily in tech talent, reportedly hiring more PhDs than any other tech company. To this day, Google has a great reputation for attracting top talent, and not by accident. People want to work there because the founders focused on hiring people as a core competency and competitive advantage.

> *A technology lead is a type of trade secret and is an advantage until competitors catch up.*

Let it be a lesson for any startup with a trade secret. To maintain a tech lead, you've got to invest in it! VCs want to see these types of startups with a healthy R&D budget (research and development) to indicate that they plan to stay ahead of the competition.

Trade secrets are not limited to technology leads. They can also include ways that we operate our business that give us an advantage over competition. Our founding team, for example, may have core competencies that others simply cannot copy. Or we might have exclusive access to better, faster or cheaper suppliers. We may also have developed an in-house business method or process, a way of doing business, that our competitors cannot figure out. Lastly, our relationships with customers and partners could be a part of a *secret sauce* that our competitors cannot easily copy.

Strategic Partnerships

As we continue through a list of potential competitive advantages, it is important to point out that not every startup will have access to every advantage. Most startups don't have network effects or tech leads and can really struggle to come up with some way to create barriers to entry. Also, even if we have advantages mentioned above, we are always in search of more barriers to protect our turf.

One tried and true business strategy to create an advantage is to set up exclusive relationships within our value network. The aim here is to make some portion of the value network inaccessible to our competitors. Perhaps we can lock in a key supplier or become the sole supplier to the biggest distributor for a particular geographic region.

> *Exclusive partnerships lock in a portion of our value network.*

These strategic partnerships can take many forms, and parties at both ends of the transaction may enter into these arrangements for a variety of reasons. Again, it will be our expertise in the value network that will aid us in finding the best partners to create the most effective barriers through partnerships.

Generally, to get the benefit of exclusivity, we will have to give up something. That is, to achieve this reduced competitive risk, we will likely need to give up some opportunity. For example, we may need to offer a reduced price or enhanced benefits to entice industry leaders to become our partners. We'd then make less per transaction but have lower risk of the competition swooping in and stealing market share.

Think like a VC...

Balance the trade-offs between opportunity and risk.

Perhaps the most famous example of creating a competitive advantage through exclusive contracts is Ticketmaster, whose team was able to secure exclusivity from large performance venues by paying multi-million dollar signing bonuses to municipalities. This strategy gave Ticketmaster a significant advantage over competitors for decades, so much so that many complained that Ticketmaster behaved like a monopoly.

Intellectual Property (IP) Law

The most traditional sustainable competitive advantage is the exclusive legal right to use our innovation, banning others from copying our success. This exclusive right usually comes in the form of a patent, though copyrights and trademarks may also have benefits in keeping competitors out in certain industries. All of these are known more broadly as *intellectual property,* or *IP*.

The laws surrounding intellectual property are very complex and generally require brilliant legal minds to interpret and debate. If we are looking at a startup that has any IP legal issues, we have a good excuse to expand the team to include an entrepreneurial lawyer on the advisory board who specializes in IP law. (Our VC firm most certainly has IP lawyers in our network.)

Patents

The traditional homerun in the department of unfair advantages is the monopoly provided by the U.S. constitution in the form of patent protection. Patents are a very interesting (and relatively new in the course of human history) economic development bargain. It's a trade-off for society. In exchange for receiving monopoly rights for 20 years, the inventor must share with society exactly how the invention works.

The theory is that society will benefit in the long run through the advancement of science by giving inventors these rather short-term incentives to keep inventing.

A patent is a social contract: a limited monopoly in exchange for sharing ideas.

To receive a patent, an inventor must come up with a discovery that is new, useful and non-obvious. A drug discovery is a classic example. Pharma companies have the exclusive right to sell branded drugs until the drug *goes generic* (when the patent expires), at which time the price drops precipitously as competitors are allowed to enter the marketplace.

While a patented drug can be a relatively straightforward example, patent protection for other "discoveries" can get very complicated. There are many vague words in the statutes that are open to interpretation: *discovery, invention, utility, new, useful* and perhaps the vaguest, *non-obvious*. It can be difficult to determine what is or is not patentable, and then beyond that, what exact protection a patent offers when it is granted. It is rarely clean-cut, which explains multi-million-dollar patent wars we occasionally hear about in the press.

> *Patents can be very difficult and expensive to defend, and the outcomes are risky.*

Further complicating the benefits of patents is the lack of any enforcement agency. There are no patent police. If a startup has a patent and believes another company is infringing upon it, the startup must bear the expense of defending the patent by suing the offender. This often leads to very expensive and risky trials.

Some high-profile cases have included Apple suing Samsung for hundreds of millions of dollars in damages over smartphone patents. Amazon received a patent for the one-click checkout that led to a multi-million dollar lawsuit with BarnesandNoble.com.

Patent protection is a complicated matter. More information about patents is readily available at the USPTO web site,[41] but again, legal advice is the best approach if we find that we have any potential patent issues.

> *Patents protect "inventions." Copyrights, "works of authorship."*

Copyrights

While patents protect *inventors*, copyrights give *creators* exclusive rights to *works of authorship*, such as books, newspaper articles, songs, poems, lyrics, drawings, movies, sound recordings, software, etc. Authors have rights for 50-100 years after their deaths before the works fall into the *public domain*, after which they are available for free use by anyone.

Copyright protection is of critical importance to content providers, like media and entertainment companies, which create original works of authorship and license them to others. Lately, streaming entertainment companies such as Netflix, Hulu, Spotify and Pandora have created new business models from exclusive licensing of copyrighted content from television networks, film studios and music companies. If you ever wondered why a certain movie, television show or album is available one month on your service but not the next, it is the result of

---

[41] www.uspto.gov, U.S. Patent and Trademark Office.

B. Founder/Industry Fit

complicated negotiations between media content companies and service providers.

Copyright law also has some implications with software companies, though it's a bit of an unusual relationship. While it is possible to copyright software code, it offers little practical protection as other companies can write similar code that accomplishes the same thing. This is akin to students paraphrasing but not plagiarizing information for a term paper. For this reason, copyright protection is rarely considered an advantage for software companies.

Trademark

A trademark is a word, slogan and/or symbol used by a company to distinguish its products from competitors' offerings. It is trademark law that prohibits us from opening our own McDonald's restaurants. Trademarks are an absolute necessity as a long-term business practice, akin to paying your taxes. All ongoing concerns should protect their brands.

However, trademarks and branding are not really strategic advantages for startups. If anything, startups are at a strategic disadvantage because we must navigate a minefield of pre-existing trademarks. This is a big challenge when choosing a company name, for example.

Trademarks are "business as usual," not an unfair advantage.

True, in a number of years, if we have executed well, there will be value in our brand, perhaps significant value. However, also true, every other company has the same opportunity. Hence, creating a strong brand (including trademarks) is no more of a strategic competitive advantage than simply doing a better job of executing our plan. In other words, there is no secret sauce here; it's business as usual.

Secret Sauce Summary

In this chapter, we've explored how to handle the competition. We began with an investigation of the competitive landscape. This was a follow-up to our work in product/market fit, where we asserted that we have a better/faster/cheaper solution. In this chapter, we went deeper into the question, *than what*? With a greater understanding of the competitive landscape, we often need to circle back and iterate the product/market fit (refine the product features or the target segment).

In exploring the competition, we need to be cognizant of founders' all-too-common failure to fully investigate competitors, sometimes going so far as to say there is no competition. Even if there is currently no direct competition, as would be the case in a "blue ocean market," the sea is still full of sharks, and we need to understand their behavior.

We discussed several strategies to build barriers to entry to keep the competition out. VCs are looking for a startup to have some sort of real or metaphorical *secret sauce* that will give the startup an unfair advantage. Creating and sustaining competitive advantages often require significant investments. Two-sided marketplaces, for example, require much more capital to get started because two types of customers must be acquired before any value is created. Technology leads are similarly expensive to maintain with continued investment in R&D. Partnerships require that we give up something (opportunity cost).

Some competitive advantages are available to first-movers, but being first is not by itself an advantage. It's an opportunity to erect specific barriers, like network effects, strategic partnerships and sticky products. Without one or more of these advantages, our success will almost certainly be limited by the entry of copycats, who will eat up market share.

> ### WHAT WE COVERED
>
> ### Secret Sauce
>
> - Macro: Comp. Landscape
> - Micro: Key Players
> - Barriers to Entry
> - First-Mover Opportunity
> - Network Effect
> - Sticky Products
> - Trade Secrets
> - Strategic Partnerships
> - Intellectual Property

Chapter Questions

1. How is "competitive advantage" different from "differentiation?"
2. Explain the double metaphor: early bird vs. second mouse.
3. What is a sticky product, and why are they important to VCs?
4. Think of a product that you use that is sticky and explain why.
5. Is a technology lead a kind of trade secret?
6. Why are patents in the constitution?
7. How is competition connected to value proposition?
8. As VCs, how much do we care about how the founding team represents the competition?
9. Why might founders compare their startup using features that are not particularly relevant to customers?
10. What are "blue ocean markets?" What does red represent in this metaphor and why do we avoid it?
11. What kind of competitive advantage did Ticketmaster masterfully utilize?

Due Diligence Advice for Students: **Secret Sauce**

Competition: Don't take your founders' word for it! Founders are often surprisingly lacking in their understanding of the competition. Put on your Sherlock Holmes hat and Google, Google, Google. Use creative keyword searches to find potential competitors. Perhaps use a keyword suggestion tool. See if there is a trade organization that has industry overview information. Learn the lexicon of the industry. Demonstrate a macro level understanding of the space as well as depth of knowledge about key players. Use 2x2, Venn or product attribute chart to summarize findings. Make sure to revisit your product/market fit after you better understand the competitive landscape.

Secret sauce: Assess both the current situation and the future potential. If the startup has a competitive advantage today, is it sustainable over time? What investment and strategy will that require? Alternatively, if a startup does *not* currently have an advantage, is there a way we can create and maintain one with our investment? This is an area of analysis in which we need to be speculative and assertive.

---

6. Business Model

How quickly (and perhaps profitably) can we grow?

Business Model Contents

Defining "Business Model"

Before we can have a coherent conversation about business models and startups, we need to talk a little bit about how "business model" became a catchall catchphrase. Coming out of the dotcom bust, "business model" evolved as the vague term of art used to describe monumental startup failings. You would hear analysts say things like, "Of course Pets.com bombed. Mailing big heavy bags of pet food is a terrible business model."

The problem with a catchall catchphrase is that it has too many variables baked in. There is no way to know specifically what fundamental business rule is being broken. What exactly is wrong with delivering heavy things? Bad margins? Limits to scalability? Supply chain? The cost of delivery as compared to the value being created? Is there some inherent weakness in the strategy to deliver dogfood to people's homes rather than sending it to retail outlets to be held in inventory before being purchased and self-delivered by consumers?

Adding to the confusion is the common conflation of "business model" with "revenue model." The *revenue* model only includes how a company transacts with customers, i.e., how it makes money. The *business* model includes much more, like building infrastructure and developing strategic partnerships.

In this chapter, we'll deconstruct the phrase "business model" from the VC's perspective. Let's start with a fundamental definition:

> *Razor Definition, Business Model:*
> *The competencies, systems and infrastructure developed by a company to facilitate interactions and transactions within its value network with the goal of creating and redistributing value.*

There is a lot to unpack there. Let's start by focusing on the last portion of the definition, which articulates the goal of the business model: to create and redistribute value. For traditional businesses, this could be reworded into the objective: *to grow and profit*. It turns out that those two outcomes, growing and profiting, are in conflict, and for venture-backed startups, the latter half of the goal (to profit) may not even be necessary.

Growth vs. Profitability

When it comes to building a business model for any company, be it brick-and-mortar, high tech startup or anything in between, there is an inherent and persistent tension between long-term growth and short-term profitability. To facilitate growth, companies must make significant investments that often far outweigh short-term profits.

As we discussed in Part I, VCs are making equity investments in startups with the primary purpose of fueling growth (see Equity to Fuel Growth,

p. 25). However, focusing on growth in the extreme is risky and can appear reckless. It takes time for a company to hire the right people and build the systems and infrastructure required to handle growth. To pour all our resources into customer acquisition creates the potential for *success failure*, wherein we succeed at attracting customers but fail at keeping them happy. We may ultimately collapse under the weight of our own growth.

At the other extreme, over-focusing on sustainable business fundamentals, like profitability, carries the risk of losing significant market share to competitors. As discussed in the previous chapter, if we

> *Startup's dilemma: grow too quickly (and become unstable) or too slowly (and lose market share).*

have sticky products, there is a first-mover advantage, and we'll want to get as many customers as quickly as possible to protect our turf.

Google, for example, was well-served by getting to market (to create value) long before it had figured out a revenue model (to redistribute value). The founders ran on the leap of faith that they would be creating immense value by organizing "the world's information, making it

> *When the product/market fit is very compelling, there is an argument for sacrificing some stability to achieve faster growth.*

universally accessible and useful."[42] Given that level of value creation, they had confidence they could figure out a business model. In late 2000, over two years after releasing the search engine, Google launched AdWords, and the rest is history.

Soon thereafter, the dotcom bubble burst and shook the foundation of the create-enough-value-and-we'll-figure-out-the-rest philosophy. When I came through business school in 2001-03, the curriculum was crowded with cases of failed dotcom business models. The prevailing thinking was that the Internet bubble was largely caused by the absence of business fundamentals.

---

[42] See a one-minute video of a young Larry Page in 2002 explaining Google's mission at http://stanford.io/2u4oflj.

Frankly, this Monday morning quarterbacking drove me crazy when I was a student and was one of the reasons I was profoundly moved by the realism of VCIC (see *Where I'm Coming From*, p. 4). In classes, we were sanctimoniously declaring the stupidity of the reckless business models of startups like Pets.com and Webvan, a grocery delivery service funded by venture capital in 1999 and bankrupt by 2001. It seemed to me that these ideas were not so much stupid as unlucky, victims of macro circumstances. (Over a decade later, I'm somewhat vindicated as opinions have shifted.)[43]

At VCIC, there was no sanctimony as we were all in it together: students, founders and VCs. These were the actual quarterbacks playing the game in real time. We were immersed in the complexities of trying to figure out the best business model for a startup, how to balance growth and fundamentals, risk and opportunity.

My traditional business school classes had been, of course, focused on *traditional* business fundamentals. In that conservative light, yes, 1999 was a year of recklessness. However, from the perspective I witnessed at VCIC, juggling all the variables that founders and VCs juggle trying to make a startup work, I saw things differently. VCs have a different set of business fundamentals, one for which the balance between growth and stability is always tipped toward growth. One for which failure is a normal part of the process. That's the hit-driven model.

> *For VCs, the balance between growth and profitability always leans toward growth.*

It took me a few years out of business school to fully grasp what had bothered me in those armchair quarterbacking case discussions. First, hit-driven industries behave differently than traditional businesses, and the volume of failures will always seem reckless to traditionalists. To this day, venture capital is regarded as gambling by many professionals in more traditional finance roles.

---

[43] "Turns out the dot-com bust's worst flops were actually fantastic ideas," Wired Magazine, Robert McMillan, 12/08/14, bit.ly/bust-now-good.

Secondly, nobody is safe from the pendulum swings of macro market conditions. When markets are soaring, even traditionalists lean toward growth. When markets crash, even VCs take a second breath. Sequoia Capital famously sent a "batten down the hatches" PowerPoint deck to its portfolio companies after the 2008 crisis.[44]

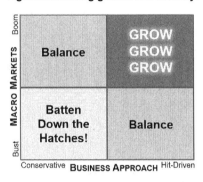

Figure: Balancing growth and stability.

Not surprisingly, VCs have come up with a couple of handy rules of thumb to help put growth and profitability into context. One is the 40% rule, stating that growth plus profitability should be 40% or higher. There are two caveats to this rule: 1) it doesn't apply to *all* kinds of startups, just SaaS (software-as-a-service); and 2) it does not apply to very early stages.[45] Still, it gives us a glimpse into the balancing act required with growth and profitability.

With the 40% rule, we could have 20% growth and 20% profitability. Alternatively, 100% growth and negative 60% profitability would satisfy the rule. In the latter, even though we are burning through cash, we are still creating equity value through growth, meaning the valuation of the startup is rising despite the fact that we are "losing money."

The SaaS Rule of 40: after reaching scale: growth + profitability ≥ 40%.

Students should take this rule with a grain of salt and definitely not try to apply it across other sectors or startup phases. Sharing economy, e-commerce, Internet-of-things and blockchain startups are all going to look a lot different than B2B SaaS. Nonetheless, the existence of the 40% rule is a glimpse into the give-and-take between profitability and growth.

---

[44] Sequoia's PowerPoint deck in a Tech Crunch article of 2008: bit.ly/sequoia-doom.
[45] As discussed in 2015 by Brad Feld (bit.ly/40brad) and Fred Wilson bit.ly/40fred.

Path to Exit

Like all investors, VCs buy low and sell high. The latter half of that equation is determined by the *exit valuation*, which refers to the valuation of the startup when it is acquired or goes public. Our primary goal for any startup in our portfolio is to maximize that exit price so that we may maximize our return to LPs.

> *How much we need to focus on business fundamentals is dictated by the exit strategy.*

When coming up with a plan to balance growth and profitability, VCs look to the exit for guidance, specifically, we try to build whatever business model will maximize the exit valuation. If we have a startup that may go public, for example, we'll need to focus on profitability to create the stability required by public markets. On the other hand, if our exit strategy is to be acquired, we'll have to figure out what potential acquirers value most. Some acquirers may be focused on getting new customers, others on gaining new technology and still others may care most about our revenue. Usually it is some combination of those three factors.

For example, Facebook acquired Instagram for $1B when Instagram had 30 million users and no revenue. Clearly, profitability was not Facebook's primary concern. More likely, Facebook had a vision for how to integrate Instagram's technology and user base into Facebook's proven system for generating revenue through targeted advertising.

> *Facebook acquired Instagram for $1B when Instagram had 30M users and no revenue.*

Let's assume this is true and look at the strategic implications. If Instagram had been grooming itself to be acquired by a major tech company like Facebook, one could argue that they would have been well-served *not* to spend any of the venture capital they had raised on developing the expertise to generate revenue through ads. Rather, the argument continues, they were best served to focus on their core technology and their user base. In other words, they were well served by focusing on growth rather than worrying about creating a sustainable business model.

[Note: I have no inside knowledge of Instagram's exit strategy. For all I know, they were trying like hell to reach profitability so that they could go public.]

Our argument is that Instagram was well-served by creating an unstable company. It is much riskier to have a company that makes no money. If there had been a stock market crash, Instagram may have run out of cash as sources of equity funding may have dried up. A company will always be more stable if it has its own source of funding (revenue). The VCs and founders of Instagram made a calculated risk. To maximize the exit valuation, they took some short-term financial risk. In this case it worked. (Not so much for Pets.com or Webvan.)

If you recall our moonshot metaphor from Part I of this book, VCs are supplying the jet fuel (cash) for the rocket (startup) to get to the moon (exit). What we are currently discussing is a rocket that has broken free of earth's atmosphere. It would be safer to fall into orbit and circle the earth (metaphor: generate revenue and become a stable company). However, to get to the moon, we must leave orbital safety and head out farther into space. We blast another round of jet fuel and point the rocket toward the moon. It is riskier, but the rewards are much higher.

Google and Instagram are famous and also extreme cases of super-fast growth with apparent disregard for profitability. This leads some traditionalists to interpret that VCs lack business fundamentals. What traditionalists are missing is the hit-driven, moonshot approach that drives VCs to focus on the path to exit rather than profitability. VCs are knowingly taking extra risk, including some spectacular failures, all with the goal of a moon landing. Rather than having, say, five regular satellites in orbit, the VC model may have one magnificent moon landing and four incidents of space debris.

The hit-driven approach of VCs emphasizes growth over stability.

Barriers to Scalability

A term VCs employ to describe their non-traditional growth-over-stability business model is *scalability*, which refers to a startup's potential to grow quickly and achieve a desired exit. The only stability required is to survive until exit. This is in stark contrast to the perspective of traditional businesspeople, for whom "stability" must always imply a "sustainable business model."

> *Scalability: ability to growth quickly with just enough stability to make it to exit.*

Perhaps the most effective approach to describing the scalability of a startup is in the negative, by identifying *barriers* to scalability. For any given startup, what are the obstacles to scale? Are those obstacles something that we can overcome with our capital (and other non-cash) contributions to the startup?

Here we are in another arena in which the founders may not be our best authorities. While they know the most about their startup, founders have often been operating in a cash-strapped environment which can blind them to opportunities made possible by large cash infusions of venture capital. Also, the scalability required for a moonshot is inherently dangerous, often more risk than founders want to take.

While VCs have a portfolio and assume some startups will fail, founders at a given startup do not have a portfolio. All their eggs are in this particular rocket ship, which will often influence them toward stability (orbit). VCs must be politely assertive in strategizing for maximum scalability (moonshot). Nobody wants to be space debris.

Assessing scalability is a two-pronged process, similar to analyzing the secret sauce of a startup. First, we assess the current situation, the current barriers to scale. Second, we strategize and speculate about the future, specifically, what barriers to scale might be removed if we invest millions of dollars. For secret sauce, we were determining what barriers to entry might be *erected* after our investment to keep competitors out.

Now assessing the business model, we're trying to *remove* barriers to scale. Again, this analysis often must come from the VC firm as the founders may not have the clearest vision in this regard.

> *Example Barriers to Scalability*
> Infrastructure Needs
> Product Development
> Long Sales Cycles
> Slow Customer Adoption
> Legal/Regulatory
> Finding Talent

Scalability and Product/Market Fit

There are two sides to scalability. Foremost is the ability to quickly acquire customers. Second is the need to build competencies, systems and infrastructure to support them. Let's start on the customer side by reconnecting with our product/market fit chapter. One of the major factors determining the speed of customer adoption is the level of pain customers feel, coupled with the level to which they perceive our solutions to be addressing their pain. Step #1 for a startup to have the potential to scale quickly is to have a compelling value prop, which is usually evidenced by impressive early traction.

A second consideration from the product/market fit chapter is market size. We need a big enough market to ensure scalability. (Metaphorically, we need a big enough pond size for our fish to grow.) In sizing the market, we need to be careful about segmentation, specifically whether we can expect scalability to behave the same across different segments.

Lastly from product/market fit we need to consider traction. Often, by the time a startup is pursuing venture capital, it has some customer adoption to tout. However, early traction in one

> *Customer-side scalability starts with a great product/market fit.*

segment is not necessarily predictive of adoption by the larger customer segments a startup may need to pursue to scale.

These product/market fit considerations are a first step toward analyzing a startup's scalability on the customer side. If we have an extremely compelling product/market fit (a homerun value prop, huge market size and terrific early traction), there is reason to have confidence that we will be able to figure out a way to redistribute that value, as Google did.

However, most startups have some level of uncertainty in their product/market fit. Something about the value prop, market size or traction is likely to give us pause. Hence, VCs have developed tools to help quantify the value that we might create as well as the expense associated with growth. On the value creation side, we have the lifetime value of customers (LTV), and on the expense side, customer acquisition cost (CAC).

Customer Acquisition Cost (CAC)

As the name implies, customer acquisition cost (CAC) is the summation of all expenses required to bring in one customer. This has always existed in theory but historically was very difficult to calculate. A company might have run an advertising campaign, for example, and then tracked the resulting increase in sales. From those numbers, they might calculate a return on investment for the campaign, but rarely in those days did you hear of a specific number for converting one customer.

The new level of granularity of calculating the cost to attract one customer has been made possible by relatively new online advertising tools, most heavily influenced by Google and Facebook. These platforms allow companies to run targeted paid ad campaigns in which the behavior of each customer can be tracked. By knowing exactly what potential customers are clicking and exactly how they are behaving after clicking, companies can rather simply derive a cost per customer.

CAC, brought to you by Google and Facebook.

For example, a startup can pay $1 per click-through to send potential customers to its website. Visitors to the site can be tracked. If 10% of those visitors convert to customers, we can mathematically determine that the startup is paying $10 per customer via that specific click-through ad campaign ($1÷0.1).

Wow, that's easy, next topic, right? This simplification tool gets complicated rather quickly, and once again we are going to need a narrative to make sense of the numbers. True, if we are analyzing a startup whose main customer acquisition strategy is paid advertising via online clicks, we'll have a pretty simple calculation for current CAC. However, that specific number may not be predictive of what the future CAC will be after the startup leaves proof-of-concept phase and heads into growth stage, or when the startup starts to pursue new customer segments.

Signing up some eager early adopters is a very different challenge than reaching the mainstream, as famously explored in Geoffrey Moore's

influential 1991 book, *Crossing the Chasm.*
Moore identified a gap in customer adoption
separating "technology enthusiasts," often
eager to adopt new solutions, and the more
conservative majority of a large market. As VCs

> *Today's CAC is not necessarily tomorrow's CAC as we "cross the chasm."*

building unicorns, we are often trying to jump this chasm.

A second challenge with using customer acquisition cost is the reality that most startups will not rely entirely on targeted click campaigns. Many startups have numerous go-to-market strategies, including traditional advertising, direct sales or strategic partnerships. Attempting to come up with one number for customer acquisition cost can be a silly exercise. In those cases, it's all about the narrative, and there are going to be key elements of understanding CAC that will get lost in the numbers.

Sales Cycles

Time is a very important part of the cost of customer acquisition cost that can be difficult to quantify. A sales cycle is the length of time it takes to go through the entire sales process with one customer. The Internet created the possibility of an extremely attractive business fundamental: very short sales cycles when we have a product online that our customers can click to buy, download and/or sign up for. CAC is perfect for those situations.

However, we may have a more complex sales process. For example, on the other end of the spectrum we could have a specialized B2B enterprise software that requires a dozen visits to our customer's headquarters, meetings with different committees and the green light from multiple decision-makers before a purchase is finalized. We could be looking at sales cycles over one year long.

> *Long sales cycles increase customer acquisition cost but also may provide a barrier to entry to keep competitors out.*

Long sales cycles are generally associated with large ticket items sold to large organizations. Government, military, education and healthcare are all sectors that have historically very long sales cycles and thus inhibit scalability. On the positive side, once we get those contracts, we have a competitive advantage as our competitors will have to deal with long sales cycles as a barrier to entry.

Despite these challenges, CAC has become an essential communication tool for startups. Founders absolutely must deal with it, i.e., provide a number, even if their startup is not a good fit for this shortcut. If this sounds familiar, we had a similar situation in

> *Despite its shortcomings, CAC is now industry standard and required by VCs.*

market size. You may recall my founder who stated that market size is just some BS number you come up with to make VCs happy. This is (partially) true. We must come up with numbers, but there also should be a compelling, coherent story about the numbers. VCs are great BS detectors.

The CAC story needs to include both the current story and future vision for customer acquisition. Some of the elements of that story include:

- How compelling is the product/market fit?
- How much do we have to educate customers?
- What is the threat of competition and how might that affect CAC?
- What are other barriers to adoption?
- What are some non-monetary influencers on CAC, such as sales cycles?

Lifetime Value (LTV)

The cost to acquire customers is an important metric, but it doesn't have much meaning unless we know the value of each customer we acquire. The earlier example with a $10 customer acquisition cost could be terrible if we are selling a $5 one-time product, or fantastic if we are getting a lifelong subscriber for a $10/month service.

There are two ways of looking at *lifetime value* (LTV) of customers in our startup. The most obvious is a current value of all revenues that will be generated from that customer. In the above example with a $10 monthly subscriber, we might estimate an average customer life to be five years, yielding a total of $120 * 5 = $600 of lifetime value. We would happily pay $10 to acquire such a customer![46]

The second way to value customers is by working backward from a potential exit. If our exit strategy is to be acquired by another company, we may be able to estimate how much that company would value our customers. In other words, we can look at how much acquirers have paid for other startups and estimate a price per customer, often called *price per user* when there is little or no revenue being generated.

> *Two ways to calculate LTV:*
> *1) NPV of future revenue;*
> *2) value at exit.*

In this scenario, if we could acquire customers for $1 each and then *get acquired* for $20 a customer, we could have a winner regardless of the amount of revenues we were able to collect. This scenario would be a strong candidate for focusing on growth over profitability with the goal of obtaining as many customers as possible.

These numbers are approximated based on the price of acquisition of other startups divided by their number of users at exit. For example, Facebook's acquisition of Instagram for $1B when Instagram had 30M users implies a $30 per user price at exit.[47] Note that the $30 purchase price from Facebook becomes Facebook's customer acquisition cost. For this price to make sense, Facebook must have a higher lifetime value for customers, and indeed, looking at Facebook's market cap (nearly $300B) divided by its total users (1.5B), it would appear that Facebook's users are worth about $200 each.

The examples above are very conveniently quantifiable. As is true with many tools we employ to simplify complex concepts, CAC and LTV are powerfully effective (when used judiciously and put in context) or potentially dangerous (when taken at face value). For example, many startups these days have figured out what VCs are looking for and are pitching high LTV-to-CAC ratios, as if they are cash machines with no impediments to scale. Just add money, turn the crank and you'll make

---

[46] Note that we do not bother with discounting net present value (NPV) with a risk rate.
[47] See 10 top price per user examples, Statista, 2016, http://bit.ly/vcr010.

a lot more money! However, as we've seen, the cost to acquire the first 1,000 customers will likely be very different from the cost to acquire the next 10,000.

The numbers do not speak for themselves. We need to connect our numbers with analysis that explains the larger context of growth. How do CAC and LTV reflect our ability to scale? How do we expect the numbers to change as we grow? What are the key variables behind the numbers? What barriers to growth can we foresee? What can we do to remove those barriers?

> *CAC and LTV: two more numbers that require analysis (a story).*

Products vs. Services

Earlier I mentioned the two prongs of scalability: acquiring customers and building the competencies to serve them. So far we've focused on customer acquisition. When it comes to building the company that will serve those customers, it can be helpful to consider the context of products vs. services.

Product companies sell *things*, such as apps, games and software. Service companies sell *getting things done*, traditionally requiring human labor, such as consultants or lawyers. The concepts of products and services are easy to confuse, as many things we purchase are actually a combination of the two. Restaurants, for example, sell food (products), but they are also selling the experience of having it cooked and served in a specific way (service). Fast food looks a bit more like a product, while a five-star restaurant provides a premium service.

Products have the disadvantage that they require an upfront investment to design and produce. However, products come with the very important advantage that, once they are ready to go, they can often scale very quickly. This is particularly true for virtual products, which have little to no manufacturing or inventory challenges.

> *With products, you can even make money while you sleep.*

For example, compare legal software to legal services. An infinite number of people could download our software with no extra effort on our part, even while we sleep. Meanwhile, if we are providing legal services, we'd need to hire more and more lawyers as we take on more and more clients.

Services have the advantage that they often do not require much in the way of upfront capital. For example, a newly minted psychologist, lawyer, real estate agent or graphics designer can print business cards and be ready for customers. They can add clients one at a time, often remaining cash flow positive. The downside of services is scalability. At some point, the psychologist/lawyer/agent/designer will hit capacity, the maximum number of clients that can be squeezed into a week, and growth hits a wall. You can't scale yourself.

Because services are easier to start, and products are easier to scale, some startups attempt to start as a service with the plan to "productize" their solutions so that they can scale. This can be a very advantageous model, allowing founders to fund the startup with income in the form of consulting services while they develop the product.

> *VCs are optimistically wary of startups attempting to productize their services.*

However, there are potential pitfalls. Not every solution is transferable from one customer to the next. If the solution were highly customized, there is the potential that each future customer will also require major customization, which may perpetuate a service model. For a traditional business, there is nothing wrong with a service model. At issue in this text is scalability. Services businesses generally cannot scale quickly enough for the growth required by venture capitalists.

Table: Ease of scale for services vs. products

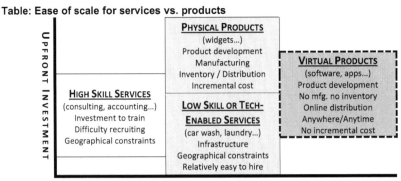

Many businesses have some elements of services and of products, and one can debate whether companies like Facebook, Twitter, Uber, AirBnb, Mint.com, Salesforce.com, eBay and TurboTax are at their heart a service company or a product company. The label is not as important as identifying the specific barriers to scale. Some impediments might be inherent to the model, and we'll have to account for them with our funding strategy. Other barriers we can attempt to remove.

In Part I, I mentioned a few "hot spaces," industries that are currently receiving a lot of venture capital: artificial intelligence, blockchain, mobility and the Internet of things (IoT). It is no accident that the first three out of four of these sectors are virtual products, which have the

> *Not surprisingly, "hot spaces" usually scale very easily.*

most attractive scalability. The last one, IoT, is also very attractive for scalability, taking common, cheap items and adding some proprietary functionality for which we can charge a premium, resulting in excellent margins.

Margins

We started the chapter with the debate between growth and profitability, noting that VCs are primarily concerned with growth. We discussed some key concepts and metrics when it comes to assessing startup's scalability, including CAC, LTV and whether the company is offering products or services. Now it is time to dig a little deeper into the profitability side of the equation, for which VCs tend to focus on the concept of *margins*.

There are several different *margins* that financial analysts can track: gross margins, net margins and operating margins. To accountants, each type of margin has a very specific definition. Gross margins refer to revenues minus direct costs of goods. Operating margins also take out overhead. Net margins take out interest, depreciation and taxes.

With startups, it is a little more conceptual, as we are projecting into the future rather than reporting past activities. For example, we probably don't have any interest or taxes since we are unable to borrow anyway, nor do we have profits to tax. That's why when VCs talk about net, we often use the acronym EBITDA: earnings before interest, taxes, depreciation and amortization.

VCs focus is generally on gross margins, which is to answer a conceptual question: how much more value can we create than it costs on a transaction-by-transaction basis. I say that this is somewhat conceptual because we really don't know yet. When we are in startup phase, we have not ironed out all of the details about how we will be transacting. We may not even know our price or revenue model yet (to be discussed in the next section).

However, in broad strokes, we should be able to take a guess. Are we, for example, taking easily obtainable cheap commodities and transforming them into a premium product, like Internet-of-things companies? Or do we have significant costs associated with each product with significant competitive pricing pressures? The former will yield healthy margins. The latter will get squeezed.

VCs need to be in very high margin businesses, ideally in the 90% range, but certainly well over 50%. These margins are not necessarily the startup's current margins. We mostly care about what margins *will be* once the startup has reached scale. We might even be thinking about future margins *after exit*, as in the ones that an acquirer might achieve after acquiring our startup.

Virtual products are a dream for margins because they have almost zero cost of goods. When Google was taking the leap of faith that they would eventually figure out a way to be profitable, part of that formula was incredibly favorable margins. There is almost no incremental cost for Google to add a customer. Same with Instagram.

Virtual products have nearly zero COGS, resulting in high margins.

In these cases, startups are creating significant value for users for almost no cost per user. This is a scalability dream! With this high margin potential, we are able to take some business model risk, such as not figuring out the revenue model yet. We may never need to monetize the value we are creating, as in Instagram's case, if our acquirer already has that competency.

B. Founder/Industry Fit

As a rule of thumb, the margins required by VCs are only possible if there is a technological breakthrough that allows a significant cost advantage over current solutions. This happened on a macro level during the dotcom boom of the late '90s. As PCs became ubiquitous and the Internet blossomed, virtual products became feasible, giving startups the opportunity to distribute near-zero COGS products, which coincidentally, thanks to the Internet, had almost no barriers to scale. A similar opportunity has arisen in the last decade with the ubiquity of mobile phones, and perhaps will again in the next decade with the Internet-of-things.

So far our discussion of margins has focused on costs, which are only half of the margin formula. On the other side of the ledger are revenues.

Revenue Model

A revenue model is a very important element of the business model, so important that the terms are sometimes sloppily interchanged. Readers of this book will not confuse the two, as revenue model is only dealing with how a startup transacts with customers. As we've already seen in this chapter, VCs have many other considerations when it comes to business model, most notably scalability.

Still, revenue is often very important, and most startups will need to demonstrate that they can generate sales. This may even be a prerequisite to receiving venture capital, as we've noted in the traction chapter. If nobody is willing to pay for it, how do we know a startup is really creating value? One of the first elements of quantifying that value creating is pricing.

Pricing

Pricing is a direct function of product/market fit. The more value being created, the higher the premium a startup may be able to charge. The challenge comes in translating the rather fuzzy concept of "value creation" into the not-fuzzy-at-all number that becomes the price that customers would be willing to pay. Pricing is perhaps one of the largest challenges facing the founders of a startup. As with other topics covered rather briefly in this book, there are semester-long classes devoted to the topic of pricing.

From the VC perspective, our main concern about pricing is the opportunity to charge and maintain premium pricing. This ties directly back to product/market and founder/industry fit. On the product side, we want our customers' perception of value to be high enough that we can charge a price that will yield VC-level gross margins.

On the industry fit side, we need a competitive advantage so that we can maintain our premium pricing without pressure from competition. If there is any indication that we may ultimately be competing on price, then we may be incurring more business model risk than we'd be comfortable with. The exception here is when we have a cost advantage, often the consequence of an innovation, so that we can provide a superior solution and win on price while maintaining our margins.

Common Practice

Beyond pricing, the next consideration for a revenue model is the type of transaction we would like to facilitate with customers. The key issue here is to keep it simple and fit into current familiar practices. Expecting customers to grasp a new way of transacting is risky business. Most industries have common practices that are deep-rooted. Ideally, our venture will sell to customers in a way that people are already familiar and comfortable with.

Common Revenue Models
- Subscription/Recurring
- Transaction/Purchase
- Fee-for-Service
- Freemium
- Rental income
- Licensing
- Commission
- Installation + maintenance
- Advertising

The advice to adhere to common practice is counterintuitive, given the preference discussed earlier to have a disruptive technology. However, disruptive technologies do not necessarily need disruptive business models. It can be attractive to take a disruptive solution and insert it into a pre-existing value distribution network. Then we can simply beat the pre-existing competition with our better/faster/cheaper solution.

However, there are times when a disruptive business model is the most attractive despite the extra risk. Back in 2003, Apple launched iTunes and disrupted the music industry. For decades, consumers had been buying albums of music. Starting in 2003, consumers began purchasing $0.99 singles. Fast-forward a decade and the music industry was disrupted again, this time by streaming-music subscription services.

> *On revenue model, the rule is to keep it simple. Being disruptive requires exceptionalism.*

Recurring/Subscriptions

Music is not the only industry that has been disrupted and moved into a subscription-based revenue model. In the B2B world (business-to-business), a similar disruption has taken place over the last decade, thanks to the cloud and ubiquitous high-speed connectivity. Companies like Salesforce.com, Amazon Web Services and Dropbox have changed the way that businesses pay for software. Prior to 2005, businesses normally purchased software up front. This was true for off-the-shelf products, like Microsoft Office and Adobe Creative Suite, as well as IT enterprise giants like Oracle and SAP, for which corporations would pay hefty installation and maintenance fees.

Over the last decade, a new model emerged and now dominates the B2B space: software-as-a-service, or SaaS. Just as consumers transitioned from purchasing music to "renting access" on a monthly basis, businesses have now been trained to subscribe to software rather than purchase it outright. This subscription model trend has been accelerated by the attractiveness of *recurring revenues.*

Recurring revenue is income from customers on a repeat and often automatic basis, like rent. The average consumer has scores of subscription accounts for things like cell phones, utilities, Internet, music, movies, cloud storage, messaging...even Amazon Prime.

The same is true with B2B, with the typical small business using SaaS subscriptions to handle many core business functions, like CRM (customer relationship management), file sharing, payroll,

> *The subscription model is the new gold standard in revenue generation.*

timekeeping, bookkeeping, email marketing, web hosting and database management.

Recurring revenues have two huge advantages. First, they can increase the lifetime value of the customers by increasing customer retention. Second, they can smooth out earnings. These benefits have motivated most companies in tech to seek out subscription models.

Microsoft Office is a classic example. The software bundle used to have a traditional transactional model: pay hundreds of dollars for the software. Upgrades would come out every few years, and customers would have to decide whether to re-up or wait until the next upgrade. These days, Office offers an annual subscription around $100/year. Their earnings are flattened, not bouncing with each upgrade, and users are along for the ride for updates.

There is one last advantage of recurring revenue: increasing the growth curve. If we sell products the old-fashioned way and want to grow, we need *more* new customers this month than we had last month. In today's parlance, that could be called *100% churn*.

Figure: Recurring vs. regular revenue growth

Now imagine we have 0% churn, and each month's revenue is in *addition* to last month's revenue, stacked on top. This cumulative effect of recurring revenue can be a significant contributor to a hockey stick growth curve.

Razor and Blade

Similar to a subscription service is *razor and blade* model, in which a platform product is sold at a discount to facilitate the sales of replaceable high-margin products. The razor is practically given away; then the blades cost an arm and a leg. Printer manufacturers use the same strategy to sell high-margin ink cartridges.

B. Founder/Industry Fit

This model is very common in medical device companies, who sell large, expensive machines at a discount followed by *replaceables* at a considerable markup. The fancy high-tech thermometers at doctor's offices, for example, may well have been free. But not so the disposable plastic covers used each time they check our temperature.

The razor/blade model is particularly popular with medical devices.

Technically, these are not exactly recurring revenues but predictable repeat customers, since they must purchase the replacement products in order to continue using the gear they purchased. But in practical terms, customers feel locked in when they own the larger piece of gear, and so the behavior is often very similar to recurring revenue.

Principle User is Payer

Another issue to consider in our revenue model is the risk associated with creating value for customers who do not make purchasing decisions. For example, if a startup is targeting me, a professor, they'd likely have to sell through my institution, a university. Creating value for a professor may not equate to creating value for an institution. Even though I may desire to purchase the product, I likely have to wait for the university to make that decision.

Similarly, targeting teenagers as consumers can be a challenge for items that their parents will be paying for. Ideally, we hope to have your users in a position to make the purchasing decisions. Back to me as an example, the startup might price its offerings within an amount that many professors can cover with their discretionary spending accounts. Then the end user is also the payer.

The ideal revenue model is a subscription with high margins being paid for by the end user.

Revenue Model Summary

Of course, not every startup even needs a price or a revenue model. If we have near zero incremental costs, we may be able to go years without knowing for certain how we will harvest the value we are creating.

We also do not necessarily care about revenue, pricing or margins if we have an exit strategy in which an acquirer will be purchasing our users and/or technology. They may want our users so that they can sell them their technology, or they may want our technology so that they'll be differentiated in their market. In either case, our pricing strategy may not have relevance in their value network.

If we are trying to build a company to go public, we will very much care about revenues and margins. We will need to reach significant levels of income, nearing $100M a year, with a *consistent upwards trajectory*, to be a candidate for an IPO.

Lastly, if we see tough times ahead, we should be thinking about a revenue model as a potential source for funding, as the equity markets may not be available to us. If for some reason we think an acquisition is going to take a very long time or that public markets may be hitting a down cycle, we may need some income just to survive.

Business Model Summary

Generally, you don't hear much of the phrase *business model* until the markets are in a down cycle, and everyone all of a sudden has a come-to-Jesus moment to start focusing on traditional business funda-mentals. However, it is not really our job as VCs to build *sustainable* businesses unless it is required for the best exit. It is our job to return capital to our investors via our unique hits-driven equity-growth investment thesis.

Hence, as VCs, we have slightly different *fundamentals* than traditional investors. Our focus is on scalability in high margin businesses with a clear path to exit. A revenue model may have little significance unless it is necessary to get to exit.

WHAT WE COVERED

Business Model

- Defining "Business Model"
- Growth and Profitability
- Path to Exit
- Barriers to Scalability
- Scalability and P/M Fit
- CAC & LTV
- Products vs. Services
- Margins
- Revenue Model

Chapter Questions

1. Why are growth and profitability negatively correlated?
2. Is profitability in an early stage startup a *primary* concern of VCs? Why or why not?
3. What are two different approaches to thinking about LTV?
4. What factors go into calculating CAC?
5. How is CAC related to market fit?
6. Create a service vs. product scorecard and rate the following types of businesses: sharing economy, social network, e-commerce, tech-enabled on-demand services, software-as-a-service.
7. In what situations is a revenue model irrelevant? Why?
8. Why are recurring revenues attractive?
9. What are some factors that make services businesses harder to scale?
10. Thinking like a VC, would you consider Facebook a service or a product?
11. Do you think Uber's business model is disrupting the taxi industry? Why or why not?

Due Diligence Advice for Students: **Business Model**

Focus on identifying and removing barriers to scale, both current and future. Use numbers when appropriate but focus on the narrative. Do not count on founders to understand our exit-driven strategy, meaning be strategic and assertive about the kind of growth-oriented business model a VC fund needs to see (whether or not the founders are pitching that model). Reconnect with product/market fit, a major determiner of customer adoption, as well as competitive threats.

VC RAZOR DUE DILIGENCE

Product/Market Fit	1. Value Proposition 2. Market Size 3. Traction
Founder/Industry Fit	4. Team 5. Secret Sauce 6. Business Model
Fund Fit	7. Growth Milestones 8. Exit Strategy 9. Return Analysis

C. FUND FIT

Up to this point in the book, we've been exploring the market and industry aspects of the value network. Now it is time to look at the mechanics of how an investment in a startup would fit into our fund, or as VCs like to say, "can we make the math work." We will explore strategies to maximize financial return.

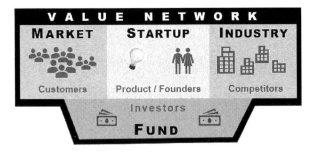

As we are looking at a startup from the VC fund perspective, it may not be surprising that many founders have not deeply considered this point of view. They understandably focused first and foremost on product/ market fit, ensuring that they could indeed create value. They may also have considered the competitive threats to that value creation. Only the most seasoned entrepreneurs, usually ones who have worked with venture capitalists before, are able to sit in the shoes of their would-be investors.

What this means in practical terms is that VCs may not get much help from the founders in determining whether the startup is a fund fit. Whereas we'd expect

slides in their pitch decks to cover the key aspects of product/market and founder/industry fit, we will have to perform much of the fund fit analysis on our own.

Further, we'll have to gauge whether the founders will be on board with the direction we would need to take to make the deal work for us. With our hit-driven investment thesis, we count on a small number of startups in our portfolio to outperform the rest. We need each investment to have the potential to be one of those hits to move the needle on our fund.

This focus on the endgame and whether a startup might be a hit for us creates a structural challenge for this book. Arguably, these chapters are out of order. Rather than starting with growth milestones, we should probably put the exit first (as we discussed in Part I, "Work Backwards from the Exit," p. 66). However, I have decided that the exit feels more natural to be at the end, but we will necessarily allude to our exit strategy as we look at the growth milestones we intend to hit along the way.

Another consideration for these sections of analysis is that they are even more future-focused than any chapter we've covered so far. In competition, we were concerned with today's threats as well as how competitors may react tomorrow. In product/fit, we wanted to understand product/market fit for the current target market as well as future segments.

Fund fit analysis is future facing, requiring strategy and foresight.

However, fund fit is *all* about the future, specifically a *new* future for a startup that only becomes possible if the startup receives our venture capital investment. This is a future that we will help create. Every venture capitalist must have a vision for how to make this happen, becoming both strategist and prognosticator.

Given the level of uncertainty in predicting the future, different VCs will have different approaches and will often disagree. This level of analysis does not lend itself to right and wrong answers. More relevant are compelling narratives, weaving numbers and story into a vision for the future. We will never know what was right or wrong. We *will* know, with the help of time, if the path chosen worked or not, but we'll never know what *might have* worked.

We'll be investigating two elements of fund fit: growth milestones and exit strategy, answering these fundamental questions:

- What can the startup achieve with a VC investment? **GROWTH MILESTONES**
- How will we ultimately get out of this investment? **EXIT STRATEGY**
- Can we make the math work? **RETURN ANALYSIS**

Fund Fit	7. Growth Milestones
	8. Exit Strategy
	9. Return Analysis

7. Growth Milestones
What can the startup achieve with a VC investment?

Growth Milestones Contents

Milestones and Risk

Perhaps the most important strategic concept for maximizing financial returns in a venture capital investment is *milestones*. Any time a milestone is hit, the underlying valuation of the startup increases, just as a public company's stock price rises when the company hits its numbers. Setting, funding and hitting milestones are imperative for creating value in a venture.

Each milestone is tied to one or more key risks. Hitting a milestone results in demonstratively lower risk, which translates into higher valuation. Though there are some shared characteristics across all startups, every industry has its own set of inherent risks. Biotech companies, for example, will have vastly different milestones than software startups. The challenge for venture capitalists is to identify key risks in a startup and determine whether there are milestones the startup could achieve to mitigate those risks. The second part of that challenge is to fund the activities required to hit the milestones.

Example Milestones

- Functional prototype
- First paying customer(s)
- Beta customer(s)
- Successful clinical trials
- Proof of concept
- Technical achievement
- Product release
- New feature release
- Site goes live
- Strategic partnership
- Critical mass
- Patent secured
- FDA approval received
- X number of customers
- X daily average users
- X dollars of revenue
- X number of page views
- X% repeat customers
- X decrease in COGS
- Hired rockstar CMO

For example, a software startup may have beta testing, new feature releases and/or strategic partnerships to forge. Biotech companies have regulatory and approval processes. Hardware companies build prototypes and release products. Young founding teams need to recruit seasoned executives; experienced founders may need to bring in young, energetic talent. Most startups will benefit from many of the achievements listed, and it will be the job of the venture capitalists to figure out which of the activities should be funded with a round of venture financing.

Use of Funds

Most startup pitches will include a "use of funds" section, which describes how the founders intend to spend the cash they are raising. Unfortunately, their explanation is often tactical rather than strategic. That is, founders often share their hiring plan or marketing spend. What they often forget to share is the outcome anticipated by those expenditures, the milestones they are planning to hit. VCs might ask, "Where does that get us?" That can be translated into, "What milestones will we achieve with this investment?"

> *Use of funds needs to include the milestones to be hit.*

As we discussed in the Growing section of the VC Job Cycle (p. 69), VCs pre-identify a series of milestones and estimate the amount of funding that will be needed for each. The amount being raised in a round of financing should only be as much as is necessary to hit specific milestones. The goal is to maximize the value of their equity from round to round.

Breaking up the funding needed into a series of rounds separated by milestones is advantageous for VCs and for founders. VCs reduce capital risk by deploying less capital up front and reserving *dry powder* for follow-on rounds. If milestones are missed in a significant way, a VC firm may choose not to participate in later rounds, freeing up the reserved capital to invest in other opportunities.

Figure: Typical example of multiple rounds of funding.

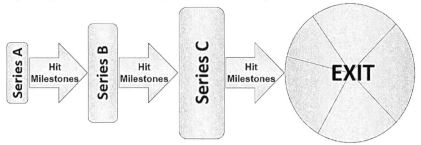

Founders also benefit from the multi-round pattern by lowering dilution and thus retaining more equity. This is a result of raising only the amount needed to get to the next milestone. After hitting the milestone, the valuation increases, and future funding is not as dilutive.

If founders had to raise more capital at the lower valuation, they would lose a higher percentage of their startup.

Hit Movie Example

The process of a producing a blockbuster movie is a good case study of how milestones create value. It starts when someone has a good story idea (which creates some value). Then that gets put on paper as a treatment (a little more value). Then an award-winning writer is found to write a screenplay (even more value). Spielberg reads the script and gets on board to direct (a lot more value). Clooney likes what he sees and signs up to be the lead (starting to sound like a hit!).

Figure: Increasing equity value in a film project.

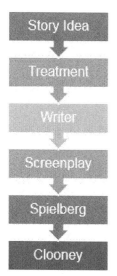

This movie concept has hit several value-creating milestones, and we haven't even started filming, not to mention editing, scoring, marketing, etc. During each step along the way, risks are being mitigated and value is being created, even though no income has yet been derived from the movie.

The last point is an important one and deserves further investigation. Notice that value is being created long before there are any customers or revenues. How is this possible? The answer is the difference between cash and equity, and understanding that difference is often the key to maximizing financial returns.

Most people, including entrepreneurs, tend to think on a *cash* basis. We see money coming in and money going out, and we calculate that the difference is our profit (or loss). We, of course, ultimately want to maximize profit. But it turns out that in a startup, where there is little or no income to balance out expenses, this pursuit of profitability can be a distraction from the real goal, which is creating the most value. Naïve entrepreneurs are racing to profitability or break-even rather than pursuing maximum return potential.

Building Equity

Cash is a liquid asset. That means we can spend it easily and quickly. You might say fluidly. We can go to the store with cash and exchange it for milk. Having a lot of cash is a type of wealth that we can all understand. We have money and we can buy what we want.

However, individuals may be wealthy and still have no cash. As an example, let's say we are poor and our grandparents leave us a beach house worth a million dollars. All of a sudden, we are much richer. We have a very big *asset*, but it is illiquid. We cannot take our house to the store to buy bread. Our wealth is tied up in equity in the house. Or stated differently, most of our net worth is equity, not cash. This creates a challenge, as we need cash to get by.

Similarly, startups are often equity rich and cash poor. Much of the value we can create with a venture capital investment will yield increases in equity, not cash. As we saw in the previous chapter, we may not even be building the capability to generate cash, depending on our exit strategy. For example, we might be close to developing a cure for cancer, which everyone would agree holds a lot of value as an illiquid asset. However, the startup could still be cash poor, and in fact has the serious risk of running out of cash before hitting the next milestone.

Another example, let's say we have two successful restaurants. If we open a third restaurant this year, the startup expenses we incur may overwhelm our profits (cash) from our other two restaurants. On a short-term cash basis, we appear to be unprofitable, and we have negatively impacted any break-even analysis. However, in the long-term, we are creating more value in our venture because we are growing our overall business and thus increasing the value of our equity.

> *Investing in growth will result in lower profitability but higher equity value.*

AirBnb Example

In Part I, we looked at some follow-on rounds for unicorns. Let's dig a little deeper into one of them, AirBnb, to see how the milestones are tied to funding. The figure below shows the Series A, B and C of AirBnb.

There have been several subsequent rounds, but we'll focus on the early stage funding.

Figure: Example follow-on rounds for unicorns.

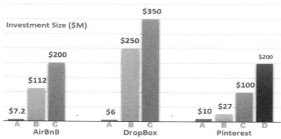

Table: Detail about AirBnb rounds of funding.

Date	Round	Amount	Pre-Money	X Increase
Jan. 2009	Seed	$20K	~$300K	-
Apr. 2009	Seed	$600K	$1.5M	0.32→1.5 = 5X
Nov. 2010	Series A	$7.2M	$100M	2.1 → 100 = 50X
Jul. 2011	Series B	$112M	$1.2B	107 → 1,200= 11X
Oct. 2013	Series C	$200M	$2.3B	1.3 → $2.3 = 2X
Apr. 2014	Series D	$475M	$10B	2. → $10B = 3.4X

In 2008, after failing to raise $150,000 from VCs or angels, the founders of *AirBedandBreakfast* famously got scrappy and sold cereal at the presidential political party conventions to raise some seed money. That scrappiness helped get them into Y-Combinator in January of '09.

The "guys" made a big impression on Y-Combinator co-founder Paul Graham, who went to bat to help them get funding. "We had big doubts about this idea, but they vanished on meeting the guys," Paul said in an email to VC Fred Wilson. Fred passed on (declined) the investment and went on to regret it.[48] The company, renamed AirBnb, secured a $600,000 seed round from Sequoia and a couple of others in April of 2009.

---

[48] Paul published an informative email chain, including the quote above, about AirBnb funding on his blog, http://www.paulgraham.com/AirBnb.html.

One lesson for other young entrepreneurs: if you demonstrate a fanatical drive to succeed in your startup, a lot of investor doubt (but not all) can be erased. It seems that in the early days, investors were much more impressed with the team's drive and problem-solving creativity in the face of scarce resources (selling cereal to raise $30,000), not so much with the idea (dudes on couches?).

> *Lesson for young founders: being scrappy (smart and creative) is highly valued by VCs.*

After the seed round, AirBnb reportedly was only making a couple hundred dollars a week. One major obstacle that the team identified was the poor quality of photographs for listings. To solve this, they used part of their funding to overcome this risk. The company began offering free professional photography for individuals who wanted to list their property. It worked and revenues took off.[49]

Before closing the A round about 18 months later, AirBnb had hit milestones of 700,000 nights booked in 8,000 cities in 166 countries. Estimating an average of $100 per booking, that's $70M in transactions, of which AirBnb takes a flat 10%, or around $7M in revenue.

The Series A was reportedly a $7.2M investment on a pre-money of $100M. This is worth chewing on: how could the company have a valuation that was 15 times higher than all of the money it had ever earned? The double answer is growth trajectory and market size. On trajectory, the team had implemented improvements, such as professional photography, that had dramatically increased the growth curve. They had removed barriers to scale, and in so doing had proven that with very little money ($620,000 so far), they could create a lot of value.

> *The largest valuation increase, 50X, occurred between the seed and A rounds: from 2.1M to $100M*

As importantly, there was still plenty of room to grow, if you defined the opportunity as the much larger hotel market. It was at this point that my aforementioned VC friend passed on the investment (see p. 133), believing it was

---

[49] From Vator.tv's series "When They Were Young," bit.ly/whenyoung.

C. Fund Fit

still "dudes on couches." The Series A investors believed in the bigger market.

Note that part of the calculation for a VC considering joining the A round is price. The Series A is priced at a very impressive $100M. Usually Series A is more in the $10-30M range, and even lower if you are not in California. A VC would need to really believe that the team was onto something big to think there was the potential for a 10X return with a current valuation of $100M. In fact, it would have to become a unicorn, as the definition of a unicorn is a $1B valuation (10 x $100M = $1B).

It only took another seven months for it to become a unicorn. The Series B was an investment of $112M on a pre-money valuation of $1.2B. This press release gives us an idea of the metrics they were using to track their success:

> "AirBnb has experienced explosive growth over the past year, doubling the benchmark of 1 million nights booked in just four months. The company now has over 2 million nights booked, receives over 30 million page views per month and has seen the number of AirBnb Social Connections triple to 54 million since launching the feature in May. As the company poises itself to meet the growing demand in international markets like Germany, the United Kingdom, France and Brazil, this investment will help position AirBnb as the leader in the broader vacation rental market in 2012."[50]

Guess who got on board for the Series B? Yes, my VC friend finally came around and concluded this was bigger than "dudes on couches." This is a classic example of why VCs split investments into rounds, each specifically designed to give enough capital to hit the next milestone, thereby decreasing risk and attracting more capital (at a higher price). My friend's firm had to pay up for the Series B, but they also got the benefit of milestones that had been hit, significantly de-risking the deal.

Quick return analysis:

- Seed investors put in $600K and enjoyed watching their shares increase in value over 500X over the next two rounds to over $300M on paper as of the B round.

---

[50] http://bit.ly/airbnb-seriesb

- Series A investors put $7.2M and experienced a 70X increase in valuation by the Series D round, worth an estimated $500M.
- Series B investors put in $100M and experienced ~7X return, valued at nearly $700M after the Series D.

I've chosen not to take this through the E and F rounds of AirBnb funding because the later rounds really don't look as much like traditional VC investing as early stage PE (private equity). The company went on to raise a Series E of $1.5B, debt of $1B and most recently a Series F of $1B. The valuation after the F round was reportedly $31B. It was while raising the F round that AirBnb announced it had turned profitable.

Negotiated and Time Limited

When working with VC numbers, it is important to stop and remember that all of the variables are both *negotiated* and *time limited*. Both the pre-money valuation and the amount being invested are moving targets. Exactly how much of an investment does a startup need to get to the next level? What is a startup worth today, when it is not even profitable? The answer is: *who knows!* Or more specifically, whatever the market will bear.

And the market can change from day to day. Selling a home is a good comparison—another transaction involving an illiquid asset. When you put your house up for sale, what is it worth? It is hard to say. There are a number of factors that can affect its valuation: typical price per square foot in your neighborhood, sales prices of other comparable homes, the value of your recent renovations, trends in your market, a crash in the world economy, etc.

The reality is that nobody knows the price until you sell it. Then you have a price, for a moment, equal to exactly what someone was willing to pay for it. That number is only good for that moment.

Just after the house is sold, as after a round of VC investing, circumstances can change quickly, and the valuation will change accordingly. That night, there could be a nearby natural disaster. The following weekend there could be a feature in the New York Times about how great the neighborhood is. The house next door might sell for a surprisingly high or low amount.

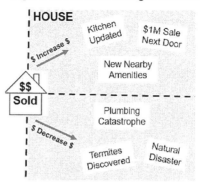

Figure: House value changes after sale

Any of these events will affect the value of the underlying illiquid asset, but we can only guess as to how much. There will not be another true *price* until we choose to put the house on the market, go through the process of showing it, negotiate a new price and ultimately consummate the transaction. Only then will we know the true valuation, and once again, only for a moment. Then the cycle continues.

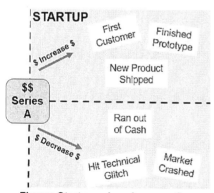

Figure: Startup value changes after round

The same happens with startups. The valuation was negotiated under a specific set of circumstances, and all parties know (and are planning on the fact) that things will change. A product will launch. A big new customer will sign. A beta will flop. The top engineer will leave. The stock market will go up. Then down.

All of these things, some internal, some external, will conceptually affect the valuation, but we will not know *exactly* what the new valuation is until there is another transaction, when we will sit down across the table again and negotiate a new price for another round of funding.

A quick insertion of mechanics: the valuation changing is more practically described as the share price fluctuating. Just as with public stocks, startup share prices go up and down. The difference is in liquidity and transparency. Public stocks are traded every minute, meaning their prices are publicly negotiated all day long. A startup's share price will only be negotiated in the next equity round or in a liquidity event, i.e., exit, and may not be public information.

The startup market is much less liquid and less transparent than homes. The transactions happen much less frequently, and when they happen, the information is often undisclosed. VCs always have an informational advantage over founders because we know the details of many private deals.

Seed Stage Valuations and Convertible Notes

As we see above, pricing a deal is a sticky proposition, and it gets stickier the earlier in the life of the startup, at the *seed stage*. How do you put a number on an idea? Enormous potential in the numerator, enormous risk in the denominator, all with made-up numbers?

One way to avoid having to negotiate valuations is by issuing a *convertible note*. Rather than spell out the terms of a round of equity, which would necessitate a potentially messy negotiation about valuation, a convertible note allows a cash transfer that will *convert* to equity during the next round, with a predetermined discount.

It is called debt, but really at its core it is unpriced equity. The purpose of this cash is to be an equity investment. If the startup does well and makes it to another round of equity, *Convertible debt is essentially an unpriced equity investment.* the debt will *convert* into new equity, and the price will be determined by the negotiations of that round. By the time the next equity round is needed, the startup should have hit milestones that help define a mutually agreeable range of valuations.

On the other hand, if the startup does not make it to another round of financing, we usually have a startup with no liquid assets as collateral, resulting in a loan that acts a lot like equity, sharing in the upside and going nearly to zero on the downside.

The issuers of convertible debt are usually angel investors. In my experience, traditional VCs were dabbling in convertible notes around 2010, but most ultimately concluded it did not fit their model. Still, a few still use debt to finance seed or pre-seed startups, and many will use convertible debt as a bridge loan for a portfolio company if the startup is running out of cash and not quite ready to raise a B or C round.

For the extra risk they are taking, issuers of convertible notes receive a discount on their equity once it gets priced, commonly 20%. Conceptually, that means that the convertible debt round investors received a 20% ROI between the debt round and the priced round.

VCs sometimes see convertible debt as the lesser of two evils: better to have convertible debt than a mispriced angel round. However, over the last few years, *valuation caps* have come into fashion. These caps limit the price of the next round. This is to protect the debt issuers. For example, let's look at a startup receiving a $500,000 convertible note. If the round had been priced at $1M, the $500,000 investment would be worth 33% of the resulting equity ($500k/$1.5M post).

However, if the same startup happened to get lucky and hit a major milestone, the next round could be priced at $10M, meaning the convertible debt issuers would get closer to 5% of the company for that same investment ($500k/$10.5M post). The 20% discount doesn't make up much of the difference.

> *Valuation caps have rendered convertible debt almost pointless because the cap becomes the de facto Series A pre-money.*

The valuation cap often becomes the default Series A pre-money valuation, meaning we might as well have negotiated an equity round to start with.

Series A Norms

When VCs say that the *math has to make sense*, they mean that they need to be able to chart out on the back of an envelope how this startup might render a great return after considering multiple rounds of financing.

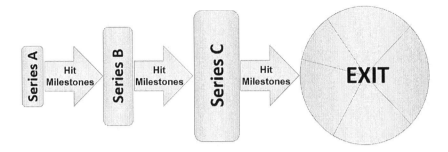

Clearly, this forward-looking calculation is fraught with broad assumptions, many of which have become *norms*. Frustratingly for newcomers, these norms are largely set by VCs and known only by VCs, though the Internet and accelerators are (slowly) changing that information gap for the startup world, much as the Internet did for real estate in a previous generation.

An example of a typical norm is that VCs don't usually take more than 50% of a tech startup in a Series A. This is a product of the underlying principle that the team is the most important component of a successful startup. Attracting amazing talent is a top priority, and sharing the equity is the proven tactic.

Another norm is that tech startups in a Series A are usually valued between $3-15M, and investment sizes are usually between $3-15M. The high side of the range (and higher) represents Silicon Valley. The low side is the rest of the industry. One study reports the average Series A is up from around $4M in 2008 to over $11M in 2018.[51] There are definitely exceptions to any norm, but having a baseline provides an opportunity to strategize about fund management.

> *Series A Norms*
> - *Take below 50%*
> - *Investment size: $3-15M*
> - *Pre-money: $3-15M*
> - *Future rounds ↑*
> - *2-3X dry powder*

Another norm is the projection that future rounds will go up, in both the amount invested and the valuations. The goal is for startups to use the VCs' cash to hit milestones, and in so

---

[51] "The rise and rise of supergiant rounds," TechCrunch, Feb. 2018, bit.ly/super-seriesa.

doing, create value. As a startup gets larger, more and more capital will be required to fuel growth.

One more norm is the practice of reserving 2-3X of the Series A investment to maintain pro rata through future rounds. Not all firms have this exact strategy, but understanding the purpose of this norm helps us appreciate how and why some firms choose to deviate from it.

Dilution and Pro Rata

As we've discussed, VCs do not look at a deal without some projection of the end game. It is from that *guestimation* that all other calculations are derived.

Let's take it one step at a time. We know that new shares are issued in each round and added to the share pool, thus diluting prior shareholders.

Figure: New shares are added for every investment round

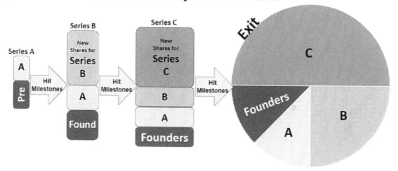

For simplicity in the example below, each round of equity is exactly doubling the number of pre-existing shares. That is, the investment size is equal to the pre-money valuation in each round, resulting in the new investors receiving 50% of the equity, and the existing shareholders being diluted by 50%.

Note that this is not a normal investment, doubling equity each round. We're just doing it this way to see what an easy example looks like.

The Series A investors here have been diluted from 50% ownership after Series A to 25% after the Series B, to 12.5% after Series C. Assuming no more rounds occur before exit, the Series A shareholders would own 12.5% at exit.

This Example
Series A: 2 on 2
Series B: 6 on 6
Series C: 20 on 20

Figure: Simplified dilution example, each round doubles shares

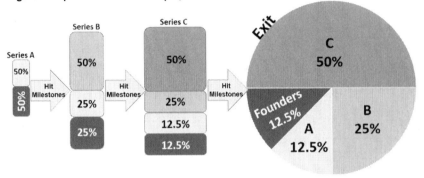

Not including special preferences, such as liquidity preferences and dividends, the proceeds at exit will be split according to the equity pie above. If this were a unicorn exit at exactly $1B, the dilution suffered by the Series A investors would amount to a loss of $375M.[52]

In the unicorn hunting business, dilution is the enemy.

Given our hits-driven model, in which we are targeting only a couple of home runs in our portfolio, we need to receive as much as possible from any hits we may have. When you're hunting unicorns, you will fight like anything to avoid dilution.

Below is a slightly more realistic (and complicated) example, in which dilution is occurring to varying degrees with each round.

In this scenario, the Series B round dilutes founders and Series A by 33%. Series C dilutes them another 25%. By exit, founders have been diluted from 60% to 30%. The Series A

This Example
Series A: 2 on 3
Series B: 5 on 10
Series C: 10 on 30

---

[52] 50%-12.5%=37.5%; 37.5%*$1B=$375M

shareholders are diluted from 40% to 20% after the B and C rounds.

Figure: Typical dilution example

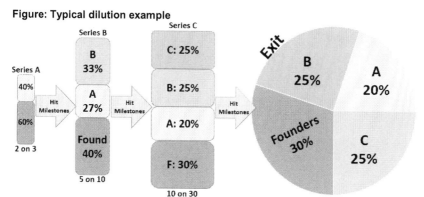

We know that the Series A shareholders will typically be reserving 2-3X capital (dry powder) to participate in follow-on rounds with the goal of maintaining a pro rata stake in this startup. In the graphic below, A^B and A^C represent the Series A investors' participation in later rounds to maintain pro rata ownership.

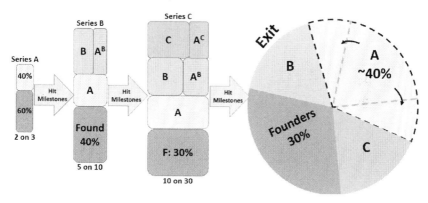

Growth Milestones Summary

The concept of funding milestones is critical to understanding how to think like a VC. We are in the business of creating unicorns, which means tackling BIG ideas, so big it can be overwhelming to realize those end goals. Milestones are the roadmap to achieving those big ideas. The "use of funds" from a round of venture capital funding should be tied to specific milestones, thereby mitigating risk and increasing the valuation for the next round of funding.

We took a look at how funding and milestones work mathematically from seed stage through numerous rounds of financing. In particular, we discussed how VCs fight their mortal enemy, dilution, by participating in later rounds. We will pick up on these concepts in the Return Analysis chapter.

WHAT WE COVERED

Growth Milestones

- Milestones and Risk
- Use of Funds
- Hit Movie Example
- Building Equity
- AirBnb Example
- Negotiated and Time Limited
- Seed Stage Valuations
- Convertible Notes
- Dilution and Pro Rata

Chapter Questions

1. Why are milestones important as we look toward an exit?
2. Why is it beneficial for both VCs and founders to spread out funding across a series of rounds before exit?
3. How are milestones and valuations related?
4. How are milestones connected to rounds of investing?
5. How can equity increase in value before any revenue has been generated?
6. What is dilution and how do VCs fight against it? Why is it a big deal?
7. What are the benefits and drawbacks of convertible notes?
8. Name several Series A norms.

Due Diligence Advice for Students: **Growth Milestones**

This section refers to *future* milestones, the ones we hope a startup can achieve with our investment. Our founders may (again) not be the best authorities on the growth trajectory we need to achieve on our way to exit. That means VCs often must come up with their own plan here for milestones. The "use of funds" for the round of funding should be tied to milestones. In other words, list the milestones and how much each will cost. Some milestones may be for the current round; others should be planned for future rounds. Be assertive: you might pick a different amount of funding to hit fewer or more milestones each round than the founders pitched.

8. Exit Strategy

What is the end game?

Exit Strategy Contents

Start with the Exit

As we've noted many times before, venture capitalists never make an investment without a vision of how to *exit* that investment. We are not buy and hold investors. Our hit-driven business model requires a liquidity event so that we can return capital to our investors, our limited partners. For VCs, success is one-dimensional. A VC is, after all, a *capitalist*, and as such has a legal obligation (fiduciary duty) to return capital to investors. There is only one definition of success for VCs: high financial returns.

> *Maximum financial return is the single goal of venture capitalists.*

There is a replicable pattern in the growth of a venture-backed company on its way to a successful exit. It is characterized by several rounds of VC financing (Series A, Series B, etc.) separated by periods during which the startup team is *deploying the capital* in an effort to hit milestones.

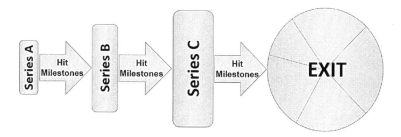

The Exit Strategy for a VC investment in a startup includes a prediction of what may happen at the end (what kind of exit, an estimation of valuation at exit, etc.). However, just as importantly, it includes a path to that end, driven by a series of value-creating milestones. The size of each round (Series A, Series B...) is not arbitrary. It should be the amount of cash needed to reach the next big milestone.

Beach House Exit Strategy Example

Back to our earlier example in which we inherit a beach house. Let's assume it is a fixer-upper and is worth a million dollars in its current condition. The best strategy to reach positive cash flow quickly would be a quick sale. Put it on the market at a reduced price and get cash fast. Perhaps we could get $800,000 in that scenario.

Or we could take the time to go through the normal home selling process with a real estate agent. That could take a few months and cost a 3-6% commission, but perhaps we'd get the full million dollars or even more. However, it is not guaranteed. It would be a higher return with a longer period and some uncertainty. Which is a better strategy?

Lastly, looking at other properties in the neighborhood, we think our house could be worth $1.5 million if we make some improvements. We estimate it would cost $100,000 and take another five months. Now we have a third option for exiting this investment. Which "exit strategy" is best? It depends.

In the above example, we have all our wealth tied up in an illiquid asset, and three different exit strategies have been proposed. The one we choose will depend on a number of factors: our appetite for uncertainty, our access to cash, our willingness to oversee a project, our interest in making more money, our need for immediate cash, etc. You might break the variables down like this:

Table: Comparing exit strategies for inherited beach house

Exit Strategy	Investment	Time	Proceeds	Uncertainty
1. Quick Sale	$0	0-1 month	$800K	~10%
2. Regular Sale	$0	2-3 months	$1M - 6%	~20%
3. Fixer Upper	$100K	5-8 months	$1.5M	~30%

My guess is that most of us would likely put the house on the market, wait the few extra months and be very happy with the million dollars. But if our sole goal was to maximize financial return, we'd find a way to raise the $100K so that we could get the extra $500,000. There are not many opportunities out there to earn half a million dollars on a $100,000 investment in five months. Think of the things you could accomplish with an extra $400,000 lying around!

VCs similarly need to *exit* startups (illiquid) so that we can return a liquid asset (cash or public stock) to our LPs. As we've discussed in Part I, the exit can come in the form of an acquisition by another company, or via an initial public offering, or IPO, in which shares of stock are sold on a public market.

The IPO is much more challenging and rare than an exit by acquisition. Going public is only a viable option to the few startups who can reach huge revenues (usually north of $100M) with significant predictability.

An IPO is only an option if a startup can achieve large, predictable revenues.

Public markets are driven by expectations, and startups are ill advised to go the IPO route unless we are very confident of the growth trajectory.

Much more common and nuanced is to pursue acquisition as an exit. When going this route, VCs and founders will identify potential acquirers early in the process to form relationships that may ultimately culminate in acquisition. An ideal exit strategy should include the following:

- Model the startup venture to be a good candidate for acquisition based on recent M&A activity: What companies are actively acquiring other companies? What strategy do they appear to be following? What metrics are they using for success? What valuations are in the market?

- Establish and achieve milestones that create the most value (and lead to highest price) for potential acquirers. Is the acquirer interested in customers, talent, technology and/or revenue?

- Begin relationships early with potential acquirers, perhaps by bringing them on as early strategic partners or strategic investors.

One key lesson here is that these strategies are not necessarily in concert with achieving maximum profits. Perhaps the most common example in this arena is the customer base as the most important asset and driver of exit valuation. Examples include unicorns exits by Instagram (acquired for $1B by Facebook), YouTube (acquired by Google for $1.65B) and Myspace (acquired by News Corp for $580M).

Now let's take a look at the theory behind the math...

Return Potential

At its core, VC return analysis is simple algebra. VCs will articulate return as an X multiple, usually over Y years on a Z investment. For example, if

VCs typically describe return potential like this: "a 10X return over 5 years on a $6M investment."

a VC fund invested $6M in a startup and then received $60M after its acquisition three years later, it could be stated "10X in 5 years on a $6M investment."

The challenge for VCs is not the algebra. It is the assumptions that go behind the numbers:

1) The total investment that will be required to get to exit, including future rounds;
2) The proceeds expected from the exit; and
3) The overall period of investment.

Total Investment

We already know that the venture capital investment process usually requires multiple rounds of financing, each designed to hit particular milestones, on the way to a successful exit. Further, we know that those multiple rounds will be split across a syndicate of VC firms. Lastly, we know that VCs reserve dry powder, or additional funds, for future rounds so that we can maintain pro rata ownership through exit. Given these parameters, we can make some assumptions about return potential from the beginning of the cycle.

Let's say we have an entrepreneur pitching an investment opportunity and requesting a specific amount of funding, say a $3M investment. VCs are not only interested in this round, but in all future rounds on the way to exit. Here is our challenge: the estimate of future funding is dependent on the exit strategy.

For example, if we think we'll ultimately go public, we may need to plan on numerous rounds of funding that may total over $100M. Alternatively, if we think we might have an early acquisition, we might only anticipate a Series B before exit.

VCs have a rule of thumb baseline strategy at this stage: reserve 2-3X the current round of investing for future rounds. In the above example, the current round is $3M (if we agree with

> *VC shortcut to estimate total investment: current round + 2-3X dry powder for follow-on rounds.*

the founder). VCs' shortcut assumption is to reserve $6-9M for future rounds.

At this stage in our algebraic problem, we can assume total investment of $9-12M. Now let's look at exit strategies.

Proceeds from Exit

Two variables will determine our proceeds at exit: our percent ownership at exit multiplied by the total proceeds of the exit. Let's start by estimating the percentage of equity we will have at exit. This will dictate the size of slice that we will receive.

VCs have another shortcut estimation here as a starting point: assume *pro rata*. That is, assume

> *VC shortcut for percent ownership at exit: maintain pro rata.*

we'll maintain the same ownership percentage that we established in the Series A.

This puts a lot of pressure on getting the first round right. In the above example, with a startup raising a $3M Series A, we would need to negotiate a pre-money valuation that would render our required percentage of ownership.

Let's take a moment to chew on that. As VCs, the variable that is driving our Series A negotiation is the percent ownership we would like to have at exit, or as Brad Feld from Foundry Group put it:

> For early-stage companies, venture investors are normally interested in owning a particular fraction of the company for an appropriate investment. The valuation is actually a derived number and does not really mean anything about what the business is "worth."[53]

Back to our $3M Series A example, we have already determined that our total investment will be $9-12M. To achieve VC returns of 10-20X, we would then need proceeds in the $90-240M range. To keep it simple, let's run with $100M as our minimum needed at exit.

Examples that Return $100M to VC Firm
- 20% of $500M
- 25% of $400M
- 33% of $300M
- 40% of $250M

Typically, early stage VC firms own between 20% and 40%. With that baseline estimate, we can estimate that the total proceeds of the acquisition for this startup would need to be between $250-500M for us to receive $100M.

As we look at the Series A, we have to ask, do we think that we can grow this startup into a $250M company, or can we get it to $500M? The answer to that question will drive our negotiations and will have more influence over our proposed pre-money valuation in the Series A than any argument about the current "worth" of the startup.

With no other information than the fact that a startup is seeking to raise $3M in Series A funding, we are able to estimate a term sheet offering with a pre-money valuation between $4.5M-12M (resulting in our

---

[53] *Venture Capital Deal Algebra*, Brad Feld, FeldThoughts, July 2004, http://bit.ly/vcrazorfeld.

ownership of 25-40%). This assumes we have faith that we can get to an exit of $250-500M.

Given this baseline case, we can extrapolate to make educated guesses in other scenarios. For example, if we think the startup could only get to a $200M exit, we might break convention and offer a $3M investment on a $3M pre-money valuation, resulting in our owning 50% of the equity after the Series A.

Percent ownership needed at exit drives the pre-money valuation negotiation in the Series A

The Math Has to Make Sense

The above example is exactly the internal calculus equity investors are making when they pass on a deal by saying, "I would have to own too much of your company for this to make sense for me." They might just as well say, "I am not going to offer you an investment because to do so I would have to offer a pre-money valuation that neither of us would be comfortable with."

Another way of saying it could be, "I cannot envision an exit for which we can all achieve the required return." Sometimes they will just say, "I can't make the math work." Recall that part of the VC philosophy is to keep the managers motivated by sharing the equity. If the earliest VCs must own over 50%, there is a very real danger that the founders will be too diluted by the time the startup reaches the Series C.

Exit Valuation

I hope you have followed me so far with this somewhat backwards logic. The percent ownership we estimate to need at the exit is the key driver during Series A pre-money valuation negotiations. That still leaves unanswered the question, how we can estimate exit valuations?

Comps

There is a quick answer: comps, or comparables. The way VCs estimate the potential exit valuation of startups is by comparing them to other

The best source for exit valuation is finding comps.

startups that have already exited. Keeping up with the M&A and IPO markets is a very important part of a VC's job. We know who is buying what and for how much. We have inside information from the private deals we and our colleagues have done.

A newly hired VC analyst will also want to use comps but may be challenged by the lack of publicly available data. Crunchbase has evolved into an excellent free source for this kind of research. Some VC firms might pay for subscriptions to proprietary databases such as PitchBook, S&P's Capital IQ, Dow Jones' VentureSource or Thomson's VentureXpert (now part of Thomson ONE).

Another option for researching comps is to Google a company name along with the word "acquisition" or "acquired." Occasionally, acquisition prices are announced in press releases, though more often prices are not mentioned.

If we cannot find suitable acquisition comps, there are some other tools that we can use to create a narrative about exit valuation. Once again, I say *narrative* because there is no single number that is the *right* answer. Rather, by investigating several options, we begin to paint a picture that an exit valuation may be in a certain range.

> *We need multiple data points to create a narrative around exit valuation.*

Multiples

A distant second tool for estimating valuation is to multiply projected income in the year of acquisition by an industry standard called a *multiple*. This is analogous in real estate to using a price per square foot for home prices. These multiples are actually derived from a pool of comparables, so in a sense this method is a more generalized version of the same process. A rule of thumb is to use financial projection for year five because earnings tend to stabilize with time.

Of course, using multiples is unreliable if we are grooming a startup to be acquired pre-revenue, or when our acquirer is more interested in our technology or userbase rather than income. Also, we must not forget that we are using a wildly inaccurate piece of data: a financial projection for five years from now. So it is with a very large grain of salt that we derive this valuation, and similar to the process of defining our market size, we'll want several data points to corroborate our estimates.

Discounted Cash Flow (DCF)

A (much more) distant third tool for determining exit valuation comes from the corporate world and has limited value when looking at startups. Discounted cash flow, or DCF, is a calculation that takes all future profits (cash flows) and converts them into today's dollars. You could think of DCF as the bird in the hand formula. Tomorrow's two birds in the bush are discounted to today's bird in the hand, using this formula:

$$DCF = \frac{CF_1}{(1+r)^1} + \frac{CF_2}{(1+r)^2} + \ldots + \frac{CF_n}{(1+r)^n}$$

You may now pretend you never saw that formula in this book because it is a trap. DCF is a terrible tool for startups. We simply have too many unknowns to use such a complicated formula. Good luck determining a discount rate, for example, let alone guessing the revenues in year 5 of a startup.

That said, I do have a Razor trick that is sort of a DCF/multiple combo. You'll notice that most of the multiples are between 5-10X. Similarly, if you used a 10% or 20% discount rate for steady cash flows, you end up with a 5-10X multiple.

Hence, if I have a startup that seems to have a legitimate path to revenue, and I believe the revenues will be a driving factor in the acquisition price (vs. users, for example), I may take *Year 5 EBITDA* and guestimate an exit valuation of 5-10X.

> *Razor DCF simplification: exit valuation = 5-10X of Year 5 EBITDA*

Exit Strategy Summary

At this point, you may well be raising your eyebrows and wondering, "Can we really just make up numbers like this?!"

The answer is, absolutely! We have to. This is exactly what entrepreneurs and VCs do all the time. Keep in mind that the goal is not to fool ourselves into doing something we shouldn't do (by being wildly optimistic), but to give ourselves tools to make better Go/No-Go decisions.

You can think of exit strategy as the success story, a vision toward which we will be steering this ship. We need to create a narrative that helps us determine what success might look like and whether we believe we can get there. For VCs, success is measured in one way: financial returns. Just as with market size, we will need numbers *and* the story around the numbers.

Our exit strategy will start with projecting the most likely liquidity event. Can we get to $100M in steady, predictable revenue, suitable for an IPO? If not, what acquirers would be most interested and what metrics might they use for a purchase price?

With those variables in mind, we can take some guesses as to whether this investment has the return potential we will require. Recall that we generally want the potential to *return the fund* with any investment, which will usually mean 10-20X potential.

> WHAT WE COVERED
>
> **Exit Strategy**
>
> - Start with the Exit
> - Beach House Example
> - Return Analysis
> - Total Investment
> - Proceeds from Exit
> - Exit Valuation
> - Comps, Multiples and DCF

To determine our return potential:
1. Estimate exit proceeds (exit valuation *x* percent ownership, pro rata);
2. Estimate how much it will take to get there (current investment *x* 3-4);
3. Calculate A ÷ B to get *X* return.

Chapter Questions

1. What does it take for a startup to be a good candidate for an IPO?
2. Prior to exit, why is it (illiquid) equity more important to a VC when growing a startup than (liquid) cash?
3. What is the minimum return required for a VC investment?
4. Why is it important to combine narrative and numbers when defining an exit strategy?
5. What is flawed about DCF as a method of determining return potential?
6. Why are milestones important as we look toward an exit?
7. Give an example of the three-step process for calculating return potential.

Due Diligence Advice for Students: **Exit Strategy**

As a continuation of the previous chapter, we are now analyzing the exit we think would be possible assuming the startup hits all the milestones from the last chapter. Our founders may (again) not be the best authorities and are often looking to us to provide significant guidance on the exit strategy. Get specific about potential acquirers. Name them. Research their M&A activity. Speculate as to what kind of company we'd need to build for them and what range of price they might pay. You may need to revisit the previous chapter's analysis using the new information you've gathered here, adjusting your growth milestones and funding to match your exit strategy.

9. Return Analysis

Contents

VC Math 101

The two most fundamental terms in a venture capital term sheet are the pre-money valuation and the investment size. Adding those two gives you the post-money valuation:

For example, VCs have offered to invest $4M on a $6M pre-money, sometimes called a "4 on 6" deal, though it is becoming more common to hear this as a "4 on 10 post," as the post-money would then be $10M.

The next level of this algebra is used to determine the ownership structure, and needs to become second nature to a VC. Pre-money divided by post gives you founders' percent ownership. The investment divided by post gives you the VCs' stake.

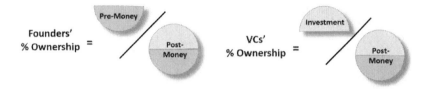

In our *4 on 6* example, we end up with:

Founders'
% Ownership = $6M / $10M = 60%   VCs'
% Ownership = $4M / $10M = 40%

Another quick example, let's say a VC firm is investing $2M in a startup with a pre-money valuation of $3M (or 2 on 3). The post-money valuation is $5M and the VC owns 40%, the founders 60%.

$$\$2M\ Investment \quad + \quad \frac{\$3M}{Pre\text{-}Money} \quad = \quad \frac{\$5M}{Post\text{-}Money}$$

$$VC\ Ownership \quad = \quad \frac{\$2M\ Investment}{\$5M\ Post\text{-}Money} \quad = \quad 40\%$$

VCs quickly learn to do this algebra in their head. Knowing the key deal terms, like *1 on 2* or *5 on 5*, VCs will immediately know that their ownership would be 33% or 50%, respectively. See the table for a cheat sheet of percent ownership for various deal terms.

Deal Terms	VC Ownership
1 on 1	1/2
2 on 2	or
3 on 3	50%
1 on 2	1/3
2 on 4	or
3 on 6	33%
1 on 3	1/4
2 on 6	or
3 on 9	25%
2 on 3	2/5
4 on 6	or
6 on 9	40%
3 on 4	3/7
6 on 8	or
9 on 12	~40%

Shark Math

I want to take a quick aside to address what I call *Shark Math*. Due to the popularity of ABC's show *Shark Tank*, many people think that equity deals should be offered as "_% of the company for $__."

As we've already discussed, this is *not* how VCs offer deals because it implies that a percentage of a pre-existing company is being sold (p. 55). With VC investing, a new class of preferred stock is being created and new shares are being sold. Nonetheless, the algebra is the same. Money comes into the startup, and the investors now own a percentage of the company.

If a deal is offered as _% of the company for sale for $__, we can solve for the valuation:

$$\frac{VC}{Ownership} \leftrightarrows \frac{Investment}{Post\text{-}Money} \quad \rightarrow \quad \frac{Post\text{-}}{Money} = \frac{Investment}{VC\ Ownership}$$

For example, let's look at a deal where 25% of the company is being offered for a $100,000 investment. Plug that into our deal algebra:

$$25\%\ VC\ Ownership = \frac{\$100,000\ Investment}{Post\text{-}Money}$$

$$Post\text{-}Money \leftrightarrows \frac{\$100,000}{25\%}$$

$$Post\text{-}Money = \$400,000$$

If you are a regular viewer of *Shark Tank*, you have heard sharks say something like, "Do you realize you are valuing your company at $400,000." This is actually a manipulation (or a mistake). Take a moment and see if you can catch what the Sharks are trying to do in the above example by claiming the founders are pricing their startup at $400,000.

What is the mistake?

The founders are actually pricing their startup at $300,000 prior to receiving the investment. The $400,000 valuation derived in the formula above is *post-money*. That valuation *includes* the investment, which the startup has not yet received. The *current* valuation should be *pre-money*, and should be $300,000. The valuation will increase to $400,000 *after the cash is received*.

In manipulating the math, the Sharks are employing a negotiation technique to make the valuation seem higher. Coming up with a valuation, also known as "pricing the deal," is often the stickiest part of the negotiation. I believe that is why I'm hearing more VCs talk about *4 on 10 post* deals, when they used to all say *4 on 6* ($4M investment on a $6M pre-money).

> *Using pre- or post-money can make a big difference in perception.*

The use of post-money vs. pre-money as the *valuation* can make a big difference in perception if the investment is for a large percentage of the company. If you take a traditional *2 on 2* deal: a $2M investment on a $2M pre-money valuation, and reframe it as a *2 on 4 post*—wow, we just doubled the value of the company!

VCIC Ventures Fund II, First Investment

Jeff and Mark were excited to announce they had closed *Fund II*, oversubscribed at $75M. The new fund had the same investment strategy as *VCIC I*, 10-12 early stage deals, typically starting with seed investments. The difference this time is that they could average closer to $6M per startup rather than the $4-5M in *Fund I*.

They have found a startup they are very excited about. A couple of Carnegie-Mellon engineering students have dropped out of school to create a co-working productivity tool. This is right in the sweet spot for VCIC Ventures: young, smart, tech-savvy entrepreneurs who already have a product in the marketplace gaining traction, but who could really use the guidance of some investors who have been there before. Jeff and Mark already have some great ideas about how to gain market share quickly.

The young founders, we'll call them YFs, have pitched that they need $100,000 to get to profitability. They say that, with their current user base and the additional customers a new marketing campaign would bring in, they would never need additional funding.

Jeff and Mark don't exactly disagree, but they have a bigger vision. True, the YFs only need about $100,000 right now to do some marketing and add some product features. However, if that investment works, *VCIC Ventures* would want to raise a $1M Series A round to start going to the next level with new product features that would appeal to a larger market.

Assuming the YFs hit the Series A milestones, Jeff and Mark think there is a potential to go big with another round of financing with the goals of reaching 100,000 paying users, 3 specific new product features and at least one strategic partnership with a major tech company. Building a company that could handle that growth would require a Series B in the $5-10M range.

At that point, Jeff and Mark could see things going a few different ways. The strategic partner mentioned above could be interested in acquiring the startup, probably in the $75-100M range, or a C round could position it well for a $200-300M exit. Another possibility is that more strategic partners may come on board, bringing the idea of an IPO into consideration.

VCIC Ventures coached the YFs about this possible bigger trajectory, including multiple rounds of VC financing, as opposed to the *$100K to profitability* strategy the YFs had pitched. *VCIC Ventures* projected, assuming milestones were hit and the economy didn't implode, that the startup could raise several rounds of funding. On the back of a napkin, they sketched out this potential scenario:

- Seed round: $100K investment on a $1M pre-money valuation
- Series A: $1M on $2M
- Series B: $5M on $10M
- Series C: $20M on $40M
- Exit: $200M

Adding all the rounds of investment above, the total raised would be approximately $26M. If they could find a buyer in the $200M-$300M range, it would be a terrific success for both the founders and *VCIC Ventures*. They estimated that the founders might retain 20% of the equity for exit, worth around $40-60M at exit.

Breaking it Down

As we've said many times already, when VCs first look at a startup, we are thinking holistically about the entire *life of the investment*, not just the Series A. We will map out in our heads a best guess as to every round of investment on the way to exit.

Figure: Typical rounds of VC investing on the way to exit

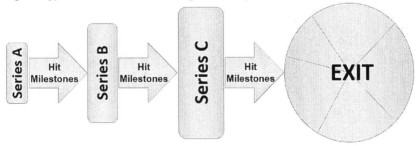

In Mark and Jeff's scenario, we start with a $100,000 seed round, followed by a Series A, B and C. Each follow-on round dilutes the ownership of earlier shareholders. In this case, each follow-on round happens to be diluting by 33% (*1 on 2, 5 on 10* and *20 on 40*). There is no magic to the 33%; it's

This Example
Seed: $100K on $1M
Series A: 1 on 2
Series B: 5 on 10
Series C: 20 on 40

mostly just coincidence. If we anticipated hitting a huge milestone, for example, there would likely be a bigger jump in valuation between rounds. I'll walk you through the math later, but for now, take a look at the effects of dilution:

Figure: Dilution through seed, A, B and C rounds

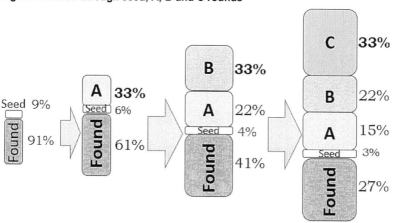

Every round projected is an *up round*, or course, as we are forecasting success. The seed investment of $100,000 on a $1M pre-money yields a post-money of $1.1M. The Series A has a pre-money of $2M. This implies that milestones must have been hit, as the value has increased approximately 1.8X.

Figure: Seed to Series A, up round by 1.8X

The seed investors' $100,000 investment is now worth $180,000 (on paper), and the $1M worth of stock owned by the founders, as determined by the seed round pre-money valuation, is now worth $1.8M. The image to the left shows the pre-money breakdown; the $1M investment is not in there yet. (Series A is a 1 on 2 round.)

Similarly, between the A and B rounds, we are projecting a healthy up round, going from a Series A post-money of $3M to a Series B pre-money of $10M, or a 3.3X increase. Finally, from Series B to Series C we see another increase of 2.7X, from a post of $15M to a pre of $40M.

Figure: Each round is an up round

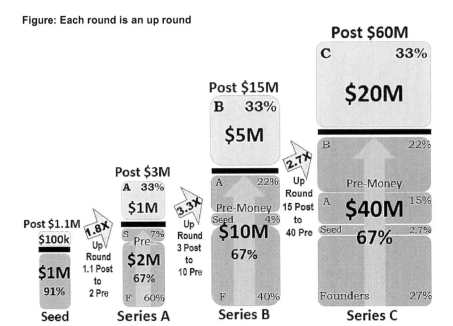

Post $60M

C   33%

$20M

Post $15M

B   33%

$5M

B   22%

Post $3M

A   33%

$1M

2.7X Up Round 15 Post to 40 Pre

Pre-Money

A   15%

$40M

Post $1.1M

$100k

1.8X Up Round 1.1 Post to 2 Pre

A   22%

3.3X Up Round 3 Post to 10 Pre

Pre-Money

Seed   4%

$10M

67%

Seed   2.7%

67%

S   7%

Pre

$2M

67%

$1M

91%

F   60%

F   40%

Founders   27%

Seed   **Series A**   **Series B**   **Series C**

Figure: Splitting the pie of a $200M exit

With the $200M exit projected in this case, the splitting of proceeds is represented in this pie chart.

The seed investors and founders, while suffering dilution, benefit from all of the up rounds. Multiply them all (1.8 x 3.3 x 2.7 x

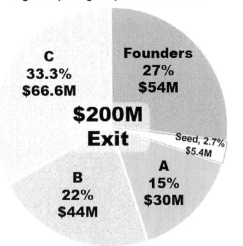

3.3) and you get just over 54X on the way to a $200M exit. Series A enjoys three bumps, 3.3 x 2.7 x 3.3, or 30X. Series B has two jumps, 2.7 x 3.3, or 9X.

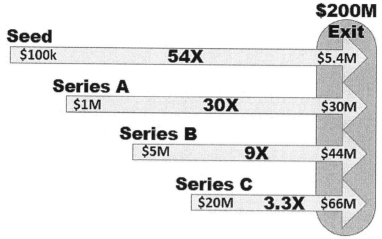

You can see why a firm would want to participate in the early rounds, with 30-55X returns for the seed and Series A. However, very little capital was put to work. If *VCIC. II* only participated in the seed and A rounds, they would not have returned even half of their $75M fund. Total proceeds for seed and A are $5.4M + $30M = $35.4M.

After the Series A, *VCIC Ventures* owned 39% (6% from the seed and 33% for Series A). If they were able to maintain pro rata through the B and C rounds, holding at 39% at exit, they would indeed return the fund with this investment: 39% of $200M = $78M.

We will now dive into the weeds of the math so that you can understand how all of this works. The algebra gets pretty complicated, and we'll use a cap table to keep up with all the moving parts. However, I will attempt to keep it all in perspective so that we don't fall too deep into a spreadsheet!

Seed Round

In the seed round, this particular startup had very low capital needs ($100,000) to hit the next milestones. Some VC firms would not bother with an early stage investment like this. They would "pass" and ask the startup to come back when they were ready for their first institutional round.

However, *VCIC Ventures'* strategy is to find early stage deals like this. The purpose of the seed investment is to get an early seat at the table for the Series A, as the returns from seed investing will not likely move the needle on the fund (see the previous section: total returns on the seed investment were $5.4M).

For the seed round, *VCIC Ventures* invested $100,000 on a $1M pre-money valuation, resulting in a 9% ownership stake.

Seed

$100k

$1M

91%

$$VC\ \%\ ownership = investment/post$$

$$\$100,000/\$1,100,000 = 9\%$$

On thn a cap table, the seed round would look like this:[54]

Figure: Capitalization table of seed round

Seed Round	Common		Seed (Preferred)		Total Post Seed		
	Shares	Valuation	Shares	Investment	Shares	%	Value
PREFERRED							
VCIC Ventures							
Seed			100,000	$ 100,000	100,000	9.1%	$ 100,000
COMMON							
Founder #1	500,000	$500,000			500,000	45.5%	$ 500,000
Founder #2	500,000	$500,000			500,000	45.5%	$ 500,000
Total	1,000,000	$1,000,000	100,000	$100,000	1,100,000	100%	$1,100,000

Pre-Money ↑   Investment ↑   Post-Money ↑

Pre-Money ÷ Shares = Share Price → $1.0

The cap table shows all the detail of creating and pricing shares. This will be very important once we've made the investment; we'll want to track things very accurately. However, at the projections stage when we are trying to make a determination about the level of investment and pre-money valuation for an early round, I would not recommend getting to the level of detail of a projected cap table. As you'll see at the end of this chapter, it is overkill for the purposes of an exit scenario analysis.

Let me repeat, the cap table is absolutely necessary post-investment. It is a critical tool for tracking equity. Where it is less helpful is when we are simply making back of the napkin projections as we decide about a current early stage investment. There is so much prognostication that

---

[54] To see a Google sheet of this cap table, go to www.bit.ly/vcic-cap-table. Go to the "Seed Round" tab.

it renders accuracy pointless, even dangerous, lest we start to have too much faith in the numbers we've concocted. That fancy cap table spreadsheet *looks* right, don't you think? The complicated formulas are working; so the numbers must be right!

Series A

Looking forward to the Series A, *VCIC Ventures* is planning to take the entire round, projecting a *1 on 2*, meaning a negotiated $1M investment on a negotiated $2M pre-money valuation. (Of course, these things could change. We're guessing about future rounds.)

$$VC \text{ \% ownership} = investment \, / \, post$$

$$Series \text{ } A \text{ } Ownership: \text{ } \$1M \, / \, \$3M = 33\%$$

If the Series A goes as planned, it would create 33% new equity, diluting all pre-Series A shareholders by 33%.

Though I have one for you below, we don't need a cap table to do this math. It's preferable to keep it simple so that we can do the math with some degree of accuracy in our heads. Taking 1/3 off the founders' 91% ownership puts them at about 61%; a third off of VCIC Ventures' seed stake of 9% puts it at 6% post-A.

$$New \text{ } Diluted \text{ } Ownership = Old \text{ } Ownership \text{ } x \text{ } (1 - \text{\% } dilution)$$

$$9\% \, x \, (1 - 33\%) = 6\%$$

Dilution hurts, but there is good news in that our diluted percentage is now worth more due to the higher valuation. Our original $100,000 is now worth around $180,000 (6% of $3M post-money).

Figure: Capitalization table for the Series A

Series A	Pre-A		Series A (Preferred)		Total Post A		
	Shares	%	Shares	Investment	Shares	%	Value
PREFERRED							
VCIC Ventures							
Seed	100,000	9.1%			100,000	6.1%	$181,818
Series A			550,000	$1,000,000	550,000	33.3%	$1,000,000
COMMON							
Founder #1	500,000	45.5%			500,000	30.3%	$909,091
Founder #2	500,000	45.5%			500,000	30.3%	$909,091
Total	1,100,000	100%	550,000	$1,000,000	1,650,000	100%	$3,000,000

Pre-Money: $2,000,000
New Share Price: $1.82
Post-Money ↑

Digging into a cap table for this round, note that the new share price is $1.82, up from $1 in the seed round. The new share price is calculated by taking the new pre-money valuation from the upcoming round and dividing it by the number of pre-existing shares:

New Share Price = Pre-Money Valuation ÷ Total Shares after Previous Round

$$\$2M \div 1.1M \ shares = \$1.82$$

To determine the number of shares that will be issued to the Series A investors, we need to take the investment, $1M, and divide it by the new share price:

Number of New Shares Issued = New Investment ÷ Share Price

$$\$1M \div \$1.82 = 550,000 \ Series \ A \ shares \ issued$$

You can see in the cap table that VCIC Ventures owns a total of 650,000 shares: 100,000 from the seed round and 550,000 from the newly issued Series A. While it is imperative to know how this works if you are going to become a VC, it is actually a bit overkill and distracting from the big picture of return analysis.

Figure: VCIC Ventures ownership after Series A

In other words, we don't really need to know that we own 550,000 shares. Instead, we can simply add up our percent ownership: 6% for seed and 33% for the Series A, totaling 39% post Series A.

As we are not planning to cash out yet, it really doesn't matter what the shares are worth at the very moment. That said, we can calculate that 39% of the post-money of $3M is just under $1.2M, which makes sense: it's our $1M Series A investment plus the near doubling of our $100K seed investment.

Coming out of the Series A, we have the approximate percentage of ownership that we'd like to maintain by reserving capital (1-3X of our Series A) for follow-on rounds.

Series B

Figure: Up round from A to B

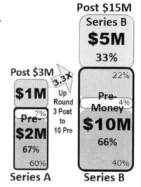

Going into Series B, we anticipate a *5 on 10* round. This implies that the startup made significant progress, increasing in valuation from Series A post of $3M to Series B pre-money of $10M, representing more than a 3X jump.

With a 5 on 10 round, the Series B investors will own 33% of the equity after the round:

Series B Ownership: $5M / $15M = 33%

Our previous ownership stake of 39% will get diluted by 33%:

39% x (1 – 33%) = 26%

Figure: Syndicating the $5M/33% Series B

Syndicate	
$3M	20%
VCIC Ventures	
$2M	13%

To maintain pro rata, *VCIC Ventures* will participate in the B round. If we were trying to maintain *exactly* 39%, we'd take *exactly* 39% of the new round. But we're VCs. Let's go with 40% of the $5M round, or $2M for *VCIC Ventures*. That will leave $3M for syndicate partners. We will split the new 33% equity 60/40. That'll be 20% for them and 13% for us.

Our total ownership stake after the Series B will be our diluted 26% from Series A post, plus our newly purchased Series B 13%, totaling 39%. So far, we've invested $100,000 + $1M + $2M. Total in: $3.1M.

Figure: VCIC Ventures equity stake after Series B

Again, we can see all the details of the shares being issued in a cap table. Our 1,650,000 shares from the previous round carry forward. The new pre-money valuation of $10M puts the share value price at $6.06. At that price, the Series B investors receive a total of 825,000 shares, bringing the total share pool up to 2,475,000, Post B.

Figure: Series B, 5 on 10

Series B	Total Post-A		Series B (Preferred)		Total Post-B		
	Shares	%	Shares	Investment	Shares	%	Value
PREFERRED							
VCIC Ventures							
Seed	100,000	6%			100,000	4.0%	606,061
Series A	550,000	33%			550,000	22.2%	3,333,333
Series B			330,000	$ 2,000,000	330,000	13.3%	2,000,000
Syndicate Partners							
Series B			495,000	$ 3,000,000	495,000	20.0%	3,000,000
COMMON							
Founder #1	500,000	30%			500,000	20.2%	3,030,303
Founder #2	500,000	30%			500,000	20.2%	3,030,303
Total	1,650,000	100%	825,000	$5,000,000	2,475,000	100%	$15,000,000

Pre-Money: $10,000,000   Post-Money

B Pre-Money ÷ Post A Shares = B Share Price: $6.06

Figure: Up round from B to C

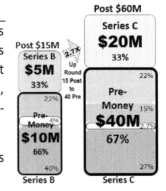

Post $60M

Series C

Ding, ding, round 4. *VCIC Ventures* has modelled a *20 on 40* round for Series C. This once again means that the startup has hit some milestones and increased valuation, another *up round*, this time from $15M post-B to $40M pre-money for C.

With a 20 on 40 round, the Series C investors will own 33% of the equity after the round:

Series C Ownership: $20M / $60M = 33%

Our previous ownership stake of 39% will get diluted by 33%:

39% x (1 – 33%) = 26%

To maintain ~40% pro rata position through the Series C, we'd need to take 40% of the $20M. However, 40% of $20M is $8M, and we cannot afford that!

Fund Fit Alert!

In this $75M fund, it stated above that we average $6M per startup in our portfolio. We've already invested $3.1M through the Series B. Another $8M would put us at over $11M, way too much exposure to one startup in the portfolio.

Let's stick with our game plan of $6M per startup and reserve $3M for this $20M Series C. Yes, we will take a hit on dilution, but *VCIC II* was not intended to be a later stage fund. We did not sell our LPs on later stage investing.

Figure: Syndicating the $20M/33% Series C

Going with $3M for us and $17M for our syndicate partners, we would end up with 5% new equity, with the rest of the syndicate getting the other 28%.

If we add 5% to the 26% we had Post B, we are now at 31%. We did not entirely avoid dilution, but we hung in there pretty well.

Once again, a cap table will show us all the details of adding a 20 on 40 Series C.

Series C	Total Post-B		Series C (Preferred)		Total Post-C		
	Shares	%	Shares	Investment	Shares	%	Value
PREFERRED							
VCIC Ventures							
Seed	100,000	4%			100,000	2.7%	$1,616,162
Series A	550,000	22%			550,000	14.8%	$8,888,889
Series B	330,000	13%			330,000	8.9%	$5,333,333
Series C			185,625	$3,000,000	185,625	5.0%	$3,000,000
Syndicate Partners							
Series B	495,000	20%			495,000	13.3%	$8,000,000
Series C			1,051,875	$17,000,000	1,051,875	28.3%	$17,000,000
COMMON							
Founder#1	500,000	20%			500,000	13.5%	$8,080,808
Founder#2	500,000	20%			500,000	13.5%	$8,080,808
Total	2,475,000	100%	1,237,500	$20,000,000	3,712,500	100%	$60,000,000

Pre-Money: $40,000,000   Post-Money

C Pre-Money ÷ Post-B Shares = C Share Price: $16.16

To the Exit

VCIC Ventures participated in every round, from seed through Series C. We took 100% of the seed and A rounds; we had syndicate partners for the B and C rounds.

Figure: VCIC Ventures equity stake by round

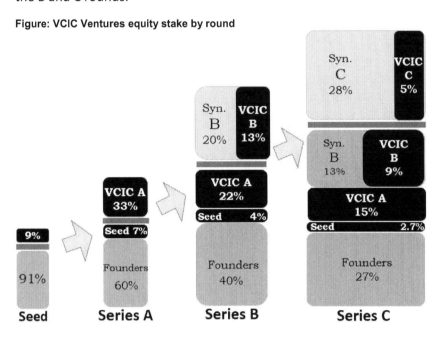

With a $200M project exit, our new equity split will look like this:

Figure: Detailed equity split for $200M exit

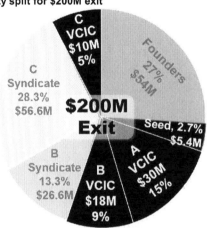

We can break down our investments, equity and proceeds in a table:

Round	Investment	Equity at Exit	Proceeds
Seed	$100,000	2.7%	$5.4M
Series A	$1M	15%	$30M
Series B	$2M	9%	$18M
Series C	$3M	5%	$10M
Total	$6.1M	31.7%	$63.4M

Ultimately, after all of this hard work going round by round and accurately calculating the dilution, we are projecting a 10X return on an average investment for our fund ($6M), that comes close to returning our $75M fund.

Back to the Forest: Rules of Thumb

We don't need to delve into all of the technicalities above to make some guesses for exit scenarios. Remember, we are doing this return analysis to inform our decision on the intial institutional round, specifically, on negotiating the investment size and the pre-money valuation for the Series A.

Rules of thumb can serve us well. First, split your overall investment over several rounds. *VCIC II* was designed with an average of $6M per startup. We modeled this exit scenario on that average.

Second, do not invest more than 1/3 of the total investment in the Series A. This is a variation of the rule of thumb to reserve 1-3X for future rounds. In this case, we only invested 1/6 in the Series A. As we look back on this analysis, we might want to increase that to get a higher percent ownership out of the gate, knowing that we'll get diluted in later rounds, which brings us to another rule of thumb.

If we expect rather large later rounds, we should also expect some dilution. In other words, we won't really be able to maintain pro rata if things get too big for our fund. We may be able to counteract that later dilution by increasing our stake in earlier rounds.

For example, if we had invested $1.5M on the $2M pre-money in the Series A, we would have received about 43% equity in that round rather than 33%. The "1.5 on 2" round would have diltued our seed stake by

43%, from 9% to about 5%. Add that 5% to our new Series A 43%, and we come out of Series A with 48%.

Would the founders balk at this extra diltuion in the Series A? Perhaps, but we haven't changed their pre-money valuation of $1M. They do not lose any value of their shares, still worth $1M post-A. Plus, they get the benefit of an extra $500,000 to put toward growing their business.

On a following page is a full capitalization table for all of the rounds discussed above, seed through Series C.

Here is how we might summarize this investment opportunity:

> "We are proposing a 1.5 on 2 Series A, reserving $4.5M for follow-on rounds. Our total in will be $6M for around 35% at exit. With a $200M exit, we'd expect proceeds over $60, which is above 10X in 5 years, nearly returning our $75M fund."

Adding the Option Pool

Recall that this team is very young, a couple of Carnegie Mellon dropouts. With such a young team, we'd likely want a pretty large option pool to attract talent. We're going to need some top-level managers who have helped grow a startup from 5 employees to 50. These students are super smart and driven, but the skills that succeed in the garage don't necessarily translate into a growing enterprise.

In the example below, we've added a 20% option pool to the Series A. Often the pool will get *refreshed* in later rounds, but just to make the point, we'll keep this math simple and let our Series A pool get diluted like all early stakeholders.

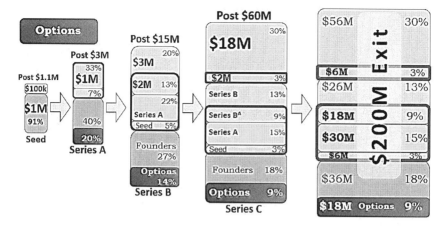

Notice that the entire option pool comes out of the founders' common stock in the Series A. This can be a bitter pill to swallow. The founders just got diluted from 60% to 40% by the addition of this pool. However, this is often more amenable to them than accepting a lower pre-money valuation.

The exit proceeds in this example have dropped for the founders from $54M to $36M. The argument VCs will make is that that is a pretty good return on investment for the $1M pre-money valuation at the seed round—a 36X return! Made possible by all that capital supplied by VCs as well as the hard work of the new employees who received the stock options.

	Common		Seed (Preferred)		Total Post Seed			Pre-A	Series A (Preferred)		Total Post A		
	Shares	Valuation	Shares	Investment	Shares	%	Value	Shares	Shares	Investment	Shares	%	Value
PREFERRED													
VCIC Ventures													
Seed			100,000	$ 100,000	100,000	9.1%	$ 100,000	100,000			100,000	6.1%	$181,818
Series A									550,000	$ 1,000,000	550,000	33.3%	$1,000,000
Series B													
Series C													
Syndicate Partners													
Series B													
Series C													
COMMON													
Founder #1	500,000	$500,000			500,000	45.5%	$ 500,000	500,000			500,000	30.3%	$909,091
Founder #2	500,000	$500,000			500,000	45.5%	$ 500,000	500,000			500,000	30.3%	$909,091
Options Pre-A												0.0%	$0
Total	1,000,000	$1,000,000	100,000	$100,000	1,100,000	100%	$1,100,000	1,100,000	550,000	$1,000,000	1,650,000	100%	$3,000,000

Pre-Money ↑   Investment ↑   Post-Money ↑   Pre-Money: $2,000,000   Post-Money ↑

Pre-Money ÷ Shares = ..re Price → $1.0   New Share Price: $1.82

Figure: Capitalization table for all rounds (bit.ly/vcic-cap-table)

Series B (Preferred)		Total Post B			Series C (Preferred)		Total Post C		
Shares	Investment	Shares	%	Value	Shares	Investment	Shares	%	Value
		100,000	4.0%	606,061			100,000	2.7%	$1,616,162
		550,000	22.2%	3,333,333			550,000	14.8%	$8,888,889
330,000	$2,000,000	330,000	13.3%	2,000,000			330,000	8.9%	$5,333,333
					185,625	$3,000,000	185,625	5.0%	$3,000,000
495,000	$3,000,000	495,000	20.0%	3,000,000			495,000	13.3%	$8,000,000
					1,051,875	$17,000,000	1,051,875	28.3%	$17,000,000
		500,000	20.2%	3,030,303			500,000	13.5%	$8,080,808
		500,000	20.2%	3,030,303			500,000	13.5%	$8,080,808
			0.0%	-					
825,000	$5,000,000	2,475,000	100%	$15,000,000	1,237,500	$20,000,000	3,712,500	100%	$60,000,000

Series B — Pre-Money: $10,000,000; New Share Price: $6.06

Total Post B — Post-Money $15,000,000; Pre-Money ÷ Shares =

Series C — Pre-Money: $40,000,000; Share Price → $16.16

Total Post C — Post-Money $60,000,000

Appendices

GLOSSARY

ADOPTION RISK — The risk that customers will not adopt a new solution. In the Razor, we mitigate this risk by demonstrating TRACTION.

ANCHOR LP — A limited partner with a large (more than 10%) stake in a VC fund.

ANGEL INVESTORS — Individuals or groups who, like VCs, make equity investments in early stage startups, but unlike VCs, do not have LPs.

BARRIER TO ENTRY — Something that inhibits competitors from getting into a market space (like very high development costs, exclusive contracts, entrenched infrastructure...). This can be a competitive advantage.

BENCHMARKING — Comparing one venture to others. Could be product attributes, growth strategy, or really any aspect of the venture planning process.

BOARD OF DIRECTORS — The governing body of a company; the CEO's boss, though often the CEO is also on the board and sometimes is chairman. Unlike an advisory board, this board has a legal (fiduciary) duty to the shareholders. In new ventures it is best to keep the board small and an odd number (Series A is often 3 or 5 members).

BOARD OF ADVISORS — A group of individuals recruited by the entrepreneur for advice. They have no fiduciary duties and may meet as formally or informally as the entrepreneur desires.

BURN RATE — The speed at which a startup is spending ("burning through") cash, generally monthly or weekly.

BUSINESS MODEL — Can refer to a whole host of issues about how a business is designed to capture the value that it creates. It answers the question: how should we set up the venture to achieve our goals? The current thinking is that it is better to use an established business model rather than create a new one. Sometimes interchanged with *Revenue Model*.

CAP EX — Capital expenditures: big ticket items needed, like factories, real estate, large equipment.

CAP TABLE — Capitalization table: a spreadsheet that shows % ownership in a venture, including # and % of shares held by founders, investors, key employees, as well as allocated to the option pool for future key employees.

CAPITAL CALL	A request for capital from the VC fund to the LPs to invest in a startup.
CARRY	The % of proceeds that a VC firm receives after the LPs have recouped their investment, most commonly 20%.
CLOSED (A FUND)	Finished fundraising and able to invest in startups
CONVERTIBLE DEBT	A loan that can convert to equity in the next round; a creative way to do an angel deal without pricing the round
CUSTOMER PAIN	The metaphorical discomfort that customers must suffer without our products, which indicates potential customer demand. The higher the pain, the lower the "adoption risk."
COMPETITIVE ADVANTAGE	Something that will give the venture a leg up on competitors, often related to IP. It usually requires a significant competitive advantage to attract VC funding.
DILUTION	The decrease in percent ownership suffered by early stakeholders as new equity is issued.
DOWN ROUND	An equity round in which the pre-money valuation is lower than the post-money from the last round.
DRY POWDER	Capital that VCs reserve for follow-on rounds, for example, often 2-3X of a Series A investment.
EARLY STAGE, LATER STAGE	Refers to the maturity of a new venture, generally associated with rounds of VC funding. The latest stage can be an IPO or an acquisition (venture gets bought by another firm).
ELEVATOR PITCH	A 2-3 minute verbal presentation that an entrepreneur should be prepared to give in case there happens to be an investor in the elevator with you.
EQUITY	Ownership in the form of shares of stock in a venture.
EXIT	An event that allows founders and private investors the opportunity to cash out by selling their shares in the venture, either through an acquisition or, much rarer, an IPO.
EXIT STRATEGY	Tactics employed to maximize value of the startup at exit.
FATAL FLAW	Something in (or missing from) the business plan that indicates to the reader that the venture will definitely not work – immediately eliciting a NO-GO decision.
FEE STRUCTURE	Fees charged by the VC fund: management fees and carry, most commonly 2/20 (2% fees, 20% carry).
FOLLOW-ON ROUNDS	Subsequent rounds of funding in a startup after an initial institutional round, i.e., Series B, C, etc.
FUND OF FUNDS	An LP that aggregates capital from other, larger LPs to invest in VC funds.

GENERAL PARTNERS (GPs)	The people who actively manage the partnership. In a venture fund, the general partners (GPs) are the VCs who do the investing.
ILLIQUID ASSET	Something that is not easy to transfer, such as a startup or house.
INSTITUTIONAL ROUND	A round of equity investment by institutional investors (VCs), not angels. The Series A is the first institutional round.
IP, INTELLECTUAL PROPERTY	Non-tangible assets that have value. Includes patents, trademarks, copyrights and trade secrets. Often used in the context of a sustainable competitive advantage.
IPO	Initial public offering, aka, "going public," refers to selling shares of the company on the open market, usually with NASDAQ or NYSE (New York Stock Exchange). See *Exit*.
IRR	Internal Rate of Return: similar to ROI, to measure return on investment. Given as an annual percentage.
LIMITED PARTNERS OR LPs	The folks who put up the money but do not take an active role in management.
LIQUID ASSET	Something that can be very easily transferred (like cash)
LIQUIDITY EVENT	See exit.
MANAGEMENT FEE	The amount a VC firm charges the LPs to run the firm (salaries, rent, travel, etc.), most commonly 2%.
MEZZANINE FUND	A later stage VC fund that invests later stage, just before exit.
MILESTONES	Specific goals, often tied to rounds of investing. For example, developing a working prototype or achieving a level of sales or hiring a CEO. Hitting a milestone generally implies you have significantly decreased risk and hence have increased value.
OPPORTUNITY COST	When choosing between two options, the opportunity cost is the value of the option you do not choose. It can be added to startup cost to determine true cost. For example, choosing to go to graduate school full-time costs $X for tuition. It also implies an opportunity cost of lost income for two years.
OPTION POOL	A percentage of ownership in the venture that is set aside (i.e., not given to entrepreneur or investors) to be given as incentives to future employees.
OVER SUBSCRIBE	Raise more money than targeted.
PAIN POINT	Refers to a very specific need that would motivate a customer to make a purchase decision.
PARTIAL CLOSE	An early announcement that some fundraising has been achieved, though the fundraising goal has not been met.

POST-MONEY VALUATION	The negotiated value of the startup just *after* investment. Investment + pre-money = post-money.
PRE-MONEY VALUATION	The negotiated value of the startup just *before* an equity investment.
PREFERRED SHARES	Like friends with benefits, "preferred" shares are a class of stock that have special rights, like liquidation preferences, anti-dilution, dividends, voting rights, etc.
PRICE ELASTICITY	A measure of how sensitive customers are to price changes. Inelastic implies that demand doesn't change much even when the price does (like gasoline).
PRICING THE ROUND	Negotiating a pre-money valuation for a VC investment.
PRO RATA	Maintain the same ownership % through future rounds, i.e., don't get diluted.
REVENUE MODEL	Part of the business model that deals only with income, i.e., who are customers and what and how are they charged. For example, recurring revenue model, razor/blade model, subscription model, etc.
PROOF OF CONCEPT	Somewhat self-explanatory, but a common phrase in new ventures that refers to ways of mitigating the risk that something won't work. Closely related to milestones and value creation.
PRO FORMA	In a business plan, this means projected financial statements, generally done by month for the first 2-3 years and by year for 5 years.
RISK PROFILE	Willingness to take risk, and correspondingly the amount of potential reward expected from the risk. For example, if one is highly risk averse, one would need a very large potential payoff to be willing to take a risk.
ROUND (OF INVESTING)	The total amount of money given to a new venture (in exchange for equity) at a given time. Rounds often have names, like: "friends and family round", pre-seed, seed, angel, Round A, Round B, Round C…
RUNWAY	Refers to the amount of time a startup has before it runs out of cash
SCALABILITY	The ability of a startup to grow quickly with enough stability to make it to exit.
SERIES A	The first round of institutional investing (from venture capitalists).
SERIES B, C, D…	Subsequent rounds of equity financing from VCs.
SWEAT EQUITY	The value of the founders' labor while starting the venture, often used in the context of negotiating pre-money valuation.

SYNDICATE	Noun: A group of investment firms who are all participating in the same round of investing in a venture. Verb: to create a syndicate.
TERM SHEET	A contract that lays out the terms of the venture capital investment. Part of the process, not the end.
UP ROUND	An equity round in which the pre-money valuation is higher than the post-money from the previous round. Opposite: down round.
USE OF FUNDS	This is the term of art for the startup's plan to spend the capital it raises from VCs.
VALUE NETWORK	The network of constituencies that may be affected by a startup, including customers, buyers, users, suppliers, competitors, employees, general public.
VALUE PROPOSITION	A brief statement that quickly summarizes a startup's differentiated solution addressing customer pain points.
VCIC	Venture Capital Investment Competition; a reality-based competition in which startups pitch to students playing the role of VCs.
VENTURE	= startup = business = firm = enterprise (older)
VENTURE CAPITAL FIRM	The legal umbrella/entity/partnership under which a group of venture capitalists organize for the purpose of raising VC funds.
VENTURE CAPITAL FUND	A partnership through which the GPs (general partners, VCs) raise funds from LPs (limited partners, institutions) for the purpose of investing in startups. Funds generally have 10-year lives. VC firms may have multiple VC funds.

PARTIAL SOURCES

- *Defense Spending, Aerospace, and the California Economy*, RAND, 1993, bit.ly/29Ao5bU
- A Brief History of the California Economy, A Modern Economy is Born, California Dept. of Finance, bit.ly/2ifTZku
- *A Rare Mix Created Silicon Valley's Startup Culture*, NPR, 2012, n.pr/HFvK3z
- *MA Won't Change Noncompete Law, VCs Pledge to Continue Campaign*, Xconomy, July 2014, bit.ly/29E2z6K
- *PBS American Experience: Silicon Valley*, 90 minutes, 2013, to.pbs.org/1ohcbBZ

- *Something Ventured*, Independent Film, 86 minutes, 2011, bit.ly/1zr1g2M
- *Venture Capitalists Oral History Project*, Regional Oral History Office, The Bancroft Library, ©2012 UC Berkeley, bit.ly/29ApOOk
- *A History of Silicon Valley*, Arun Rao, Omniware Group, 2013, bit.ly/29mOVXo
- *How Much Does Venture Capital Drive the U.S. Economy?*, Stanford Business, 2015, stanford.io/1GiVrcH
- *Proven Templates for Creating Value Propositions That Work*, Nov. 2011, Tor Grønsund, bit.ly/1ljQcw3

Recommended Reading
- *Venture Deals, Be Smarter than Your Lawyer and Venture Capitalist*, Brad Feld and Jason Mendelson, Wiley, 2013
- *The Lean Startup: How Today's Entrepreneurs Use Continuous Innovation to Create Radically Successful Businesses*, Eric Reis, Crown Business, 2011
- *Business Model Generation: A Handbook for Visionaries, Game Changers, and Challengers*, Alexander Osterwalder, Jon Wiley and Sons, 2010
- *The Startup Owner's Manual: The Step-By-Step Guide for Building a Great Company*, Steve Blank, K&S Ranch, 2012
- *Zero to One: Notes on Startups, or How to Build the Future*, Peter Thiel, Crown Business, 2014
- *The Startup Game: Inside the Partnership between Venture Capitalists and Entrepreneurs*, William H. Draper III, St. Martin's Griffin, 2012
- *The New Business Road Test: What entrepreneurs and executives should do before launching a lean startup*, John Mullin, FT Press, 2013
- *The Hard Thing About Hard Things: Building a Business When There Are No Easy Answers*, Ben Horowitz, HarperBusiness, 2014
- *The Little Book of Venture Capital Investing*, Louis Gerken and Wesley Whittaker, Wiley 2014

Acknowledgements

I'd like to thank the following students and colleagues who have generously given time and input in helping me write this book: Anne Bennett Osteen, Grahme Taylor, Jeff Reid, Rangoli Bhattacharjee, Baris Guzel, Philip Kim, Margot Lester, Keegan Emrick, Riyad Omar, Brandon

Berkowitz, Brian Johns, Tamala Grissett, Shannon Dwyer, Sarah Igoe, MD, Jim Spaeth, Gideon Katsh and Rachel Grossberg.

I would also like to thank some of the VCs and other professionals from whom I have learned immensely through the years, often as guest speakers in my classes or judges at VCIC events: Bruce Boehm, David Jones, Jimmy Rosen, Matt Barber, Mel Williams, Jayson Punwani, Barry Gonder, Chris Bartholomew, Scott Kupor, Dan Primack, Greg Bohlen, Jason Mendelson, Don Nelson, Don Herzog, Jason Caplain, Lister Delgado, John Cambier, Stephanie Nieman, John Glushik, Noel Sinozich, Patrick Dunnigan, Rik Vandevenne, Scott Albert, Mark Rostick, Bill Starling, Don Rose, Dave Neal, Chris Heivly, Ted Zoller and Clay Hamner.

About the Author

Patrick Vernon has been directing the world's largest venture capital competition since he was the president of the MBA Entrepreneurship Club at the University of North Carolina's Kenan-Flagler Business School in 2003. After graduating, Patrick joined UNC Kenan-Flagler, largely to run the Venture Capital Investment Competition (VCIC), which has grown to include over 80 universities representing 13 countries on 3 continents.

In 2006, Patrick began teaching at UNC, and by 2008 had a full course load of entrepreneurship and venture capital classes for undergraduate and graduate business students. The first iterations of this book were used as the course pack for early versions of his BUSI 506 class, renamed *Entrepreneurial Strategy: How to Think Like a Venture Capitalist*.

Prior to business school, Patrick spent a decade in Los Angeles as an artistic entrepreneur. With his *folkadelic party rock* band, the Zookeepers, Patrick performed over 500 shows across the American west. The Zookeepers recorded and released four CDs.

Printed in Great Britain
by Amazon

75776937R00163